PENGUIN BO

THE PENGUIN HISTORY
Volume Four

Gerald R. Cragg was born in Ontario, grew up in Japan, and was educated at the University of Toronto and at Trinity and Westminster Colleges, Cambridge. He was a minister of the United Church of Canada (a union of Congregational, the Methodist and Presbyterian churches), and served in rural, town and city churches. He was professor of theology at McGill University, and in 1958 he became professor of church history at Andover Newton Theological School. For a number of years he was a participant in the work of the World Council of Churches, particularly of the Commission on Faith and Order. His publications include *From Puritanism to the Age of Reason*, *Puritanism in the Period of the Great Persecution*, *Reason and Authority in the Eighteenth Century*, and *The Cambridge Platonists*.

GERALD R. CRAGG

The Church
and the Age of Reason
1648–1789

PENGUIN BOOKS

PENGUIN BOOKS

Published by the Penguin Group
Penguin Books Ltd, 27 Wrights Lane, London W8 5TZ, England
Penguin Books USA Inc., 375 Hudson Street, New York, New York 10014, USA
Penguin Books Australia Ltd, Ringwood, Victoria, Australia
Penguin Books Canada Ltd, 10 Alcorn Avenue, Toronto, Ontario, Canada M4V 3B2
Penguin Books (NZ) Ltd, 182–190 Wairau Road, Auckland 10, New Zealand

Penguin Books Ltd, Registered Offices: Harmondsworth, Middlesex, England

First published in Pelican Books 1960
Reprinted with revisions 1967, 1970
Reprinted in Penguin Books 1990
5 7 9 10 8 6 4

Printed in England by Clays Ltd, St Ives plc
Set in Monotype Baskerville

The Penguin History of the Church

(formerly *The Pelican History of the Church*)

GENERAL EDITOR: OWEN CHADWICK

1. *The Early Church*. By Sir Henry Chadwick, Honorary Fellow and former Master of Peterhouse, Cambridge and Regius Professor Emeritus of Divinity, Cambridge University.
2. *Western Society and the Church in the Middle Ages*. By Sir Richard Southern, formerly President of St John's College, Oxford.
3. *The Reformation*. By Owen Chadwick, Chancellor of the University of East Anglia and former Regius Professor of Modern History, Cambridge University.
4. *The Church and the Age of Reason, 1648–1789*. By Gerald R. Cragg, formerly Professor of Church History at Andover Newton Theological School, Boston, Massachusetts.
5. *The Church in an Age of Revolution*. By Alec R. Vidler, formerly Fellow and Dean of King's College, Cambridge.
6. *A History of Christian Missions*. By Stephen Neill, formerly Professor of Philosophy and Religious Studies at the University of Nairobi and Assistant Bishop in the Diocese of Oxford.
7. *The Christian Church in the Cold War*. By Owen Chadwick, Chancellor of the University of East Anglia and former Regius Professor of Modern History, Cambridge University.

CONTENTS

 1. Introduction: The New Age   9
 2. The Church Life of France under Louis XIV, 1648–1715   17
 3. The New Age and Its Thought: 1648–1715   37
 4. Restoration and Revolution in England, 1660–1714   50
 5. The Watershed in English Thought, 1660–1714   65
 6. Covenanters and Moderates in Scotland   81
 7. Germany: Orthodoxy, Pietism, and Rationalism   93
 8. Russia and the Eastern Churches   107
 9. The Hanoverian Age in England   117
10. Methodism and the Evangelical Revival   141
11. England: The Rise and Fall of the Cult of Reason   157
12. Christianity in the New World   174
13. The Church in France, 1715–89   193
14. Church and State in the Age of the Enlightened Despots 209
15. The High Noon of Rationalism, and Beyond   234
16. Christianity and Culture in the Baroque Age   256
17. Epilogue   279
    BIBLIOGRAPHICAL NOTE   285
    INDEX   289

1

Introduction: The New Age

THE Peace of Westphalia (1648) ended a generation of war and a century of strife. It was the end, not only of the Thirty Years War, but of religious wars in general. During the next century and a half the peace of Europe was often broken; there was warfare among the nations but religion seldom provided the pretext. The failure of Louis XIV to keep a Catholic dynasty on the throne of England was a belated postscript to the era of religious struggles. Both sides forswore propaganda by the sword, and henceforth doctrinal disputes were settled within states, not between them. Consequently matters of faith ceased to be an important irritant in international affairs. Pope Innocent X objected to the clauses of the treaty which affected Catholics, and registered his protest in the Brief *Zelo Domus Dei*. He pronounced the clauses 'null and void, accursed and without any influence or result for the past, the present, or the future'. But rhetoric is easier to command than respect. Europe paid no attention to his outburst; political problems, it was apparent, could now be settled without reference to the opinions of ecclesiastics and theologians. The pope's influence had dwindled to the point where he could no longer effectively participate in the political affairs of western Europe. In Germany he was treated as a foreign potentate; the Inquisition excluded him from direct participation in the affairs of Spain; in France Mazarin carefully kept him at a distance. His deposing power was extinct. His interdicts had become so ineffective that he dared not use them. The new period therefore opens with the international prestige of institutional religion in eclipse. In matters of belief the Peace acknowledged within each state the increased power of the secular prince. As religious sanctions lost their authority, the law of nations correspondingly increased in prestige. The work initiated by Hugo Grotius was continued and expanded by Samuel Pufendorf; it was generally conceded that the relations between sovereign states must be subject to control, but the principles which the new period invoked were more secular than those which had served an earlier age.

Religious differences no longer justified contention between nations. They ceased to divide fellow citizens to the degree that had once been universal. An increasing tolerance was characteristic of the age. This was not always or immediately apparent. Hungary rescinded lenient regulations and replaced them with punitive measures against dissent. Louis XIV revoked the Edict of Nantes, the safeguard of Huguenot liberties, and attempted to create religious uniformity in France. When the French seized the Palatinate, they subjected the Calvinists to such ruthless pressure that neighbouring Protestant princes threatened reprisals against their Catholic subjects unless Louis desisted. The Archbishop of Salzburg expelled some 15,000 Protestants from his principality. In Switzerland religious strife continued until the Peace of Aarau (1712). Suspicion persisted long after violence subsided, but the nature of the problem changed. Religious rivalry became a factor in the complex task of maintaining a balance of political power between contending groups. In England the failure of persecution, reinforced by powerful political considerations, led to a policy of modified toleration. Henceforth, when repression was applied, the motive was more often political than religious. In many countries heresy was still a punishable offence, but by the beginning of the eighteenth century erroneous beliefs were more often ignored than penalized. Toleration might seem insecure, but the persecuting spirit was ineffectively though sometimes fervently invoked. In most countries religious hostilities gave way to a growing awareness of class divisions. Occasionally social distinctions corresponded to denominational cleavages. In England the alliance of squire and parson tightened, and nonconformity was largely restricted to the middle classes. Elsewhere the divisions in society were often reflected in the life of the church. By interest and outlook the French hierarchy was more closely linked with the upper classes than with the lower orders of the priesthood, while the country clergy were increasingly sensitive and sympathetic to the aspirations of the common people.

Stability was at a premium. The turmoil of the decades before 1648 consolidated the desire for peace. Louis XIV's ambitions were considered dangerous because they threatened to disrupt the balance of power and shatter the security so precariously maintained. In the second part of our period (1715–89), the quest for stability was pursued consistently and with reasonable success. The policies of Walpole in England and of Dubois and Fleury in France afforded Europe one of its longest intervals of unbroken peace. This prevailing attitude affected the way in which the church and its task were regarded. The general temper of the times encouraged men to seek a comfortable and prosperous life, enlightened in outlook yet buttressed by traditional authority. It was natural to invoke the support of the church for the existing order. In stable times religious institutions are usually conservative in attitude; they readily become the guardians of established ways. In the eighteenth century they were deeply involved in the structure of society. Stability was as necessary to the churches as to the nobles or the peasants. Ecclesiastical income came from semi-feudal dues such as tithes, and social disruption was certain to result in serious loss. Yet the ideal of a corporate life which this view presupposed was beginning to crumble. It was assumed that the proper way to deal with needy persons was to reintegrate them in the common life, but the theory was increasingly difficult to apply. Though the church was still the principal agent of social welfare, it could no longer meet the demands which were laid upon it. In France its work in education and in health was exposed to mounting criticism. It was everywhere powerless to remedy the basic needs of the peasants when the dislocations of capitalist agriculture overwhelmed them.

One of the chief issues confronting the age was the problem of authority, and it affected the church at every turn.

The relations of church and state were settled in a way uniformly unfavourable to the church. The Erastianism of Hanoverian England kept the church in decorous subjection. Elsewhere its independence was more openly curtailed. Rulers interfered in its affairs, expropriated its wealth, and altered the structure of its life. In Roman Catholic countries the ties with Rome were deliberately relaxed. The movement in favour of national churches, dependent on the curia in name alone, made considerable headway. In some of the autocracies, the church was reduced to the status of a department of state.

The authority of the church was challenged in many spheres, but nowhere so seriously as in the intellectual realm. The new psychology, which described the human mind as a blank sheet of paper on which experience inscribed knowledge, was an attack on the view long current in the church. The veiled suggestion that ethical culture was an adequate substitute for Christian faith was an indirect assault on the church's authority. People wanted freedom to think and act as they pleased. To Voltaire and those who shared his views, the Enlightenment offered emancipation from 'prone submission to the heavenly will'. Liberty was interpreted in many ways, but it was assumed that it conferred at least the right to take your religion moderately. At first, avowed attacks on authority were rare. In his early works Voltaire refrained from explicit reflections on either church or government, but his praise of Quaker resistance to both dispelled any doubt about his meaning. Traditional authority was also weakened by the oblique criticism of men like Pierre Bayle. The exaggerated deference paid to Newtonian physics had a similar effect. Soon the bolder spirits found this cautious approach to authority too diffident. Attacks became more avowed and more venomous. The leaders of enlightened thought grew more outspoken in their criticisms of the church and its faith. And when the arrogance of rationalism finally provoked a reaction, the alternative was not necessarily any more favourable to Christianity. Rousseau, it has been said, invented nothing but set everything ablaze. The champions of Enlightenment began by advocating stability; they ended by ushering in the French Revolution.

The fascination of this period lies primarily in the intellectual developments which it witnessed. By the middle of the seventeenth century we stand on the threshold of the modern world. The issues which occupied men's minds and the spirit in which they were debated carry us from an atmosphere still predominantly medieval to one which is essentially modern. Science registered dramatic triumphs, and by the end of the eighteenth century educated people everywhere accepted the Newtonian interpretation of nature. The working of the human mind had been explored by Locke in a way that seemed both satisfying and exciting. Locke believed that God is the ultimate source of wisdom and authority, and regarded Christian morality as a supremely wise and rational code of conduct. Of greater significance, however, was his conviction that reason teaches us to understand the law which governs nature and unfolds the pattern of belief which a thoughtful man can derive from it. Locke did not challenge the need or the value of revelation, but the relative position he assigned it implies that it confirms what can be appropriated in other ways. Locke's successors made explicit what is latent in his thought. The role of reason was magnified, that of revelation was depressed. The scriptures were subjected to intensive and often to unsympathetic scrutiny. Miracles were challenged. Prophecy was reassessed. Christian thought faced a threat which might have stripped it of all its uniqueness and its authority. In this struggle lies the perennial interest of this period. At the outset the new thought was cordially disposed toward the Christian faith. Gradually the balance shifted from what God has revealed to what man has discovered. In due course the sufficiency of reason was confidently affirmed, and the whole content of Biblical theology was relegated to a marginal status of comparative insignificance. In England the challenge was met with vigour and determination. A series of able writers demonstrated that the church could still out-think its critics, and the works of Berkeley and Butler occupy an honoured place in the history of English thought. In any case, the challenge of reason proved self-destructive. Hume showed that extreme rationalism leads to complete scepticism. In philosophy a new approach to the problem had to be discovered. Meanwhile Wesley shattered the facile supposition that religion is merely an intellectual hypothesis. He recalled men to the fact that faith is a divine power, and one which can transform human lives.

On the continent the pattern was slightly different. English thought – particularly the physics of Newton and the psychology of Locke – became part of the intellectual background of the age. The cosmopolitanism of the eighteenth century is shown in the international status of certain basic convictions. Many of them were derived from the English Deists. The typical cosmopolitan was Voltaire, who popularized a view of reason which had been largely discredited in the country of its origin. Faith in reason might appear to be an epitome of eighteenth-century thought, but its very confidence provoked a reaction. Rousseau and the romantics repudiated the desiccated intellectualism of the rationalists, but the new emphasis was as dangerous to the faith as the old. On the continent the reply to unbelief was more hesitant than in England. The French apologists were unconvincing, and by their attitude most churchmen showed that they were primarily interested in other things. In Germany, the evangelical movement known as Pietism proved that arid rationalism and a bleak type of scholastic orthodoxy were not the only alternatives open to man's inquiring spirit. Admittedly it failed to combine zeal and intelligence in a way satisfying to both, and consequently it bequeathed to the next century the fundamental problems with which it would have to wrestle. In Immanuel Kant, however, Germany produced a thinker uniquely qualified both to epitomize the age which was ending and to anticipate that which was to come.

Reason and authority represent one kind of tension, 'enthusiasm' and 'formalism' another. The period began in reaction against the kind of zeal which had hitherto produced uninterrupted turmoil. Civilized man, it was assumed, would be wise to adhere to his beliefs sedately and in a reasonable spirit. Pope's famous line reflects the basic conviction of the age: 'For modes of faith let graceless zealots fight.' 'Enthusiasm' was equated with fanaticism, and was everywhere suspect. But fortunately ardour could not always and everywhere be suppressed. Thus we have a succession of movements which prove that, beneath the sophisticated surface of the Age of Reason, zeal still survived. The Jansenists in France stood opposed to the Jesuitism so popular in high places. Quietism was a mystical protest against excessively intellectual ways of apprehending the divine. In England the sobriety of Augustan Anglicanism confronted first the dwindling ardours of later Puritanism, then the fresh zeal of early Methodism. In Germany the pietistic spirit reacted against the rigidities of Lutheran orthodoxy.

It is clearly a grave injustice to treat this period as the preserve of a dull and prosaic Christianity. It is equally foolish to ignore its manifest defects. Reform was an urgent need, but the attempts to achieve it usually failed. The power to make necessary changes was lacking. Glaring weaknesses in its organization hindered the English Church from fulfilling its mission. In the Restoration era the predominant desire was to return to the situation which the Puritans had so rudely disrupted and even a suggestion of change seemed treasonable. When Hanoverian times awakened thoughtful men to the need of modifying the existing system, politicians refused to run the risks of any kind of change. Ecclesiastical life was so intimately intertwined with the structure of politics that few who occupied the places of power were willing to alter a system wherein the very defects proved convenient. No one gave more than a passing thought to the plight of the church, and when the French Revolution broke up the European scene, the very mention of reform became abhorrent. In France the most urgent political and fiscal changes were blocked by interest and inertia. When the state could not save itself, it is scarcely surprising that the church, tied to a disintegrating system, was blind to the need for change.

Only when an autocratic ruler decided that enlightened absolutism presupposed reform did it prove possible to modify the structure of the church. The programme which Joseph II initiated in Austria is the best example of what this approach to the problem could accomplish. It is also the best explanation of why such changes were so ephemeral.

The period from the Peace of Westphalia to the French Revolution was not a heroic age. Nevertheless it included many figures who command our genuine respect. During its course many of the important movements in modern Christianity have their rise, and many of the problems which distinguish the modern era first assume their familiar form. Here is the key to much that has happened since, and to many of the issues which still confront us.

2

The Church Life of France
under Louis XIV,
1648–1715

THE second half of the seventeenth century was the Age of
Louis XIV. He established a new type of kingship, absolute
in power and resplendent in dignity. In subtle ways he
created the atmosphere which pervaded Europe, and the
standards which he established profoundly affected the life
of the church.

His personal rule did not coincide with his reign. When
he came to the throne he was a minor, and power rested in
other hands. Cardinal Mazarin was the dominant influence
in the state, pursuing with skilful persistence the policies
inaugurated by his great predecessor, Cardinal Richelieu.
The Peace of Westphalia crowned Mazarin's efforts, but for
a decade the full fruits of victory were withheld. By 1659,
however, he had achieved his purpose; at home he had laid
the foundations of royal supremacy, and abroad he had
humbled the Catholic empire of Spain. Neither of the great
churchmen who directed the destinies of France allowed his
religious convictions to dictate his foreign policies. Both
believed that at home there must be an end to attempts to
use religious loyalties to create a state within the state.
Richelieu curbed the power of the French Protestants by
stripping them of some of their constitutional safeguards.
Disunity was rife within the Catholic Church; Richelieu
aimed to create a uniformity which would subject all reforming impulses to royal control. Mazarin consolidated
what his predecessor had done. Thus the lines along which
policy might develop had been clearly indicated; it remained
for the king to show what he could achieve.

In 1659 Louis XIV came of age. Two years later, Mazarin

died and the king announced that henceforth he himself
would direct national affairs. The religious history of his
reign reflects the consequences of his exalted view of royal
authority. The king was absolute. National strength demanded unity; this presupposed uniformity, and consequently dissent could not be tolerated. So the Protestants
were repressed, and royal policy achieved a Pyrrhic victory
in the revocation of the Edict of Nantes.[1] The king's authority embraced every aspect of the nation's life; the church
was not exempt, and rival pretensions to authority over it
would need to be closely scrutinized and if necessary resisted.
So came the renascence of Gallicanism, with the consequent
tensions between the king and the pope.

Political considerations might have suggested to Louis that
his Protestant subjects could profitably be left in peace. The
Huguenots had once been a serious problem, but they had
lost the political aspirations and the aristocratic alliances
which had formerly made them so formidable. In 1662,
Louis acknowledged that they had given incontestable proof
of 'their affection and fidelity'. They were no longer a
menace to the Catholic Church. Some of their pastors were
able orators and learned scholars, but few were conspicuous
for proselytizing zeal. Moreover, the Huguenots had shown
that they were an economic force of great importance.
Instead of being encouraged or even tolerated, they were
subjected to increasingly severe persecution. This was a
reversal of the policy which had served France so well in the
past, which had brought her diplomatic advantages and
commercial benefits, and had placed her in the forefront of
European progress. It was at variance with the trends which
would characterize the new age. The responsibility for the
change lay in part with the king himself. His theory of
government made it impossible to treat dissent as unimportant; he believed that national strength demanded a unified

1. The edict which closed the French Wars of Religion in 1598, allow-
ing the Protestants to exercise their religion in certain places, giving them
full civic equality with Catholics, and certain garrison towns as safeguards
within the constitution.

people with a single official faith. The disposition of the king was strongly fortified by the desires of the church. The Catholic Church in France seemed to be at the peak of its power. Its clergy were eminent for eloquence, learning, zeal, even for social sympathies. But they regarded the continued existence of the Huguenots as an affront. They had always resented the Edict of Nantes, which was the charter of the Protestants' rights. The higher clergy were engaged in intermittent controversy with the papacy about their distinctive privileges, and found it desirable to emphasize their anti-Protestant zeal. Here the king assured his bishops of his support; he, too, had his differences with Rome; each could encourage the other by attacking Protestant pretensions.

At the outset the king and his clergy merely proposed that the Edict of Nantes should be interpreted in the most stringent sense and its benefits curtailed as severely as possible. The church asked, not that 'Protestantism be crushed by a single blow', but that 'it should be enfeebled and gradually starved by the retrenchment of its liberties'. As a first step, the assembly of the clergy suggested in 1660 that commissioners be appointed to investigate the administration of the Edict, and from that point onward the liberties of the Edict were steadily removed. Each year some ancient privilege was rescinded, some new burden imposed. In 1666 a royal edict set forth in some sixty clauses the various ways in which Protestants could be harassed. Scarcely an aspect of their life remained untouched. Conversions to Catholicism were encouraged by a variety of expedients. Economic inducements were offered to those who apostasized. Protestants were excluded even from the humblest grades of government service. All the while the king solemnly affirmed that the essential provisions of the Edict of Nantes remained unchanged. If his policy was creating concern at home, it was causing consternation abroad. Colbert warned him of the serious economic results that would follow. The Great Elector of Brandenburg registered a vigorous protest. For the moment Louis called a halt; he even revoked the edict of

1666. But the harrying of Protestants continued, and daily their insecurity became more manifest.

Ten years later Louis reverted to his repressive policy. He was free from foreign distractions, and his outlook was insensibly changing. The influence of Mme de Maintenon (subsequently his unofficial wife) fortified the vein of superstitious zeal in his character. His private morals improved; the gaiety and splendour of his court gave way to a sedate preoccupation with religious observances. The king had much to atone for; as a contemporary remarked, he was eager 'to do penance for his own sins on the backs of the Jansenists and the Huguenots'. Since his conversion had 'no root in reason and bore no fruit in charity', there was nothing to halt his progress as a persecutor, and he eagerly advanced toward one of the political blunders of his reign. Measures against the Huguenots increased in number and in severity. Their facilities for public worship were drastically curtailed. Their share of the burden of taxation was sharply increased. Their ministers could live only in certain places and for limited periods. Endowments given for the support of their poor were seized for the benefit of Catholic institutions. Their hospitals, schools, and colleges were closed. Their churches, in great numbers, were destroyed. Their members were barred from the learned professions. Homes were invaded on the pretext that children (who were thereupon abducted) wished to become Catholics. Restrictions on personal freedom were more vexatious than the destruction of property; both culminated in the infamous *dragonnades*. Soldiers quartered on Protestants were allowed a latitude which made ruin or even death the only alternatives to conversion. Thousands gave verbal adhesion to the Catholic faith. Those who were able to flee sought refuge abroad, and the great exodus of Huguenots began.

In theory the Edict of Nantes was still law; the enactments, nearly two hundred in number, which had been passed during the last twenty years, merely clarified the manner of its operation. Every influence in high circles now encouraged Louis to take the final step. He was assured that few Protestants persisted in their heresy; one more effort, declared the Jesuit Maimbourg, and 'the disastrous conflagration which has wrought such ruin in France and of which little more than the smoke remains, will soon be utterly extinguished'. The king was eager to be convinced, and in 1685 revoked the Edict of Nantes. All the remaining privileges of the Huguenots were rescinded. Their ministers were exiled, but lay people attempting to leave the country were subject to the severest penalties. Those who quietly submitted, it was said, would not be disturbed. But such assurances proved valueless. The *dragonnades* were revived. Multitudes were sent to the galleys. In spite of all precautions, thousands escaped to other lands. Goaded beyond endurance, the Huguenots of the south rose in rebellion; for twenty years the fighting in the Cévennes valleys distracted France's concentration from other objectives and drained away her resources.

While the existence of Protestantism challenged the king's authority at one point, the claims of the pope challenged it at another. Absolutism could not tolerate dissent nor acquiesce in intervention by a foreign power. The pope was an Italian prince as well as a spiritual leader. What kind of authority could he exercise over the French church? The form which the Roman primacy had assumed inevitably aggravated in all Catholic countries the problem of the relation of church and state. In France it was further complicated by a body of traditions and convictions known as Gallicanism. The antecedents of Gallicanism can be traced back to the Middle Ages, and parallel manifestations can be found in many other countries. France was unique not only by virtue of her strength and her pre-eminence, but also because of the type of relationship which still prevailed between the national church and the Roman see. Elsewhere the challenge posed by the Reformation had promoted centralization; local autonomy usually resisted it, but for most of the Roman Catholic world the canons of the Council of Trent had given authoritative sanction to this trend. In France, however,

only the doctrinal findings of that Council had been accepted, and the relations of church and state were still
governed by the Concordat of 1516. Though the Concordat
still guided the relations between France and the papacy, it
reflected an outmoded state of affairs, which elsewhere the
church was ceasing to sanction.

By the middle of the seventeenth century it was clear that
the issue was certain to increase in gravity. As soon as
Louis XIV assumed control of national affairs, he showed
that he regarded the church as an appropriate instrument
for advancing his political ambitions. A ruler who claimed
unlimited authority regarded Gallicanism as an appropriate
theory for regulating ecclesiastical affairs. In addition, public
opinion welcomed a new emphasis on the rights and dignities of the French Church. The unification of the country
under Bourbon rule had intensified national pride; a heightened self-consciousness within the church inevitably followed.

Gallicanism was a theory admirably adapted to existing
needs. Behind it lay the force of a strong tradition, yet it had
not been too rigidly defined. It took its stand on 'the Gallican Liberties' – certain ancient rights in which Frenchmen
took a patriotic pride. These 'liberties' stipulated that papal
bulls might enter France only with the permission of the
Crown; that judicial decisions of the Vatican had no legal
force in France; that French subjects could not be cited
before a Roman tribunal; and that the civil courts of France
could legitimately deal with church affairs whenever the
laws of the land appeared to be infringed. Gallicanism,
however, was much more than a reaffirmation of customary
Privileges. It owed part of its appeal to a reaction against
the centralizing tendencies at work in the Roman Church.
Ultramontanism seemed to many Frenchmen to be his-
torically indefensible and theologically unsound. It also
threatened to produce administrative changes of a revolutionary character: Frenchmen had been accustomed to
settling their ecclesiastical disputes at home, and they believed that their own courts could handle such matters more

wisely and effectively than a foreign tribunal which commanded little confidence. Moreover, Roman theologians
like Bellarmine had linked papal infallibility with a body of
political theory which many Frenchmen intensely disliked.
The Ultramontanes affirmed that the interests of the church
took precedence of all others; since the pope was the only
judge of such matters, he could override the will of all temporal rulers whenever church affairs were at stake. Gallicanism, therefore, naturally developed a two-fold emphasis.
Theologically it declared that the infallible authority of the
church was not committed to the pope alone, but was vested
jointly in the pope and the bishops, and that consequently
the final decision lay with a general council. Politically it
denied the right of the pope to interfere with the temporal
rights of sovereign rulers, no matter how serious the provoca-
tion might be. This led naturally to a reaffirmation of the
divine right of kings, a doctrine which Bossuet set forth with
great cogency in France. Gallicanism was thus a position
which could be held in a variety of ways. The French
bishops were primarily concerned to defend the collective
mind of the church, and to protect the autonomy of the
national church against an autocratic and infallible papacy.
The *parlements*, with their strong legal bent, were determined
to prevent the intrusion of an alien authority. But the lines of
demarcation were never rigidly drawn. In spite of attempts
to make Gallicanism a unified and comprehensive doctrine,
reconciling the duties of the good citizen and the good
Catholic, it was usually held with primary emphasis on one
aspect or the other. Indeed, some of the French Jesuits
showed that under the influence of national and patriotic
fervour it was possible to be an Ultramontane in theology
and a Gallican in political theory. The absence of sharp
definition suggests that Gallicanism should be regarded as
an atmosphere rather than as a system.

In the latter part of the seventeenth century, an infallible
papacy faced an absolute monarchy; the theoretical claims
of both had been hardening, and conflicts were bound to
arise. Some of these were relatively trivial in character,

some were precipitated by the overweening pride and autocratic methods of Louis XIV. The crucial dispute of the reign concerned the 'regale' – the royal right to the temporalities of a vacant see. What might seem a simple claim had been magnified by generations of crown lawyers into an extreme and extensive system. The issue became acute because Louis, in the interests of absolutism and uniformity, wished to extend the 'regale' to the sees of provinces which he had added to the possessions of the Crown. Bishops who had hitherto been exempt from this imposition protested and appealed to the pope. In 1681, the assembly of the French clergy conceded Louis' claims, and extended the 'regale' to all his domains. When the pope ignored this action, the king temporarily shifted his ground, and demanded that his clergy define more explicitly the position of the Gallican Church. The result was the formulation of the famous Four Articles of 1682: (1) the pope has no power in temporal matters; (2) general councils are superior to the pope in spiritual affairs; (3) the generally accepted laws of the French church are inviolable, and the papacy must conform to them; (4) in matters of faith, the pope's decisions become irreversible only when ratified by a general council. These affirmations were set forth with all the grandiloquence that Bossuet could impart to them, and Louis at once commanded that they be accepted by the clergy and constitute a part of the education of the French priesthood. As a result Frenchmen increasingly invested the king with the quasi-divine authority which he claimed, and in the process the political theory characteristic of the *ancien régime* steadily assumed more explicit form. Moreover the rift between the king and the pope inevitably widened. The pope refused to yield, and retaliated by declining to institute the new bishops whom the king appointed. In exasperation Louis seriously toyed with the idea of a schism. In 1689, however, his bitter antagonist, Innocent XI, died. The new pope was prepared to be conciliatory and the king had no desire to be permanently at enmity with the head of the Church. Louis had good reason to welcome a *rapprochement*. He faced the cumulative results of serious reverses abroad, and needed to strengthen his position by means of any alliances he could make. In 1693 he capitulated. The Gallican articles were revoked, but with a secrecy in marked contrast with the fanfare which had marked their promulgation. Indeed, they were withdrawn so unostentatiously that they continued to represent the convictions of many Frenchmen, and throughout the eighteenth century Gallicanism remained a force in French life.

As far as a fuller elaboration of theory was concerned, the reign of Louis did little to resolve the ambiguities which beset the relations of church and state. But the practical application of Gallicanism was always apt to outstrip its theoretical development, and in seventeenth-century France the doctrine tended to be a decent cloak for the determination of an autocratic monarchy to treat the church as a department of state. Louis regarded the clergy as civil servants. He expected them to be subservient to his wishes, and he had the power to make and keep them so. He could reward the deserving with comfortable sinecures; he could ruin the recalcitrant by burdening their revenues with pensions for his courtiers.

If Gallicanism sought to safeguard the autonomy of the church of France, Jansenism sought to achieve its purification. The latter controversy was more complex than the former, both in its causes and throughout its course; it was even more productive of passion and of lasting bitterness. It arose out of the writings of Cornelius Jansen (d. 1638), a Dutch theologian who was Bishop of Ypres at the time of his death. He was appalled at the aridity of prevailing systems of theology. He contended that the stoical self-sufficiency which marked most popular morality ignored the helplessness of man and forgot his absolute dependence on his Maker. The ceremonialism which was rampant in the church merely hid from the people the essential fact that a man can be saved only through the love of God creating faith. This love becomes effective through conversion, and conversion is dependent on the good pleasure of God. Thus

Jansen's teaching on grace implied the doctrine of pre-destination. Vehement in opposing Jesuitism, he was no less emphatic in repudiating Protestantism. He was seeking a Christian position which would be genuinely 'evangelical but not Protestant, Catholic but not Jesuitical'. He found his inspiration in St Augustine, whose doctrine of grace had been obscured by the medieval preoccupation with merit. Into his work *Augustinus* (1640), he distilled a lifetime of thought and study.

Though Jansenism was an active force in the Low Countries, it achieved its greatest influence in France. An intimate friend of Jansen, du Vergier, Abbot of St Cyran, popularized its views, among which he particularly stressed the love of God and man's need of conversion. Even more important than his teaching was his gift of enlisting able disciples. He attracted several members of the brilliant legal family of Arnauld. Through Angélique Arnauld, Prioress of Port Royal, Jansenism established its intimate connexion with this famous nunnery.

The Jansenist controversy thus began with a particular doctrine of grace (theologically a complex question) and involved the baffling mysteries of election and predestination. But it was not enthusiasm for such abstract matters that explains the furore which Jansenism created. Gallican clergy, the higher nobility – even at court – and men of learning were drawn within the orbit of the party. Morally its impact was powerful. In a corrupt period it was austere and stringent in its demands; in a servile age it maintained a dignified self-respect; at a time when conformity was a passion, it remained a body of independent opinion, as feared as it was formidable. To such a group the government of Louis XIV could not remain indifferent.

Yet the actual controversy was little concerned with the things to which Jansenism owed its true appeal. By 1648, the doctrinal issue had been effectually obscured. It is true that five propositions taken from the *Augustinus* were censured in 1649 by the Sorbonne, and were forwarded to Rome for condemnation. The general tenor of these propositions reflected a twofold emphasis detected in Jansenist teaching by its critics: (1) without the assistance of a special grace from God, men cannot perform his commandments; (2) the operation of grace is irresistible, and men are therefore subject to a determinism either of a natural or supernatural kind, though neither is violently coercive in character. Latent in these was a theological pessimism repugnant to the dominant schools of thought. But theological considerations had already yielded place to others. A consistently important element in the conflict was the opposition between the Jesuits and the Jansenists. Antoine Arnauld, for many years the foremost leader of the Jansenist party, had attacked Jesuit methods in a particularly damaging way. In addition, the contestants were drawn into a struggle in the Sorbonne between the members of the 'regular' and the 'secular' clergy – i.e., between those who were members of the religious orders and those who were not. Gallicanism and Jansenism became intertwined in various ways. To complicate the situation, the papacy was not primarily concerned about the theological aspect of the matter. Seventeenth-century popes often gave the impression that they were more interested in power than in doctrine, and Alexander VII in particular was anxious to assert and confirm his authority. Almost from the outset, therefore, partisan and political prejudices eclipsed the genuine religious concerns and embittered the controversy. For the space of nearly twenty years hardly a month passed without some clash between the Jesuits and their civil and ecclesiastical allies on the one hand, and 'the defenders of grace' on the other. Then, after a brief interval, the struggle was resumed, and continued through most of the eighteenth century.

The course which the debates assumed threw the Jansenists on the defensive; for years Antoine Arnauld and his colleagues conducted a skilful rearguard action. The Jansenist position was tactically strong, since it could not readily be overthrown; it was morally weak, since it bore little relation to the fundamental religious concerns of its adherents. Its opponents had seized on certain heretical propositions

assumed to be found in the *Augustinus*; but were they? This
apparently simple question of fact was capable of almost
endless debate. Were the offending words used in the book
in the sense that their critics assumed? And was this really
a matter for papal definition? The Jansenists had suffered a
serious reverse when the Sorbonne condemned the propositions. In due course, Arnauld's opponents decided to deprive him of his university degrees. They succeeded, but
their manoeuvre precipitated the intervention of the man
who immortalized the controversy. Pascal's *Provincial Letters*
originated in an attempt to fend off Arnauld's deprivation,
but they widened into an attack on the whole system of
moral casuistry practised by the Jesuits. The brilliance of the
Letters, their union of devastating wit and intense moral
earnestness, created a profound effect. The Jesuits and their
sympathizers claimed that Pascal was not properly qualified
for the task he had undertaken; he had been furnished with
extracts from works of casuistry (i.e., on the way to resolve
moral problems) but he did not understand the basic principles of moral theology. But the practice of the Jesuits had
made them vulnerable to attack, and a system which
offends a sensitive conscience cannot hope to be exonerated
by an appeal to a complex theory. As far as the cultured
public was concerned, the *Letters* brought irrevocable discredit on the Jesuits.

The fate of Jansenism was decided, however, in a very
different court of appeal. The alliance of the French crown,
the papal curia, and the Society of Jesus proved decisive. In
1660, the period of persecution began. Louis XIV instructed
the General Assembly of the Clergy to devise a means of
extirpating the heresy. Early in the following year the clergy
suggested that the holding of any benefice in France should
be made conditional upon the signing of a formula con-
demning the five crucial propositions. Every attempt was
made to circumvent the wiles of the Jansenists and to evade
the intricate 'questions of fact or of law'. Many of the
Jansenist leaders went into hiding, the nuns of Port Royal
were exposed to the full fury of official displeasure. There is

probably no parallel in monastic history to their resistance, on a doctrinal issue, to their bishop, to the clergy of their national church, to their king, and to the pope; but it has been remarked with equal truth that there is no precedent for the attempt to make doctrinal heresy depend on the question whether or not certain words could be interpreted as conveying a certain meaning when found in a certain book.

The king discovered that his wrath, though unbounded, was not irresistible. In 1665 he turned to the pope. Alexandder VII, who had suffered many things at Louis' hands, seized his opportunity. The Constitution (*Regiminis apostolici*) which he issued treated the dispute as purely one of insubordination towards the Holy See, and the formulary it imposed was framed in appropriate terms. The complex interrelation of the various problems of this period is reflected in the fact that four bishops who had resisted the king on the 'regale' were equally resolute in opposing the pope.

The year 1668 brought a lull in the controversy. Careful negotiation devised formulas by which those who had resisted either the pope or the king could submit with dignity. The agreement initiated a decade of comparative calm known as the 'Peace of the Church' (1669-79). Many women of high social standing were drawn to Port Royal. But the 'peace' was at best precarious, and it was not permanent. Death robbed the nunnery of some of its most effective protectors, Louis' zeal for orthodoxy rekindled his anger against Jansenism, and the position of Port Royal became increasingly insecure. But Jansenism, though quiescent, was by no means dead. Quesnel's *Réflexions morales* – a most popular work by one of the leaders of the party – helped to keep it alive, and round this book the defenders' intrigues began to thicken. Early in the eighteenth century, a tactless academic question precipitated an explosion. A Jansenist posed to the Sorbonne the problem whether the condemnation against the *Augustinus* might be received with 'respectful silence'. This implied a passive outward acquiescence in a law which might inwardly be repudiated as wrong. The whole controversy erupted with astonishing violence. Louis proposed to the pope that they should collaborate in eradicating Jansenism for ever. In 1705, accordingly, Clement XI explicitly condemned 'respectful silence'. The king proceeded to further severities. The nunnery of Port Royal was desecrated. Nor was this enough. As foreign disasters multiplied upon the king, his zeal became a kind of superstitious frenzy. He again sought the assistance of the pope, this time against Quesnel's *Réflexions*. In 1713 appeared the famous Bull *Unigenitus*, which condemned over a hundred propositions culled from the work. A more drastic condemnation of everything that Jansenism had ever advocated could scarcely be conceived, but the severity of the Bull aroused a corresponding reaction. Fénelon, who approved of *Unigenitus*, admitted that many Frenchmen believed that it condemned St Augustine, St Paul, and even Jesus Christ himself. The Bible-reading which Bossuet had so carefully fostered was blighted by the Bull. And the wave of sympathy which it awakened meant that throughout the eighteenth century Jansenism persisted as a disturbing ferment in French life.

Jansenism began as a reaction against the Jesuits and all their ways. As a movement of protest it did not stand alone. The Jesuits were an aggressive body, and their vigour invited opposition. They were moulded by a discipline of military rigour, and were committed to explicit and practical objectives. They favoured a type of belief as precise and compelling as mathematical proof, and in their regulation of religious practice they exalted expediency above all other considerations. They pressed the plea of utility to the point where many theologians felt compelled to protest. The great controversy about the proper limits of utilitarianism concerned moral theory, and particularly the regulation of the confessional. What standards should priests apply to penitents? Should they be lax or stringent? The Jesuits argued for a flexible attitude; severity defeated its own ends by repelling those who needed the church – and who might in turn be useful to it. In urging confessors to be lenient, they appealed to the doctrine of Probabilism, which stipulated that a priest should grant absolution if there were any good grounds for doing so, even if there were also other and stronger reasons for refusing it. Such grounds required definition, and so there arose an elaborate system of casuistry, designed to shield the penitent from the confessor's zeal. 'Casuistry' was originally a word free of sinister implications; it owes its unhappy connotation to the methods advocated by the Jesuits. Their critics contended that the Jesuits debased morality: they encouraged people to take their standards ready-made from their confessors and to abandon the duty of facing their own responsibility, while the custodians of morals were compelled to adopt a lax view of Christian conduct. Prevailing tendencies were opposed to Jesuit theories. Dominican theologians had developed a counter theory (known as Probabiliorism) which stressed the duty of a stricter attitude. In 1665, 1666, and 1679 laxist views were condemned by the papacy. The Jesuits were commanded to permit in their seminaries both the criticism of their favoured position and the exposition of alternative views. In France the weight of theological opinion rallied behind the critics of Probabilism. Pascal was stern in his denunciations, and many others were equally severe. Bossuet was particularly cogent in his criticism, and his prestige invested his condemnation with immense authority. By the end of the century, the discredit of the system seemed to be virtually complete, and in 1700 the French clergy, led by Bossuet, formally censured Probabilism. This was not the end of the matter. Throughout much of the eighteenth century a bitter controversy raged between the Jesuits and the Dominicans, and subsequently a Probabilism with safeguards re-established itself as a dominant moral theory in the Roman Church. There seems little doubt, however, that in the reign of Louis XIV the controversy relaxed moral restraints at a time when the inducements to licentiousness were already strong.

By the end of the seventeenth century the cult of reason had made sufficient progress to warrant a protest. The formalism which had invaded religious practice and the ceremonialism which marked the worship of the age predisposed

dissatisfied souls to respond to the movement known as
Quietism. The mystical revival aroused considerable interest
in France, but its inspiration came from foreign sources. In
Spain the tradition of St Teresa was still strong, and something both of its teaching and of its atmosphere was carried
to Italy by Michael de Molinos. His activities aroused a
mixed response. The bishops, even the cardinals, were
divided in their attitude. The Jesuits vigorously attacked
Molinos' methods of spiritual direction. His personal morals
were not above reproach. His views were condemned by the
pope. He was arrested by the Inquisition; sixty-eight propositions from his works were condemned, and he was sentenced to perpetual imprisonment. But some of his books,
particularly his *Spiritual Guide*, were extremely popular. The
soul, he taught, attains Christian perfection when it is wholly
at rest in God. When it abandons all effort and resigns itself
to complete passivity, it loses itself in God, and takes no
interest in its own well-being.

This doctrine was introduced into France, and was expounded by a number of minor mystics. Certain convictions
were common to all the French Quietists. The believer, they
taught, must become a stranger to the world; then he would
experience the continual presence of God and live a life of
unbroken prayer. They found their incentive in disinterested
love of God, their method in the exaltation of passivity, their
goal in the abandonment of the will to God. Their contemplation was so inward and personal that they sometimes
appeared to undervalue the external proofs of Christian
life, even vocal prayer. They conceded to the church a
limited and temporary role; it could bring the soul to the
outer boundaries of Paradise, but those who aspired to true
holiness must look beyond its ministrations to a life of immediate fellowship with God. Such views were certain to
find critics as well as advocates. Under normal circumstances
Quietism would have caused scarcely a ripple on the surface
of French life; Mme Guyon gave it both notoriety and
importance.

This remarkable woman came of a good family and

possessed great personal charm; her critics claimed that she was also a person of undisciplined zeal and of unbalanced character. Her initial efforts were unquestionably indiscreet, but she soon showed that she could commend her views in high places. She won adherents at Court; she even gained the support of Fénelon. In her writings – particularly in her *Short and Easy Method of Prayer* (1685) – she elaborated her views. Contemplation, she claimed, was the essential activity of the Christian life. In rapt contemplation of God, the soul, losing all concern for its own well-being, grows indifferent alike to reprobation and to eternal felicity. There is no need to ponder the great truths of the Gospel, not even the life and death of our Saviour, since these are not the proper objects of pure contemplation. The one thing needful is to yield 'to the torrent of the forces of God'.

Such teachings could not pass unchallenged. Fénelon, who sympathized with her emphasis though he did not share all her views, invited Bossuet to pass judgement on her case. After an interview with Mme Guyon, Bossuet administered a stern warning. He was also the moving spirit in a commission of inquiry which condemned the teachings of Molinos and La Combe, and by implication those of Mme Guyon herself. Not content with this, he began a treatise which would indicate the proper limits of mysticism. But Fénelon anticipated him by publishing his *Explanation of the Maxims of the Saints* (1697). Fénelon was anxious to conserve the values in Quietism and to guard against its possible abuses. This, he felt, was not an impossible task. The two most distinguished leaders of the French Church were thus openly at variance on a doctrinal issue. Fénelon appealed to the pope, and the pope condemned his views, though in the mildest possible terms (1699). Fénelon at once submitted, and thereafter played little part in the public affairs of the Church.

Though this might seem a controversy of little consequence, its results were serious. It forms an excellent illustration of the complexity of religious issues under Louis XIV; Jansenism, Gallicanism, the rivalries of political parties, and the jealousies of factions at Court all became involved. Issues were blurred, and it became difficult to recognize their true character. The spectacle of an open breach between the two most honoured spiritual guides of the French episcopate confused the faithful and encouraged those who favoured greater laxity.

The age of Louis XIV was entangled in continuous theological debate, but an account of its controversies does not exhaust the record of its religious life. At the outset of the reign there was some disposition to look abroad for spiritual inspiration. Spanish and Italian schools of devotion had their disciples, but neither the torrid fervour of the one nor the sentimental dilettantism of the other accorded well with the cool and critical character of the mood which prevailed in France. But there were indigenous movements which were healthier in tone and far more permanent in their effect. St Vincent de Paul (d. 1660) was deeply distressed at the benighted condition of the country *curés*, and he founded the Lazarists (Priests of the Mission) to evangelize the neglected areas of France. Poverty and its consequences were prevalent in rural districts; to alleviate them he established the Sisters of Charity. In important respects he deviated from normal practice. Religious orders had usually demanded as large a measure of independence as they could achieve; St Vincent de Paul insisted that his workers be subject to the bishops. The conventual life, isolated from the world and devoted to prayer, had formed the accepted pattern for women with a religious bent; the Sisters of Charity were founded to work in close contact with their neighbours.

St Vincent de Paul was not alone in his concern for the training of the clergy. The need was great, and little had been done to meet it. The average *curé* was usually poor and often astonishingly ignorant: some did not even know the common formula of absolution. Those who desired a theological education had little chance of getting it. Theology was wholly ignored in most of the provincial universities, and diocesan seminaries, recent in origin, were still few in number. The

French Oratory had been founded to train clergy, but its distinction as a centre of learning restricted its wider effectiveness. It numbered among its members some scholars of great eminence, but it did not fulfil its founder's hope that it would help to train a better educated country clergy. The Congregation of Saint-Maur was a home of critical and historical studies, and Mabillon's labours in church history earned it a distinguished reputation, but it, too, was restricted in its scope. The task of educating the ordinary clergy was largely discharged by two orders founded in 1642 and 1643 – the Sulpicians and the Eudists. They emphasized piety, not learning, and they notably improved the standards of the priesthood. Similar to them in spirit, though committed to a different task, were the Christian Brothers (founded 1680) – an order of celibate laymen who provided teachers for the humblest type of school. The first half of the seventeenth century had seen the establishment of a variety of other orders; many of these were still in the first flush of their enthusiasm, and played an important role in the rejuvenation of church life.

No account of the age of Louis XIV could pretend to be complete if it ignored the influence of the leading preachers of the capital. Sermons were one of the few means of moulding public opinion; they were almost the only vehicle of criticism in matters of high public concern. This was not without its perils: the preacher was tempted to prostitute his pulpit to political ends, and even to use it for his personal advancement. In a self-conscious and literary age, sermons often became over-elaborate in structure and highly stylized in form. Prominent court preachers in particular sometimes subordinated their message to their method of presenting it. Such artificiality was attacked by St Vincent de Paul and by other leaders of the religious revival, and was rebuked by the example of Bossuet, one of the most splendid ornaments of the French pulpit. In his preaching, he aimed to combine theology and ethics in such a way that theory would fortify practice. A passion for the Gospel and a concern for Christian conduct were held in skilful equipoise, and both were reinforced by the magnificent rhetoric with which he clothed them. In the latter years of the reign, Bossuet seldom preached in Paris, and his place as the leading preacher of the capital was taken by the Jesuit Bourdaloue. It was of his sermons that Fénelon remarked that they were superb arguments about Christianity, but they were not religion.

3

The New Age and Its Thought:
1648–1715

THE middle of the seventeenth century might seem an unpromising date for the beginning of a new era in western thought. Europe had been convulsed by strife. Much of it had been devastated by the civil wars of Christendom, and its people, in sheer exhaustion, turned back to the familiar ways that promised stability and peace. The turbulence of recent years confirmed the gloomiest views of man's inherent nature, and the collapse of morality suggested that anarchy had undermined the spiritual vitality of western Europe.

The modern period, however, had already begun. Bacon had pointed to the scientific method which would rule the future, and Descartes had unfolded the principles of thought which inaugurated the new age in philosophy. Men's minds would no longer be governed by assumptions which were an inheritance from medieval and classical times. Descartes died in 1650. Most of his life belongs to the period before the Peace of Westphalia, but his influence was so powerful that it is impossible to understand the new age without examining his contribution to its thought. By birth Descartes was a Frenchman, and he was educated in Jesuit schools. By choice he was a soldier. Military life gave him unequalled opportunities for studying human nature, and in the long winters which separated one campaign from the next it afforded him the maximum leisure for reflection. He spent a great deal of his life in Holland, a country pulsating with vitality after its bitter struggle with Spain, vigorously consolidating its mercantile empire, and standing at the summit of its intellectual, artistic, and scientific eminence.

His predecessors had tacitly accepted a wide variety of

beliefs about matters human and divine. Descartes began by postulating that our approach to knowledge must be governed by doubt: we reject everything which, when tested by pure reason, appears uncertain. By the proposition, 'I think, therefore I am', he established his primary principle. Thought cannot doubt itself; and no other statement about ourselves is comparably free from contradiction. The criterion of truth is the clearness and distinctness of the idea. We deduce this from the character of our fundamental conviction. No idea is so clear as the idea of God. Since it is not derived from sense experience, and is not fashioned by our own act, it must be an innate idea, implanted in us by God himself. To think of God is to imply his existence; that which is perfect would be less than perfect if it did not exist. Perfection includes veracity; on this depends the reliability of our perceptions of the world around us, and so we can be sure of the existence of other beings and of other things.

Bit by bit Descartes constructed his system of knowledge. It embraced physics and mathematics as well as metaphysics, and it was not finally divorced from practical application to daily life. He provided something new and exciting: proofs of God, of freedom, and of immortality impressively reasoned yet comprehensible to ordinary minds. Part of Descartes' appeal lay in the unity into which he bound all the diverse ingredients of our life. It will be seen at once that his system of thought contained various elements which were destined to play a decisive part in later developments, and which had an important bearing on religious reflection. It exalted reason, and reason in a form different from, and far more attractive than, that which scholastic dialectics had allowed it. Moreover it recognized the fact of doubt and assigned it a regulative place in human thought; so far from being the final sin it became the primary virtue. Descartes was not primarily concerned with questions of faith; he ignored them merely because he was preoccupied with the area where faith and reason overlapped. Most of his successors followed his example; as a result reason ap-

peared the chief means of attaining belief, and the succeeding age was satisfied with what Descartes considered a par-
tial approach. His most dramatic achievements were in the
field of mathematics. He helped to fashion the tools which
would make possible man's scientific conquest of nature. His
thought was coloured by this fact; so was the thought of the
ensuing period. It has not always proved to be a liberating
influence.

Cartesianism – the system of thought founded by Descartes – was immediately recognized as a challenge to the
Aristotelianism which still held sway in most European
countries. The Dutch universities, then in a brilliant phase of
their development, were deeply divided in their loyalties but
the new thought provided an invaluable stimulus to investigations of many kinds. The university of Louvain, in Flanders, declared itself opposed to Descartes. In France the
Jesuits resisted the new system, the Oratorians supported it.
Gassendi, a Christian who was an Epicurean, a priest who
rigidly separated religious faith and philosophic speculation,
proved a formidable antagonist. The immediate influence of
Cartesianism can best be studied in the thought of three
great figures: Malebranche, a disciple of Descartes; Spinoza,
who was deeply influenced by him; and Pascal, who was
strongly opposed to him.

Malebranche, an Oratorian with a congenital aptitude
for metaphysics, claimed that it was Descartes who had
awakened him to his true vocation. For him, to be a Christian
was to be a philosopher; to be a philosopher was to be a
Cartesian. If there were apparent discrepancies, he would
reconcile them. He aimed to prove that the individual and
the universe were comprehended within the living unity of
an order in which faith and reason are both fulfilled. Within
this whole, God achieves his purposes through the uniformity of the laws which he has established. These laws are the
product and the expression of reason; and reason becomes so
all-embracing that it finally includes even God within its
orbit. In Malebranche we have clarity allied to order, a
faith in logic combined with mysticism, and issuing in the

conviction that we can be so closely united to God that we
see life as he sees it.

With Descartes, belief in God, though central to his system, was formal and correct in character; in both Malebranche and Spinoza, it had become a passionate conviction. Pantheism is present in both, latent in Malebranche,
explicit and avowed in the Jew Spinoza. Malebranche believed that Cartesianism provided the perfect expression of
Christian truth; Spinoza was convinced that all traditional
beliefs must be abandoned. It seemed to him that religion
had ceased to be an inward persuasion, and consequently it
no longer governed men's conduct. The church had become
the prey of greedy and ambitious men, so that envy and
malice had driven out the spirit of love. A new beginning
must be made, and reason must provide the point of departure. Spinoza believed that there is only one substance – the
infinite being. Because it is infinite, no predicates can be
applied to it, since all our attempts to describe the infinite
prove at best to be mere negations. Yet we can attribute
thought and extension to God, and consequently the divine
is made manifest to man in two ways: through mind and
through material things. All that exists, exists in God, and
man himself is a mode of eternal being. Spinoza believed
that men tend to start with themselves, and, being preoccupied with their petty concerns and their selfish nature,
merely fashion God in their own likeness. We ought to
reverse the process: begin with God, and reintegrate man
into the eternal, for thus man is merged with the universal
order.

Few things are more impressive than Spinoza's conviction
that in complete union with God the mind of man achieves
imperturbable tranquillity. To his contemporaries, however, Spinoza represented the final word in destructive
criticism. He conceived infinitude in a way that excluded
personality, and with it purpose and design. Religion ceased
to provide the highest form of personal relationship, and in
consequence both man's freedom and his happiness had to
be redefined. They were nobly conceived, but not in a way

that is really congruous with the Christian understanding of
full personal life. Man's political institutions and his religious
literature were also exposed to searching examination.
Spinoza's purpose was constructive, but many people refused
to believe it. And this confirmed the impression that Cartesianism was potentially a dangerous system. Spinoza had
learned from Descartes the geometrical and rational method
which he used to fashion his semi-scientific, semi-religious
pantheism. He developed a naturalistic conception of cosmic
law which challenged the prevailing theology at a variety of
points. The Cartesian scepticism, it appeared, was an acid
which bit deeply into traditional beliefs. The disciples of the
new system – men like Malebranche and Fénelon – did not
always pause to ask whether the Cartesian conception of
God was really congruous with the pattern of Christian
faith, and whether the religious views they were encouraging
might not finally prove detrimental to the very interests they
were trying to promote.

No such confusion existed in the mind of one of the most
brilliant figures of the period. Blaise Pascal was the most
determined opponent of the new philosophy, the man most
fully persuaded that the Cartesian picture of man and the
universe, though it had much to commend it, was fundamentally false. He combined marvellous mathematical and
scientific gifts with a religious faith of unusual depth and
intensity. He had – what many of his facile contemporaries
lacked – a profound sense of the tragic mystery of life.
Furthermore, he showed a remarkable capacity for systematic thought and literary gifts of the highest order. It is not
necessary to consider his contribution to mathematics and
science, nor even his merciless exposure of Jesuit casuistry
(cf. Chapter 2). The Jesuits, with their ambiguous moral
flexibility, were the chief enemy within the church; the
free-thinkers, relying on Descartes' philosophy, were the
great menace from without. To refute them he began to
collect material for a work in defence of Christian truth.
Because of his early death (1662), he never completed it, but
his fragmentary jottings form that disjointed but singularly

penetrating work, the *Pensées*, and from it we can deduce the pattern of his thought.

Descartes had felt that it was sufficient to establish the authority of reason, and to show that it contains within itself the elemental truths of religion as well as of science. But for Pascal this left the basic issue undecided, since reason is a neutral force, which may be subordinated to ends which are either good or bad. It is necessary to penetrate to the truths of Christianity. Faith, no less than reason, is requisite, and faith is the gift of God. Demonstration can never supplant grace, and it is grace which helps a man remove the barriers which cut him off from God. That the natural man lacks the means of achieving full life Pascal never doubts. He regards as self-delusion the free-thinkers' conviction that man, by his inherent aptitudes, guided by his own scientific knowledge, can fashion for himself an abundant life. This naïve oversimplification rests on assumption, not on evidence. The scientists should study the facts; and the facts reveal a disconcerting picture of inner chaos. Man's reason ends in irrationality; his good will is entangled in animosity; justice and force are distinguishable and yet prove to be inseparable. Human life is not progressing steadily through sweetness towards light; it is entangled in contradiction and confusion. To explain this evidence Pascal suggests a hypothesis: in man we are dealing with a twofold nature. We see the consequences of man's fallen condition; we also recognize the operation of divine grace. As a rational support for the hypothesis, Pascal advances two types of argument. He points to history: against all the rules of probability, Christianity established itself in the world, and has since maintained itself in a manner which strongly supports its claim to a divine origin. In the second place he appeals to experience. What we discover in moments of inspiration presupposes a reality which it is absurd to challenge, and which points to a relationship with God into which Christ brings us even in this present life.

The penetrating power of Pascal's thought and the brilliance with which he presented it made a profound impression not only on his contemporaries but on countless readers from that day to this. For our purpose it is chiefly interesting to note (as M. Boutroux pointed out) that the problem of 'religion and science' has now emerged, and has already elicited three characteristic responses. Descartes finds that our knowledge of both the natural and the supernatural is rooted in human reason; they have a common source, and neither has an overriding authority. Others, of whom Gassendi is typical, tend to magnify science; they regard it as essentially self-sufficient, and they banish religion to the position of a peripheral interest. For Pascal, religion is not an interest detachable from the rest of life. It illuminates our nature and experience. It draws into a unity the scattered elements in our life. It guides our minds and controls our science, because it alone can unfold the full mystery of nature. It answers the questions which reason can only raise, and it brings us to that fulfilment of life towards which science in its more limited way is struggling. It cannot be set in opposition to reason or science, because it includes yet transcends both. If our thought starts from God and finally rests in him, we have found the means by which the fragmentary powers of our being are harmonized in the service and appropriation of all truth.

In Leibniz, who died in 1716 just after the first phase of our period had ended, we have a further example of the bewildering versatility of the great figures of this age. He was a mathematician and scientist, a philosopher and theologian, a historian and jurist, a statesman and diplomat, an economist and philologist. In many of these fields his contributions were of permanent importance; in some they stamp him as one of the great creative forces in the intellectual history of Europe. To many of his contemporaries he was best known as an advocate of Christian reunion. He felt that the internal divisions of Christendom were as needless as they were disastrous. Tolerance which advanced no further than mutual forbearance would accomplish little, but Leibniz believed that Catholics and Protestants were actually agreed on certain basic truths, a kind of common rational foundation, and that this was a sufficient basis for cooperation. He believed that he had developed a system of philosophy compatible with the theology of all the churches, and many of his characteristic views were elaborated as a result of his attempt to bring the churches together. Leibniz was alert and ingenious, but he underestimated the complexities of ecclesiastical negotiation. He was neither the first nor the last to discover that churches may theoretically desire unity and yet may find it impossible to reach acceptable common ground. Leibniz did not fully realize that Catholicism was willing to discuss but not to concede and, though a Lutheran himself, he did not really understand the genius of Protestantism. So, though the negotiations involved him in protracted discussions with men as eminent as Bossuet, they achieved no concrete results.

Leibniz was a true son of his age. 'Our reason,' he wrote, 'illumined by the spirit of God, reveals the law of nature. . . .' The existence of God is the key to knowledge and the postulate of morality. Moreover, it is necessary for the realization of the monads – those units of existence out of which the universe is constructed. Leibniz was fascinated by the dynamic nature of the world, and he realized that causation probably lay near the heart of the matter. But he lacked the means to pursue that insight, and relied perforce on his monads which gave him a mechanistic universe created and governed by a benevolent God. In its unity and harmony the universe is thus the fulfilment of the divine purpose, and consequently must be the best possible world. If God created a world to reveal his perfection, he must have chosen for his purpose the one best suited to that end. Leibniz was then obliged to reconcile with this conclusion the disconcerting fact of the existence of evil. He distinguished imperfection and physical suffering from moral evil (wherein lies the crux of the problem) and indicated the role which each plays. He offered a variety of solutions, none of them wholly convincing, but all tending to the conclusion that even with evil as an ingredient, this world is better than any conceivable alternative. Because the problem is acute, the answers

seem lame, and Voltaire could ridicule them without mercy.
'If this is the best of all possible worlds,' he asked in *Candide*,
'then what are the others like?' But Leibniz's influence was
too great to be dissipated by satire. His philosophy, systematized and expounded by his disciple Wolff, dictated the pattern of thought in German universities for years to come, and
in theology he paved the way for the Enlightenment.

The religious thought of a century – especially of a century marked by such decisive changes – cannot be represented by a brief catalogue of its more eminent thinkers. New
forces were transforming the intellectual outlook of western
man. Not all were specifically religious in character, but most
of them directly or indirectly modified religious beliefs.

The later seventeenth century was a period of rapid
scientific advance. Interest in the study of nature was
general, and most European nations contributed to the expansion of knowledge. Holland was pre-eminent, and among
a host of able Dutch investigators three men of genius stand
supreme. By his patient and detailed study of insect life, Jan
Swammerdam laid the foundation for the science of ento-
mology. Anthony van Leeuwenhoek, by his researches in
physiology, unfolded the structure of the eye and of brain;
he greatly enlarged our understanding of the circulation of
the blood, and, thanks to the improvements he effected in
the microscope, he opened up a whole world of minute and
hitherto unknown organisms. Christian Huyghens was another of the brilliantly versatile men who seemed able to
take the whole field of knowledge as their province. In an
age of mathematicians he had few peers. His mechanical
genius was responsible for the micrometer, for the first pen-
dulum clock, and for a great increase in the range of the
telescope. With finer instruments he could achieve better
results, as he proved in astronomy when he discovered the
rings of Saturn. These were men of humble and reverent
mind, but the impact of new knowledge on old patterns of
thought was raising questions that religious thinkers would
have to face. A new class was beginning to emerge: men of
sceptical outlook, impatient of all restraint. An extreme

representative was Cesare Vanini, a Neapolitan priest who recognized no God save nature. But in general he reflected a vaguely critical spirit; he did not advance a series of anti-Christian propositions.

The seventeenth century was learning other lessons besides those concerned with the structure of the universe. Men were discovering the world in which they lived. Travel introduced a fluidity which brought new experiences and which often called in question old beliefs. Travel literature had an astonishing vogue. As regards accurate reporting, some of it left much to be desired, but, imaginary or true, it served equally well as a vehicle for new ideas. Many a traveller brought back the ideas with which he left home, but when embellished with exotic illustrations they carried far greater weight. The meaning of freedom, the nature of justice, the rights of property – fundamental concepts in every age – were seen in a new light because they had been set in a new social context. This could be done, of course, without submitting to the tedium of travel, and *Gulliver's Travels* is the most celebrated example of social criticism masquerading in the guise of a travel diary. A whole new world of values was introduced. New patterns of virtue were brought to light. The Egyptian, the Chinese, the Persian, the Siamese, even the virtuous savage – all might be pagans, but it was discovered that they were true philosophers. They proved to be models of wisdom and virtue, even though they had never heard of the Christian faith. Is not truth far more relative than we imagine? 'The climate of each particular race', remarked Chardin, 'is, in my judgement, always the primary cause of the inclinations and customs of its people.' Travel steadily eroded old convictions. 'Some', said La Bruyère, 'complete their demoralization by extensive travel, and lose whatever shreds of religion remained to them. Every day they see a new religion, new customs, new rites.'

As man's horizons widened, the centre of his interest changed. Trade was expanding and comfort was on the increase. Economic and political realities were concentrating attention on this world, not on the next. Men were absorbed in the present and forgot the future. The rise of new political institutions and the extension of political authority posed questions about power which were wholly secular in character. The relation between church and state, so long defined in terms of the divine right of the ruler, was still expounded along traditional lines by churchmen like Bossuet, but often political developments embarrassed the theorists. No one questioned that state churches were the best way to relate the beliefs of the community to its corporate life, but princes were treating the churches in a way certain to embarrass all who had the true welfare of the church at heart. High ecclesiastical office increasingly became a reward for political services rather than a recognition of spiritual qualifications, and the ties between the throne and the altar were already operating in a way that made the clergy not the spokesmen of reform but the champions of reaction. In most countries the limits of religious freedom were contracting. Toleration was revoked in Hungary in 1678 and in France in 1685, and in Catholic countries there was little sign that before long the tide would begin to flow in the opposite direction. In Calvinistic countries there was greater freedom, because the state was inclined to leave the churches to deal with heresy without the benefit of government intervention. The Huguenot refugees who swarmed into Holland found themselves at the centre of a vehement theological debate, conducted with complete freedom of expression. The French Protestant leaders had been shrill in denouncing persecution in their own country, but disliked the consequences of unlimited toleration. The liberty they found was as much a result of secular indifference as of Christian insight and courage.

The atmosphere of the age encouraged the critics of the churches to venture on more and more explicit assaults on traditional beliefs. It was not enough to praise the enlightened Chinese and his pagan virtues. At the outset the attacks were peripheral. Men did not directly criticize the Bible, but raised questions about chronology. The period was greatly puzzled about the age of the earth. The Bible

seemed to provide an inspired account of the essential events
since the Creation, and patient men had deduced from it a
chronology of history. But the results refused to tally with
the evidence which the studies of other sources (Egyptian,
Persian, Chinese) provided. Ingenuity worked marvels of
adjustment, but to no avail: there were not enough years to
accommodate all that had happened. But far more serious
issues were raised by Richard Simon (1638–1712), an Oratorian priest and a student of Biblical documents. As a good
Catholic, he felt he had found a means of confounding the
Protestants, who relied on the Bible, but his superiors quickly
detected that the missile which he had flung at their
enemies was something of a boomerang, certain to return
and work discomfiture in their own ranks. He was therefore
expelled from his order. His work is one of the earliest examples of the true critical study of the Bible. He and his age
lacked the insight to use it fruitfully, but he had devised a
method which has long since been accepted as an indispensable tool of Biblical investigation. Bossuet might be distressed at Simon's findings; the church might discipline a
presumptuous priest, but it could not suppress his work. And
others were active in the same field who were beyond ecclesiastical discipline. As Spinoza's writings became better
known, it was seen that his penetrating comments on the
Bible presupposed a new approach. Possibly more influential than either Spinoza or Simon were the pioneering efforts
of that many-sided and greatly gifted man, Hugo Grotius.
But the task of popularizing these results fell to other hands.
Pierre Bayle, one of the group of exiled Huguenots who had
found a haven in Amsterdam, seized on these critical results.
With his marvellous flair for popularization, he not only
expounded Simon's theories, he expanded them. His *Dic-
tionary* proved a mine from which Deists and sceptics could
quarry material for their attacks on the Bible and on the
faith which it sustained.

Bayle insisted, of course, that his purpose was not destructive. He had an insatiable intellectual curiosity and an
irrepressible itch to write. He was not an original thinker,

but in one area after another he suggested avenues of investigation which others (Voltaire or Diderot) would subsequently pursue. But whatever his purpose may have been, the spirit which he fostered was critical, and it was not subservient to any constructive ends. To a greater extent, perhaps, than any other man, Bayle created the sceptical spirit which was to prevail throughout so much of the eighteenth century.

Because that spirit was new, the best way of meeting it was not immediately apparent. Pascal had suggested at least one way (and a powerful one) of countering its ravages, but he was dead and his projected work existed in fragments only. Bossuet, growing old, was aware that the intellectual climate was changing. In his younger days, his resplendent oratory had made him famous and his attacks on Protestantism had brought him wide acclaim. But he was now faced with a challenge which could not be met by authority alone, and he had not the requisite means at his disposal to meet it in any other way. Patiently he began to master Hebrew in order that he might understand the new methods of Bible study. He was aware that Bayle and Le Clerc and others were raising new questions to which new answers would have to be found. Meanwhile he was exposed to the incessant attacks of Jurieu and the Huguenot exiles. It was not merely a great career which was coming to an end in faltering indecision; the magnificent confidence of which Louis XIV in his prime had been the symbol was forsaking the apologists of the age to which he had given his name. Men no longer thought in terms of a hierarchical disposition of life, of disciplined order, divine right, divine providence, and the stability of a classical period. They were prepared to think in terms of movement and change. Bossuet had been the spokesman of the day that was ending; the new day would greet Voltaire as its prophet.

4

Restoration and Revolution in England, 1660–1714

By 1660, the impetus of the Puritan revolution had spent itself. It had produced no leader to replace Oliver Cromwell. It had no policy; beyond a desire to perpetuate its own power, it had no plans. It had failed to solve the constitutional problems of the English people, it had failed to satisfy their religious aspirations, and by regimenting the details of their daily lives it had aroused general exasperation. Military rule had been both expensive and oppressive. The Restoration took place because the majority of Englishmen were weary of experiments and wanted to return to familiar ways.

So the English people welcomed back a Stuart king, and everyone knew that with the monarchy would come the restored church. With patient care the exiled Anglicans had prepared for such a day. The Laudian leaders who had shared the misfortunes of their king had both a policy and a plan. At the outset it was necessary to proceed with caution. The Presbyterians had played an important part in the Restoration, and appeared to be firmly entrenched in positions of power. In the Convention Parliament they were a party to be reckoned with, and it was not desirable that they should take alarm. The initial pronouncements of the king were gracious and conciliatory. From Breda in Holland he had issued a Declaration which promised consideration for 'tender consciences', and many who had rejoiced at the Restoration but had anticipated its results with alarm had taken fresh hope. He now appointed leading Presbyterians to royal chaplaincies, and offered them high preferment in the church.

The interval of uncertainty continued for two years. The

general nature of the new regime was emerging, but at many points its detailed character could not be foreseen. Cautiously the religious settlement went forward. The bishops were restored, and once more took their place in parliament. Vacant sees were filled with men of strong character, of considerable learning, and often of pronounced views. Displaced clergy repossessed their livings, and the ejection of Puritan ministers began. The old forms of worship were reintroduced. The task of renovating churches and cathedrals commenced. Key positions were quietly conferred on staunch churchmen, and meanwhile negotiations with the Presbyterians continued. Richard Baxter had indicated that he and his friends were ready to find their place in an episcopal church reformed of certain abuses, and the resettlement of the church went steadily forward. When the Presbyterians in parliament took alarm, strategic concessions were offered them. By the Declaration of 25 October 1660 the king promised them almost everything they desired. The Synod which was to consider Puritan requests for modifications of the Book of Common Prayer finally met at the Savoy. It assembled with little prospect of success. The bishops saw no need for concessions, and were rapidly reaching a point where none was necessary. In Baxter, the Puritans had a leader of learning and sanctity, but temperamentally quite unfitted for delicate negotiations. After fruitless and often bitter debate, the conference broke up without achieving anything, and the initiative passed to other bodies. To Convocation was committed the task of revising the liturgy, to parliament the duty of determining the regulations that would govern its use.

What emerged was a Prayer Book which offered few concessions to Puritan scruples, and a new law which effectively excluded them from the Church. The Act of Uniformity stipulated that only those who had received episcopal ordination could officiate in the church; it imposed an oath abjuring the right of resistance to constituted authority and repudiating the Solemn League and Covenant; it demanded that all incumbents and schoolmasters should swear 'unfeigned assent and consent' to all that the Prayer Book contained, and this acceptance was to be publicly declared before St Bartholomew's Day, 1662.

The result was a substantial exodus from the Church of England and the beginning of modern dissent. Before the Civil War, separatists had been inconsiderable groups; now nonconformists became a substantial minority in English life. Those who preferred ejection to conformity acted from a variety of motives. Some could not accept reordination; some would not repudiate oaths which they had taken; some could not conscientiously use certain rites (or even phrases) imposed by the Prayer Book. Most of them were sincere and high-minded men; many of them were scholars of distinction or preachers of marked ability. They represented a loss which the church, confronted with the problems of Restoration society, could ill afford.

The passing of the Act of Uniformity marks the end of the first phase of the new reign, and we can pause and notice some of the problems which faced the restored regime. The relation of church and state had apparently been settled. The two seemed to be united in the most intimate bonds. The church was effusively royalist, parliament vehemently Anglican. Non-resistance and passive obedience became the distinguishing doctrines of the Church of England. But the events of the next reign showed that the nature of the tie might need re-examination. Another issue still in an indeterminate state was the exercise of the royal prerogative in ecclesiastical affairs. The king claimed rights which parliament refused to recognize. At first the church spoke with an uncertain voice on the matter, but under James II its attitude hardened, and the question proved fatal to the Stuart line. One problem, however, had apparently been settled. In weighing the desirability of inclusiveness against uniformity, the Restoration church had chosen the latter. It would be less marked by internal differences than in the past; the price was the forfeiture of its old right to speak for the entire nation. Yet even here the issue was not irrevocably closed. The possibility of a wider measure of comprehension was

repeatedly raised during the reign of Charles II; it became
a practical project of some importance in 1689, and developments under Queen Anne showed that the position which
the nonconformists could claim in the national life was by
no means wholly settled. But the results of the Act of Uniformity began to operate at once, and with time they became
more and more pronounced. The Act created a cleavage
which cut across English life, and which affected politics and
social contacts as well as the relationships of religious bodies.

The Act of Uniformity was merely one part of a wider
programme for suppressing the nonconformists. The Corporation Act (1661) had already debarred them from holding
municipal office; the Five Mile Act (1664) was directed
against the ministers, and the Conventicle Acts (1664 and
1670) against the people who attended their services of worship. Collectively this legislation forms the Clarendon Code,
named after Charles's great Chancellor, but the responsibility for fashioning this engine of repression rests with the
ardently Anglican House of Commons. Clarendon's position
at court grew steadily less secure, and he could maintain
himself only by cooperating with the headstrong majority
in the lower House. Their policy was partly dictated by
revenge: the squires who had suffered during the Interregnum were eager to repay their enemies in kind. In part it
was prompted by fear. The Puritans had been overthrown,
but no one knew when they might again give evidence of the
prowess which had so recently proved irresistible. The air
was thick with rumours. A nervous imagination could detect
a plot in the most improbable quarters, and there was some
genuine restlessness which gave ground for vigilance. Each
fresh alarm stimulated the desire to reinforce the safeguards
against rebellion. The very terms in which the new laws
were framed showed that political motives were stronger
than religious ones.

Such fears gradually subsided, but while they lasted they
unduly deflected attention from the primary religious task
of the restored church. A violent reaction against Puritanism
endangered even elementary moral standards. Laxity at

court was imitated in polite society as well as on the stage. Some of the Anglican bishops (Archbishop Sheldon among them) courageously rebuked the king for his evil life, but the church was too much part of the new regime to regard it with the detachment necessary for an effective protest against current ways. Religion, moreover, was deeply involved in political manoeuvres. Charles II, who had little of the fanatic in his nature, and who believed that tolerant measures would unify his realm, wished to fulfil his promises to mitigate for the dissenters the harshness of the new laws. Early in 1663 he tried to do so by a declaration of indulgence, but there were strong objections both to his purpose and to the instrument by which he proposed to achieve it. Charles was too shrewd a tactician to push his measures to extremes; he drew back, but for ten years kept the objective in view. When the Earl of Clarendon fell in 1667, political leadership passed to men more interested in political expedients than in religious programmes. There was little persecuting zeal among the members of the Cabal, who hoped that a more lenient policy would broaden the basis of their support. Some of the king's ministers were crypto-Catholics; Charles had turned to an alliance with France, and the secret treaty of Dover prepared the way both for renewed war with Holland and for the king's conversion to the Catholic faith.

On the eve of the Dutch war, Charles issued the Declaration of Indulgence of 1672. Protestant dissenters who secured the necessary licences would be free to worship publicly in places registered for the purpose; the Roman mass might also be celebrated, but only in private. The new experiment was in force for the better part of a year. Hundreds of non-conformist ministers secured licences for themselves and for the places where they preached. The first period of bitter persecution was over, and in the breathing space which they now secured they established their corporate life so firmly that it could not subsequently be eradicated. They had qualms both about the legality of the respite they enjoyed and about the real purposes they detected behind the king's policy. But their doubts were as nothing compared with the general indignation which the Indulgence created. Religious jealousy doubtless played some part in this; many Anglicans were indignant at the liberty the dissenters enjoyed. Much of it was constitutional. When Parliament assembled, the House of Commons insisted that the Declaration must be withdrawn. If the king genuinely wished to relieve nonconformists, he must do it in a legal way, and they would cooperate with him, but the royal prerogative could not be invoked for this purpose. An act to benefit dissenters was introduced; in the tangle of political manoeuvre it was never passed. But the House did pass a bill to exclude papists from positions of public trust. The Test Act was a reaction not only to what the king had done but to what it was suspected he wanted to do. Rumours were abroad about the secret clauses of the Treaty of Dover, and the act was primarily a religious expedient to secure certain political ends. It was intended more as a safeguard for the state than as a benefit to the church. It used a sacramental test to bar Romanists from office, and it had disastrous effects on the church. By it nonconformists also had to qualify for any positions they might occupy, and the necessity of receiving certificates from the clergy became an offensive and impolitic abuse. By the Test Act, a selfishly Anglican parliament prostituted the sacred rites of the church to political ends; it raised up hundreds of enemies to the Church of England, and decisively committed the dissenters to political opposition.

It also anticipated a yet more spectacular development. Fear of Rome always lurked just beneath the surface of English life. It had been aroused by developments abroad and by suspected tendencies at home. The discovery of the Popish Plot whipped national feeling to a frenzy. There was a plot, though not the one that Titus Oates professed to have uncovered. But people in a hysterical mood are in no position to weigh evidence. The king, who realized what a charlatan Oates really was, was in no position to check the process of judicial murder which took scores of innocent people to their death. Charles, who had returned with the aid of the Earl of Danby to a specifically Anglican policy, had to steer cautiously among the various cross-currents of political life.

It seemed, indeed, as if a mood of wild irresponsibility had taken possession of English life. Party feeling reached a new intensity of bitterness. Under the Earl of Shaftesbury, the Whigs, in close alliance with the nonconformists, stood opposed to the Tories supported by the Church of England. Shaftesbury was a daring political leader of consummate tactical skill, but with little sense of responsibility and no restraint. He showed in three successive elections that he could carry the country. His party proposed to ease restrictions on the dissenters. They also proposed to change the succession by excluding the Duke of York (now a professed Catholic) from the throne. Their plans were frustrated; Charles dissolved parliament, turned to the Tories, and with their aid governed for the remainder of his reign. The Tories used their power with as little restraint as had the Whigs. The full force of their fury fell on the nonconformists. Persecution was now more closely related to political forces, less directly the consequence of religious views. The discovery of the Rye House Plot (1683) gave fuller scope to forces already at work, and the last years of Charles II found the nonconformists exposed to persecution as ruthless as any they had known. Meanwhile Anglican pulpits rang with protestations of loyalty and with extravagant expositions of the doctrine of non-resistance.

For twenty-five years the Church of England had been too effusively the handmaiden of the state. The strain of hardness which entered English life after the Restoration had affected the church. But this is only one side of the picture. The external pattern of church life had been restored. The life of ordered worship had been resumed; the heritage of beauty in churches and cathedrals had been rescued from neglect and restored to use. Wren was using, with magnificent effect, the unique opportunity offered by the Fire of London. Purcell and others were proving that church music was a living art. Seldom has the bench of bishops been adorned by so many men of eminent distinction. Sheldon was not the kind of man who aroused warm affection, but few would dispute that he stood in the tradition of the resolute ecclesiastical statesmen of the past, and he was unswerving in pursuing the good of the church as he saw it. Sancroft, his successor at Canterbury, was a man in whom gentleness and wisdom were combined with sanctity. Cosin, Sanderson, Wilkins, Pearson, Gunning, Ken, Morley – all were men who lent lustre to the church, and many of them were leaders of whom any generation would be proud. Theological scholarship, though unduly distracted by controversy, flourished. The church still contained laymen devoted to its worship, and who adorned their profession by their lives.

The nonconformists also suffered, though in very different ways, from their involvement in the political struggles of the time. This was the period of the great persecution, and though repression may have been bitter, it unquestionably refined and purified their faith. Puritanism appears to least advantage just before the Restoration. In the years that followed it rediscovered its soul. The persecution which it suffered was intermittent, but it could be intense. At the outset, it was often inspired by malevolence or spite, but as the period progressed, bitterness exhausted itself; the spirit of toleration was on the increase, and magistrates were reluctant to harry honest and inoffensive folk. They might, of course, be compelled to act against their will, since the laws encouraged informers and put great power in their hands. Under a variety of statutes, the nonconformist could be brought before the magistrates. He might be fined, or sent to prison, or his case might be held over to the next assizes. He was likely to face a good deal of abuse in court, and he might suffer acute privation in prison. The fate of the prisoner was by no means uniform. If the gaol was not overcrowded and the gaoler proved sympathetic, he might be relatively comfortable. But often the space was crowded beyond endurance; heat and cold, filth and disease made conditions almost intolerable, and a vindictive gaoler could devise additional refinements of suffering. Thousands died;

many were released with shattered health to face the fact
that imprisonment often involved financial ruin. The dis-
traint of goods could have the same effect. A man's tools, his
stock in trade, all his household possessions could be seized
in satisfaction of the fines levied upon him.

In such times, meetings for worship were held surrepti-
tiously and dispersed if warned of the approach of danger.
The Quakers, indeed, refused to make concessions; even in
the most perilous times they met openly and without disguise. They drew to themselves the full impact of persecution; they not only suffered its extreme violence, but finally
exhausted the venom of their antagonists. Not all dissenters
felt called to so uncompromising a witness, but all were
compelled to reassess their position. In the process they were
forced back on those elements in their faith which could sustain them in such an ordeal, and it is no accident that some
of the noblest expressions of Puritan belief were written
under the shadow of persecution.

During the brief reign of James II the politics of the realm
were governed by the religious question. The attempt to
exclude the heir to the throne on the grounds of his Catholicism had failed. Tory churchmen were too deeply committed
to the principle of legitimacy and to the doctrine of non-
resistance to permit them to contemplate so drastic a step
as a break in the succession, but many wondered how a
Catholic head of the established church would use his
power. James's initial statements were judicious and conciliatory. He would maintain the rights of the established
church and respect the faith of his people. He easily survived the rebellions of Monmouth and Argyll, though both
leaders emphasized their role as religious deliverers. James
soon made it clear, however, that he intended to use his
power to promote the advancement of his faith. He could
not achieve his ends without help, and at first he relied on
the Church of England, while maintaining severe pressure
on the Protestant dissenters. When the Anglicans objected
to his manifest intentions, he believed that he could persuade
the nonconformists to join him, both in emancipating all

forms of dissent, and in punishing the Anglicans for their attitude. Only an obtusely unimaginative man would have believed that either of these manoeuvres could succeed; and only a stubbornly stupid one would have pressed to extremes the methods he employed. He insisted that Catholics should be free to serve him in both the army and the state, regardless of the Test Act. To gain his ends he undertook to remodel all the basic institutions – church, corporations, and even parliament. With tactless zeal he tried his persuasions on all who might help him to revoke the legislation which obstructed his purpose. He made little progress, but he aroused no fatal opposition till his attacks on the church (and by implication on property) had awakened general alarm. He tried to secure control of the universities, and his behaviour regarding Magdalen College, Oxford, showed that no legal rights were now immune from invasion. He made his fatal blunder when he committed Archbishop Sancroft and six other bishops for trial because they had declined to support his demand that the Declaration of Indulgence (1688) should be read in all churches. The acquittal of the bishops was the occasion for an unparalleled popular demonstration of loyalty to them – and, by implication, of hostility to the king. But James had pressed matters so far that men of both parties were convinced that the foundations of religious and political life were jeopardized by his rule, and an invitation was issued to William of Orange to come to England to defend its basic liberties against its king.

The Revolution of 1688 had important results for English religious life. The old relationships between church and dissent would clearly have to be changed. James's rash policy had drawn Protestants closer together than they had been at any time during the past generation. A measure of toleration was inevitable. Public opinion was ready to support it, and the political situation made it necessary. Archbishop Sancroft and other leading churchmen believed that the moment was auspicious for an attempt to bring back the moderate nonconformists to the church. The Toleration

Act was passed; the Comprehension Bill was not. Henceforth dissenting ministers who registered their places of worship, took the necessary oaths, and accepted the doctrinal portion of the Articles of Religion could preach openly and without molestation. The penal acts were not repealed; their operation was merely suspended.

With this illogical compromise the nonconformists had to be content. The immediate prospect of persecution was removed. In due course they would discover that Toryism, in its moments of resurgence, could threaten their security, but meanwhile dissent had achieved legal recognition and enjoyed the good will of a Calvinist king. The immediate result was a great outburst of nonconformist activity. Hundreds of new chapels were built. Work expanded and new congregations sprang up. But vitality showed itself in disruptive ways as well. Soon after the Act of Toleration the Congregationalists and the Presbyterians established the Happy Union – a measure of cooperation among London churches that was to supersede denominational rivalries, and which through its Common Fund was to assist needy ministers and struggling congregations. This unanimity augured well for the future, but it was short-lived. The nonconformists, indeed, seemed intent on wasting their new freedom in fratricidal fights. They quarrelled about the methods and beliefs of a Northamptonshire minister called Richard Davis. They embarked upon a long and bitter controversy which centred on a distinguished Presbyterian minister named Dr Williams. The debate was between two schools of Calvinists; its subject matter has some bearing on doctrinal developments in the next century and on the decline of the Presbyterians into Unitarianism, but its temper reflects the exhaustion which resulted from long years of suffering.

The Church of England also had its troubles. The Revolution created acute problems for a church that had vehemently championed the principle of legitimate succession and the duty of unquestioning obedience. When new rulers were installed (by act of parliament, not by divine right) what

became of old obligations? If you had sworn allegiance to
your lawful king, could you swear allegiance to anyone else
while he still lived? Most churchmen felt they could; those
who did not were responsible for the Non-Juring Schism.
Those who withdrew were a small but select body, and the
church (standing on the eve of the eighteenth century) was
weakened by the loss of saintly and disinterested men. Nor
could the church submit without serious disturbance to the
sudden repudiation of a cherished and distinctive doctrine.
Moreover, the Schism was precipitated by an assertion of
the authority of the state over the church. The oaths were
enforced by the state, and sees which were not canonically
vacant were filled. The most serious result of the Revolution
was the creation of an Erastian outlook which held unchallenged sway for more than two generations.

The turbulence of a combative era soon found other out-
lets. The Trinitarian debate – the forerunner of the incessant
doctrinal controversies of the next few years – began to
engage men's attention. The Jacobite sympathies of many
Tories predisposed William to fill vacancies on the episcopal
bench with Latitudinarian Whigs. Many of them were able,
and some of them very distinguished, men, and they made
conscientious bishops. Tillotson, Stillingfleet, Burnet, Tenison – such men might be open to criticism, but they were
surely above contempt. But the church was now divided
into two wrangling factions: Latitudinarian Whigs and High-
Church Tories. The great debate about Convocation and its
rights, which spanned three reigns, was complicated by the
interplay of many issues, but in part it was a manoeuvre to
vex the Whig bishops whom William III had appointed.

The close of the seventeenth century witnessed an emphatic protest against the influences which had dominated
social life for a generation. Restoration drama was blatantly,
almost cynically, licentious; Jeremy Collier's *Short View of
the Immorality and Profaneness of the English Stage* (1698) challenged the prevailing profligacy and marked a reaction which
produced the more sober tone characteristic of the age of
Addison. Since the Revolution, vice had claimed a latitude

as wide as it had enjoyed before it. The response of the
church was to foster the growth of societies designed to fight
evil and promote good. Religious societies cultivated the
devotional life, and channelled charitable zeal into constructive activities. The Societies for the Reformation of
Manners (1691) were formed to bring vice to justice and to
see that the statutes against it were enforced. The Society
for the Propagation of Christian Knowledge (1698) provided missionaries for the plantations and parochial libraries
both at home and abroad. Closely related to it was the Society
for the Propagation of the Gospel (1701). In organizing such
societies Thomas Bray was an indefatigable worker, but his
efforts were reinforced by a rising tide of humanitarian zeal
which was active in many directions – in concern for soldiers
and sailors, for the sick, the poor, and the prisoners. This
practical philanthropy mitigated the worst effects of the
intolerance which was the most serious blight on the life of
the age.

The reign of Queen Anne saw a vigorous revival of
polemics. But the period was not wholly arid, and the
creation of 'Queen Anne's Bounty' was one of the few disinterested acts in an age in which advantage was the determining consideration in official dealings with the church. By
relinquishing her claim to 'first fruits and tenths' (certain
dues which the crown could claim from the church), Anne
established a fund to augment poorer livings. It was one of
the few attempts in the eighteenth century to remove the
anomalies which disfigured the life of the church. But for the
most part church life was caught in the maelstrom of political agitation. The resurgence of Tory confidence showed
itself in the continuing Convocation controversy and in re-
current efforts to revive the persecution of nonconformists.
The Occasional Conformity Bills – repeatedly passed by
Tories in the House of Commons and regularly defeated in
the Lords by the Whig bishops – were designed to lock the
back door by which dissenters gained a limited access to
public life. Success eluded the 'high-flying' Tories until the
Sacheverell incident brought them to power. Sacheverell

was a clergyman of little learning (though an Oxford don), but he was a popular preacher who fully appreciated the power of unbridled invective in an explosive atmosphere. A government exasperated by his attacks on Whigs, dissenters, and by implication on the Revolution settlement, brought him to trial. In the upheaval of public opinion which it inspired, the Tories came to power. Party feeling was given free rein. The Occasional Conformity Bill was passed, and the Schism Act, attacking the dissenting academies, aimed what it hoped would be a fatal blow at nonconformist life. Under a queen who was frankly favourable to their cause, with Oxford and Bolingbroke as their leaders and Swift as their great publicist, the Tories seemed secure. Tory church-men hoped to rule the country in the interest of the Church of England. They failed for a variety of reasons. Changes, both constitutional and intellectual, made any revival of Laud's policy impossible. The urgent issue was the succes-sion to the throne, and here the Tories were hesitant and divided. They were unwilling to abandon the Stuart (and Catholic) claimant, but they were unable to induce him to accept feasible terms. Their indecision proved fatal; the Tory High Church party, after a brief moment of triumph, collapsed. It is not the fate of a particular faction which is important. During Anne's reign the church apparently possessed great political influence; what had happened was that the church had become inextricably bound up with political life. To achieve its ends it had come to rely too largely on political means. When the control of the state passed to the Whigs, the control of the church went with it. Thus the Erastianism which was to be so marked a feature of the Hanoverian Church was not a new phenomenon; it was merely a familiar fact reappearing in a different guise.

During the reign of Queen Anne a spirit of partisanship prevailed throughout the country; it disfigured the life of the church and seriously weakened its witness. Disputes between churchmen were the reflection and counterpart of conflicts between parties. The worthier elements in the corporate life of the church were obscured. 'High Church' and 'Low

Church' became watchwords of political faction. 'Church principles' were fiercely debated not only in parliament and in convocation, but in lampoons and pamphlets, in coffee houses and taverns. The turbulence in which the church was involved invaded its own life, and the obscuring of its true concerns augured ill for the days to come.

5

The Watershed in English Thought,
1660–1714

THE Stuart Restoration in England was initially a conservative reaction. Innovation was at a discount; not only in
political life, but equally in theology, worship, and church
government, the patterns bequeathed by the past had a
powerful appeal.

Many of the leaders of religious thought were men trained
in an earlier period, and they perpetuated its outlook and
its temper. Their days of active authorship might be over,
but they now advocated their views with the authority conferred by high office in the church. Jeremy Taylor and John
Cosin represented many of the finest qualities of an earlier
school of thought: loyalty to ancient standards, reinforced
by profound learning and guided by spiritual insight.
Taylor proved that respect for tradition could be harmonized
with a living faith, and that deference to authority was compatible with a generous latitude in interpretation. The new
age did not conspicuously amplify this strain of thought; it
is fortunate that at least it reaffirmed it as an integral part of
the heritage of the Church of England. Among Restoration
churchmen a common loyalty to Anglican practice did not
imply theological unanimity. Calvinism, so strong at the
beginning of the century, had been discredited by its association with the revolutionary movement, but it had its representatives even among the restored bishops, as George
Morley of Winchester proves. The Catholic strain was more
strongly represented. Henry Thorndike was a stout defender
of Catholic practice in its Anglican form. This did not imply
any sympathy with crypto-Romanism. The Laudian school
had always opposed papal pretensions, and Thorndike's
work, *The Reformation of the Church of England better than that*

of the Council of Trent (1670), continued a polemical tradition
of long standing. One of the notable features of the Restoration period was the vigour of its anti-Roman writings, and
in this the representatives of all schools played their part.
Isaac Barrow, the Master of Trinity College, Cambridge,
was a scholar of encyclopedic range, but to his contemporaries his attack on papal supremacy represented his strongest
claim to fame. In the anxious days of James II's reign, a
systematic defence of Anglicanism against Roman claims
was inaugurated by churchmen of liberal views, and early in
the next century the major works in this series were reissued
by Bishop Gibson as *A Preservative Against Popery.*

Calvinism had suffered an almost total eclipse in the
Church of England; it persisted, though probably with
diminished vigour, among the nonconformists. Life for the
successors of the Puritans had become straitened and difficult. The struggle to survive under persecution absorbed
much of their time and energy. For the most part they
remained loyal to the Calvinism in which they had been
trained, though some of its harsher features were modified
and its confidence was chastened by defeat. Richard Baxter
is one of the great figures in the final phase of Puritanism,
but he deviated from strict Calvinistic orthodoxy sufficiently
for his name to be frequently used to designate a position
intermediate between Arminianism and Calvinism. In the
Restoration era many of the great leaders of the Interregnum
were still active, though their scope was severely restricted.
Thomas Goodwin and John Owen were the chief representatives of the Independent tradition. Some of their ablest works
antedate our period, but both continued to be prolific
writers. Goodwin's sermons provide the finest examples of
that great teaching medium, the Puritan 'lecture'. Owen
contributed some notable pamphlets to current debates on
toleration and on popery, and during this period published
many of his massive doctrinal works. The controversies of
the times naturally demanded a great deal of thought and
effort. The arguments against episcopacy and an imposed
liturgy reappear; so do the attacks on vestments and cere-

monies. Even predominantly theological writers like John
Howe were drawn into the debate about nonconformity,
but polemics represented only a part of the literary output
of the later Puritans. John Bunyan, who on occasion showed
himself a formidable debater, issued a steady stream of doctrinal and expository works. He combined great practical
wisdom with a power to make the Bible startlingly relevant
to the daily problems of ordinary people. In his allegories,
however, he discovered an incomparably persuasive medium
for commending the Puritan view of life. *The Pilgrim's Progress* is one of the supreme works of the period, but as an
exposition of Puritan convictions *The Holy War* is hardly less
important. In *Mr Badman* we have a graphic picture of
seventeenth-century life as seen by a great Puritan who
knew the common people intimately. John Milton, old and
blind, produced in *Paradise Lost* the greatest of English epics,
and set forth his own variant of the Puritan view of God and
man and the universe. The Quakers were deeply involved
in the struggle for religious liberty. They were the most
uncompromising of the noncomformists, but their theological position, no less than their distinctive witness on
oaths, social conventions, and violence, set them apart from
their fellow dissenters. In addition to their innumerable
tracts on the iniquities of persecution, they used with great
effect the narrative of personal religious experience. George
Fox's *Journal* is pre-eminent though not unique. Few works
of any period are so instinct with spiritual vitality. The
reader can understand why Fox was a perplexity and an
offence to his contemporaries; he can still sense the vitality
of his confident affirmation, 'the power of the Lord was over
all'. Fox's *Journal* is a powerful apologia for the Society he
founded and a revelation of the amazing religious vigour
which animated his witness and his work.

Though traditional patterns of thought persisted, the distinguishing feature of the Restoration era was the far-reaching intellectual changes which it initiated. Evidences of a
new spirit appeared without delay. The Cambridge Platonists were a group of scholars who stood slightly apart from

the main stream of contemporary thought, yet profoundly influenced its course. They were products of the University of Cambridge; most of them were teachers there throughout their lives. Many had gained a position of some influence before the Restoration, but they had little sympathy with the Calvinism which had been so influential in the university. In effect the Cambridge Platonists turned from the way in which religious problems had been conceived and debated. The prevailing theology had become dogmatic and theoretical; the Cambridge Platonists showed that a broader and simpler system was necessary. They believed that preoccupation with abstruse doctrines did more harm than good. Their attack on Calvinism was directed more against the spirit which it encouraged than against the convictions which it held. They sought a middle way between the Laudians on the one hand and the Calvinists on the other, and they were opposed to the bitter and factious spirit of both.

The Cambridge Platonists adopted a mediating position which they hoped would prove to be a reconciling one as well. With great skill they held together a number of elements which are often allowed to drift apart. Faith and knowledge, reason and revelation, right doctrine and sound morals, were in no sense incompatible with one another. They defined reason as the discipline of thinking exactly about the things which are real; they also regarded it as the process by which the whole personality is unified in the pursuit of truth. They were receptive to knowledge no matter what guise it might assume, but it had to prove its power to liberate man's mind and enrich his spirit. Since reason reinforced faith, philosophy was an ally of theology. It helped to clarify the meaning of the infinite; it confirmed our confidence in God's existence. It showed us that it was more important to understand *what* he is than *that* he is. Above all, it was an instrument to show that the world is unintelligible except in terms of a wise and holy God.

Faith in revelation was not incompatible with confidence in reason. Man's faculties have been impaired by the Fall, and unless God disclosed himself certain truths would always elude us. Moreover, in the Cambridge Platonists there was a strain of mysticism which preserved them from the narrow rationalism to which the succeeding generation succumbed. Sanity was the mark of this mysticism. The Cambridge Platonists rose to an apprehension of God in and through nature, not beyond it. In the words of John Smith, 'God made the universe and all the creatures contained therein as so many glasses wherein he might reflect his own glory. He hath copied forth himself in the creation; and in this outward world we may read the lovely characters of Divine goodness, power and wisdom.'

The Cambridge Platonists saw 'the use of reason' and 'the exercise of virtue' as the twin spheres in which we enjoy God. Morality is closely related to religion. It is supported, and its demands are enforced, by the few great essentials of faith. Right and wrong, freedom and self-determination, are rooted in the nature of things. From this sense of moral obligation arose many of their characteristic affirmations. They believed that Christianity lays a serious responsibility upon each individual who submits to its constraint. 'Christianity is a divine life, not a divine science', and it is our duty to meet its demands with a humble awareness of what our duty entails. For the same reason they opposed undue centralization in either church or state. The concentration of power robs the individual of initiative; without initiative, responsibility is ineffective. Furthermore, they realized that responsibility presupposes toleration: unless a man is free to follow the dictates of his conscience he is not able to achieve the moral integrity which is required of him.

The contribution of the Cambridge Platonists must be seen in the light of the growing desire to find a convincing restatement of Christian truth. They did not question the essential validity of the Christian interpretation of life, though they believed that its beauty had been obscured by the rigid theological abstractions often substituted for it. What was needed was a restatement from within. This was what they offered to their contemporaries. Their reinterpretation was conservative in character and aimed at preserving the full significance of the Christian tradition. In this it differed from the destructive radicalism of the Deists. In form it was abstract and philosophical; it presented doctrine in general, not in concrete, terms, and it was concerned with values, not with facts. Here it stood in sharp contrast with popular Calvinism, which was often graphic and almost pictorial. It appealed to the Platonic tradition, though for generations Aristotelianism had dominated academic speculation. In opposition to Hobbes's materialism, it asserted the essential congruity of Christianity and idealist philosophy, and it initiated a tradition which powerfully affected English thought for the next two centuries. In all this the Cambridge Platonists believed that they were asserting the Christian faith in a form at once intellectually defensible and spiritually satisfying, able to protect religion against the twin perils of atheism and superstition.

The appeal to reason was strengthened by the force of the reaction against the 'enthusiasm' (fanaticism in our terminology) of the Puritans. It reinforced the tradition which relied on critical, elaborate, closely reasoned statements of the faith, like Bishop John Pearson's *Exposition of the Creed.* It gave added authority to the writings of Isaac Barrow – so closely argued, so mathematical in their lucidity, so clear and precise in their presentation, so weighty in the estimation of Locke and Warburton and all others who wished to think about the problems of belief. Barrow was representative, too, in his ethical seriousness; for him, as for many of his contemporaries, reason and morality were closely allied. The tendencies represented by these men found full expression in the group of writers known as the Latitudinarians. Many of them had been taught by the Cambridge Platonists, and they maintained the tradition that sought intermediate ground between the Calvinists and the school of Laud. They are distinguishable from their predecessors not merely by the absence of any mystical strain but by a far less imaginative approach to the life of faith. The contrast is partly due to the different setting of their lives. The Cambridge Platonists were university teachers in a day

when Cambridge was still a world unto itself. The Latitudinarians were prominent churchmen, the occupants of some
of the most influential pulpits in England. They naturally
allowed added weight to practical considerations; relevance
seemed more important to them than theory. They valued
reason: it was a part of their heritage, it gained increased
prestige day by day, and its authority was the great defence
against unregulated inspiration. It was equally natural for
them to define it in terms that made it indistinguishable from
common sense. They appealed to considerations which any
intelligent person could appreciate and assess. This approach
set a high value on the kind of religion which reason can discover for itself. The increasing vogue of natural theology was
a consequence of the rationalistic temper of the time. God's
existence could be demonstrated; his attributes could be determined by an examination of the universe; man's status
and destiny could be inferred from an unbiased study of
man's nature. The witness of reason is sufficient to convince
us of the reality of our moral freedom and the certainty of a
future life. Reason, it is clear, is the true corrective of over-
confident dogmatism and the best means of dispelling superstitious beliefs. The fact of revelation was not disputed, its
value was not intentionally depreciated. The usual practice
was to construct a reasonable pattern of belief, and then
prove that revelation coincided with it. Reason and revelation were invoked in turn; each was used to establish the
other. Edward Stillingfleet, later bishop of Worcester, defended Mosaic history by proving that it conformed with the
canons of reason, and in this he was representative of many
others. He insisted, of course, that 'the immediate dictates
of natural light are not to be the measure of divine revelation', but his warning was promptly forgotten.

For any thoughtful person in the seventeenth century the
problem of authority was urgent. It was involved, directly
or indirectly, in every controversy of the age. In theology
the appeal to antiquity had been considered weighty. The
Latitudinarians did not repudiate the authority of classical
and patristic authors, but they used their works with caution.

The Bible still held its position as the chief and ultimate court of appeal. Scripture was interpreted by reason, of course, and the way in which it was used underwent a subtle but perceptible change. The Latitudinarians stood halfway between the unquestioning reliance on authority which was characteristic of the early seventeenth century and the rationalism of the early eighteenth. This change was related to another important development. Science was daily commanding greater interest because it was daily registering greater triumphs. The Latitudinarians were intelligently interested in its progress and sympathetic to its claims. Some of them were members of the Royal Society and actively promoted its work.

As concerns doctrine, the position of the Latitudinarians was slightly indeterminate. Their love of clarity tempted them to oversimplify all profound questions. The terms in which they defined reason, together with their active interest in practical problems, persuaded them that essential beliefs were few and simple. Their views were so nebulous that they were often accused of falling into heresy. Their theological vagueness was partly the result of their preoccupation with matters which prompted less debate but promised greater results. Tillotson (later archbishop of Canterbury) believed that 'the great design of Christianity was the reforming men's natures', and he went on to define the specific steps that could be taken to this end. A strong ethical emphasis was characteristic of all the Latitudinarians. They constantly stressed man's moral duty. They not only counselled upright behaviour, they themselves were indefatigable in every good work. Unfortunately their moral zeal lacked dignity and urgency. Everything they did or said was moderate in tone; their religion was genuine but never ardent; they stood for a temper rather than a creed. Their outlook was reasonable and dispassionate, magnanimous and charitable. Their virtues easily degenerated; their good will subsided into mere complacency. They represent an important transitional stage between the embittered struggles of the seventeenth century and the very different controversies of the

eighteenth. But in addition they served their own generation faithfully and well. In an age too apt to acquiesce in
debauchery they insisted on the primacy of moral standards.
With new intellectual interests constantly emerging, they
insisted that the church should keep abreast of contemporary
thought.

In the second half of the seventeenth century a new understanding of the physical universe became increasingly available. New discoveries revealed the nature of the universe,
but the assimilation of new knowledge was neither easy nor
fast. The Copernican interpretation made slow headway
against the apathy of those content with traditional views.
Even in the universities the old system of thought was reluctant to yield. The change which took place in the latter
years of the century profoundly affected religious thought,
and was in large measure promoted by convinced Christians.
The task of interpreting the new science was undertaken
most successfully by two prominent Latitudinarians: Thomas
Sprat, bishop of Rochester, and Joseph Glanvill, rector of
Bath. Faith, they claimed, cannot be destroyed by knowledge. The scope of science is great. It is concerned with
God, man, and nature, but with the first 'only as the power
and wisdom and goodness of the Creator is displayed in the
admirable order and workmanship of the creature'. In
other words, scientists deal with natural phenomena, but
they approach them in a reverent and religious spirit. Consequently religion will benefit, and cannot suffer, from their
efforts. The accepted pattern of belief will not be destroyed.
Its meaning will be illuminated by the fresh insights which
new discoveries inspire. However much the disciplines of
science and theology agree in their results, they differ in
their methods. Therefore they must not be confused, and are
best kept apart. This was the position adopted by Sprat.
Robert Boyle, the great chemist, agreed with him. But
Newton, an even greater physicist, thought otherwise. Faith
and knowledge are so closely related and they illuminate
each other so profoundly that their relationship can never be
too close.

The brilliant advances of the new science were achieved by men of deep religious conviction. Both Boyle and Newton wrote extensively on theological subjects. Scattered references throughout their scientific works indicate the inferences they drew from their discoveries. In addition they wrote books which were specifically biblical, devotional, or theological in character. They believed that the natural universe, being the handiwork of God, clearly indicates its creator's existence and suggests his character. Wherever you look in nature you find order and beauty, and the scientists regarded this as one of the most cogent proofs of God's existence. Newton argued from the law which governed the stars in their courses, John Ray from the evidence he found in the structure of plants and animals. Neither had any doubt that nature demonstrated the creative power of God. Having established to their satisfaction the existence of God, the scientists defined his nature in strictly traditional terms. But their technical work complicated their theological task. After creating the world and fixing its laws, had God any further function to fulfil? Did science leave room for Providence? Boyle believed that God kept the world from disintegrating. Newton assigned him two specific tasks: to prevent the fixed stars from collapsing in the middle of space and to keep the mechanism of the world in good repair.

The new science was regarded as a powerful bulwark against the new atheism. By his will Boyle endowed a lectureship for the defence of Christian truth, and the first series was delivered by Richard Bentley. Bentley, though the greatest classical scholar England has produced, recognized the significance of Newtonian physics and based on it his *Confutation of Atheism*. Enlightened theologians were clearly beginning to take the results of the new science for granted; they saw that their task was to draw from its principles the correct deductions. In other and more subtle ways, the changing outlook affected the approach to religious problems. Science strengthened the tendency to give reason an ever larger role in theological discussion. Though the leading scientists believed that they were scrupulously loyal to traditional beliefs, they slightly modified the discussion of subjects like miracles and scripture, and these changes paved the way for the drastic revisions which the Deists demanded. The scientists also refused to argue from presuppositions; they insisted that we must begin with evidence. Theology had long been content with 'general terms' as its point of departure, and as a result had become abstract and remote. In the long run the new emphasis proved salutary; its immediate result was to discredit traditional theology as a discipline. In their investigations, the scientists were discovering satisfactions hitherto available only through conventional religious channels. They believed that they were engaged in a crusade against ignorance and superstition, and in prosecuting it they discovered that they were bound in a genuine kinship with all who pursued the same ends. In addition the new discoveries helped to open up for ordinary people a new world of experience. They found, as the title of Ray's famous work suggested, that *The Wisdom of God* (is) *Manifested in the Works of Creation*, and they verified the truth of his statement that 'the treasures of nature are inexhaustible'.

John Locke epitomized the intellectual outlook of his own age and shaped that of the next. For over a century he dominated European thought. His work, in conjunction with that of Newton, created a new mentality among intelligent people, and instantly affected religious thought. Sometimes he referred to theological matters in passing comments, sometimes he gave them his concentrated attention. The spirit in which he dealt with Christianity is more important than what he actually said about it. He made a certain attitude to religious faith almost universal.

Locke never minimized the importance of belief. In his greatest work, *An Essay Concerning Human Understanding*, his argument moves steadily toward the conclusion that beyond question God exists. Our awareness of ourselves is one of the simplest and surest elements in experience, and from it Locke deduces as a firm consequence the conviction that there is a God. This is 'the most obvious truth that reason discovers';

'its evidence' is 'equal to mathematical certainty'. The emphasis here is no less significant than the result. Belief is the consequence of rational proof. Locke not only showed how reason functions, he made its role, even in religion, appear inevitable and altogether right. In conjunction with Newton's work, he made it seem transparently clear that the evidence of reason runs through all things. The calm and dispassionate ease with which he proved his points accounts for his phenomenal success. Reason, it seemed, could resolve all difficulties and banish all mysteries. The effect on theology was revolutionary. In Mark Pattison's words, 'The title of Locke's treatise, *The Reasonableness of Christianity*, may be said to have been the solitary thesis of Christian theology in England for the greater part of a century.' The seventeenth century therefore ended with a confident affirmation of belief in God. But the God which it offered is notably impersonal. He is the suitable product of rational proof.

Locke's strong emphasis on reason naturally raised the question of the status of revelation. He did not doubt its reality or its importance, but he reinterpreted it in conformity with his general picture of the religious life. What revelation confirms is the essentially reasonable character of Christianity. It shows that few dogmas are necessary; they are simple, and intelligible to ordinary men. Christianity has one essential doctrine: Jesus is the Messiah. Locke thus carried simplification to its extreme limits; most of the structure of traditional theology was casually dismissed as irrelevant. Some authority was still necessary, and Locke found it in Scripture, particularly in the Gospels.

In his emphasis on right conduct Locke also spoke for his generation. A simple form of faith often needs to be supplemented by a vigorous type of ethics. Locke believed that moral standards must be fortified with strong inducements. Few people are sufficiently disinterested to follow righteousness without reward. Philosophers may commend the beauty of virtue, but most people will follow it only if attracted by rewards. Fortunately very solid advantages accrue to the man who does what is right, and thus interest reinforces ethics. Locke even found that the ministry of Jesus was based on a careful calculation of rewards and punishments; but it must be remembered that Locke lived in an age which had few qualms about being good for the sake of advantage. At every point, indeed, Locke spoke to a generation peculiarly disposed to receive his message. The high esteem which it accorded to reason made it ready to accept his version of a religious faith which conformed to all the canons of common sense. He bequeathed to the next age his version of Christianity and fortified it with the prestige of his interpretation of the mind of man.

Locke's influence can be detected in many quarters. Its most disconcerting manifestation was seen in the increased popularity of Deism. This school of thought reached its apex in the first half of the eighteenth century, but it first became a serious threat to orthodox Christianity in the closing years of the seventeenth. In England its earliest important exponent was Lord Herbert of Cherbury (brother of George Herbert, the poet), who summarized the main tenets of Deism in five fundamental truths: God exists; it is our duty to worship him; the proper way to do so is to practise virtue; men ought to repent of their sins; rewards and punishments will follow death. Herbert believed that this simple creed embraced all the essentials of Christianity. His five points were amplified by Charles Blount, with whom Deism assumed the guise of an attack on traditional beliefs. Revelation, he implied, was a disguise for superstition, and Christ was little better than the pagan wonder worker, Apollonius of Tyana. For a variety of reasons, Deism had considerable vogue. In a society where morals had collapsed, many found comfort in applauding any attack on the revelation which supported the Christian ethic. The vogue of reason in religion heightened the appeal of Deism as a system that was simple and rational. The immense popularity of Archbishop Tillotson's sermons told in favour of a type of faith which stressed practice, minimized theology, and leaned heavily on reason.

The initial phase of Deism ended with the publication in

1696 of John Toland's *Christianity Not Mysterious*. The school
now entered on its period of greatest activity and widest
influence. Toland was an Irish writer of facile rather than
profound gifts. The importance of his best-known book lies
in its ability to exploit familiar ideas. Toland presupposed
Locke's views and expanded them, but he was more than
Locke's echo. He clearly defined his aims. 'I prove first,' he
said, 'that the true religion must necessarily be reasonable
and intelligible. Next I show that these requisite conditions
are found in Christianity.' He further presupposed the necessity of revelation. But he defined all these key concepts in
terms acceptable to the prevailing intellectual climate. Reason was the cardinal reality. Revelation merely provided
supplementary information. It operated in a sphere governed
by rational considerations, which justified Toland in concluding that Christianity can contain nothing either contrary to reason or above it. Mystery was effectually banished.
Many of his ideas subsequently appeared in more extreme
forms, but meanwhile we have the essentials of Deism already developed: the primacy of reason, the supplementary
and subordinate role of revelation, the elimination of wonder, the curtailment of the supernatural, and the equivocal
position assigned to Scripture. We even have the hatred of
priestcraft which became so consistent an obsession of the
Deists.

In the sixteenth and seventeenth centuries political theory
carried important theological implications. The Restoration
period saw the divine right of kings reach a peak of apparently unassailable authority and then suddenly collapse. The
antecedents of the theory ran back to medieval times. Early
in the seventeenth century it had been championed by
James I, but it was the Civil War which lifted it to the status
of an official Anglican doctrine. It seemed to be the surest
defence against revolutionary views, and the cult of Charles,
King and Martyr, gave it an almost sacrosanct authority.
The divine right of kings was commended in innumerable
works. It was inculcated by preachers so different in outlook
as South, Stillingfleet, and Tillotson. It was enforced by

books of practical devotion like *The Whole Duty of Man*. It was taught at the universities as the distinguishing mark of a Church of England man. The practical consequence of divine right was passive obedience. Resistance to constituted authority was forbidden. If the king embarked upon courses repugnant to his people, they could suffer in silence but they could not oppose him, because 'rebellion is as the sin of witchcraft'. This theory, so widely advocated, so fervently embraced, collapsed when confronted with its actual consequences. James II pursued policies hateful to his people and certain to overthrow their liberties. His subjects suddenly realized that their favourite theory belonged to a departed age. To forsake it was a painful experience, and some refused to do so. The great apologist of the Revolution of 1688 was John Locke, and with his writings political theory virtually ceased to be a branch of theology.

In the early part of the seventeenth century, few people believed in toleration – a few theorists and a few sectaries. On the whole both Laudians and Puritans assumed that the triumph of their side would result in the proscription of the other party's views. Oliver Cromwell adopted toleration (except for Papists and Episcopalians at one end, and Quakers and other extreme groups at the other), but in tumultuous times toleration was a policy difficult to apply. With the Restoration, Anglicanism of a particular type triumphed and the Act of Uniformity, with its concomitant laws, was intended to regulate religious practice – and the expression of religious thought. Less than a generation later, the attempt to regiment religious conviction was abandoned. Persecution had proved ineffective; it did not coerce its victims and became an offence even to its advocates. Old hatreds died; new forces, social and political, exposed repression as a useless political instrument and an indefensible religious one. The increasing authority of reason made repressive zeal seem as 'enthusiastic' as the fanaticism of the sectaries. A steady stream of controversial literature had attacked the views of those who defended persecution, and had established, step by step, the claims of toleration. The

case had really been won when the political consequences of
the Revolution made it impossible for either of the parties
responsible for it to harry the clients of the other. Here,
again, Locke provided the theoretical defence of the toleration which would rule the outlook of the coming age.

The importance of the Restoration era lies in the intellectual changes which it witnessed. Within little more than a
generation we pass from an atmosphere still predominantly
medieval to one which is essentially modern. The prevailing
outlook changed. Questions emerged which still command
our interest. We still discuss the place of reason, the nature
of authority, the character of the universe, and we do so in
the spirit which first appeared in the latter part of the
seventeenth century.

6

Covenanters and Moderates in Scotland

SCOTLAND hailed the restoration of the Stuart line with relief and rejoicing. Recent troubles had been due to the nation's loyalty to its king and its covenants. The king who was now restored had promised to uphold the government of the church as established by law, but he had no sympathy with Presbyterianism, and gave little heed to men like Lauderdale who counselled him to maintain it in a moderate form. Yet the Presbyterians were unquestionably the strongest religious party in the country, even though they had forfeited the support of the nobility and were deeply divided among themselves. Early in the new reign Charles II served notice that he would grant no quarter to extremists: Argyll and Guthrie (the lay and clerical leaders of the Covenanters) were tried for treason and executed. In 1661 a 'Rescissory Act' rescinded the proceedings of all parliaments since 1633, and enabled Charles to treat episcopacy as the established form of church government. Episcopacy was not popular with Scotsmen; it was compromised in their eyes by past associations, but so widespread was weariness of strife that the change might have been accepted if it had been pressed with wisdom and moderation. These qualities, so sadly lacking in the past, were conspicuously absent in the years to come. The reintroduction of lay patronage touched Scottish susceptibilities at a sensitive point. Hundreds of ministers were ejected from their livings because they refused to comply with the new conditions, and their places were filled by men ill qualified to win the favour of the people. In its attempt to crush dissent the government imposed ruinous fines, and to collect them quartered dragoons on the recalcitrants.

Within three years of the Restoration a relationship had been created between the rulers and the people which explains the miseries of the remainder of Charles II's reign. Sporadic attempts were made to win over the malcontents, but the concessions offered were too half-hearted to effect their purpose, and they were promptly replaced by the ruthless severity which was the government's normal response to disaffection. This was the 'Killing time' which assumed an almost legendary status in the story of the Scottish church. Small companies of Covenanters, meeting on the moors or in the glens, were harried by dragoons and scattered without mercy. In the turbulent south-western counties disaffection was endemic, and from time to time flared up in open rebellion. These risings were ineffective because ill prepared. Among the Pentland Hills in 1666 and at Bothwell Brig in 1679, the insurgents proved no match for disciplined troops. Such outbreaks were stamped out with savage severity, and intensified the bitterness which poisoned Scottish life. This turbulent period achieved two results. Episcopacy was fatally discredited by the policies with which the government supported it, and thereby its ultimate fate in Scotland was sealed. But Presbyterianism was also profoundly affected. As a form of church government it strengthened its hold on the loyalty of Scotsmen, but the spirit which claimed to dominate the state was broken. The extreme Covenanters (represented by such groups as the Cameronians) maintained themselves as a dwindling body of irreconcilables, but most Scotsmen were at length prepared to worship as conscience dictated under a government free from constant interference from the church.

The brief reign of James showed that Scotsmen of all types were opposed to his policy of promoting Catholicism, and there was considerable relief when William of Orange arrived. The new king was sympathetic towards Presbyterianism, but he soon realized that there were political arguments (English as well as Scottish in origin) for maintaining episcopacy undisturbed. But the attitude of the Scottish bishops made it relatively easy for him to leave the question of church

government to be settled by the Scots alone. The bishops,
bound by their oath to James, refused to acknowledge the
new king. But Scotland had had enough of the Stuarts;
when the bishops refused to repudiate James most of their
supporters repudiated them, and prelacy was abolished in
1689. In the following year, the Presbyterian system was
reintroduced, and gradually assumed the form which was
henceforth to distinguish it. The system of church courts,
culminating in the General Assembly, was fully restored.
Within its own sphere, the church was free and autonomous;
the state abandoned any claim to make appointments or to
interfere with policy, and the jurisdiction of the church was
correspondingly defined. The two provinces were separated,
and a fruitful source of conflict removed. The link between
the two was the king, represented by his High Commis-
sioner, and early in the reign the ingenious procedure was
perfected whereby even the thorny question of summoning
and dissolving the General Assembly could be regulated
without compromise of its rights by either side. Thus the
bitter feud regarding the prerogative of the prince and the
freedom of the assembly was amicably settled. The Westminster Confession of Faith was recognized as the authoritative interpretation of the doctrine of the church, but other
documents (and notably the Covenants) were quietly ignored. The State restored the Presbyterian system without
committing itself to any doctrine of the divine and exclusive
claims of that system. The rights of patrons of livings were
restricted, but this change was temporary; after the union
of England and Scotland the parliament at Westminster
overruled this decision, with results that were both persistent
and unhappy. But the Act of Union also provided that the
Presbyterian Church of Scotland should be the national
church of Scotland, and the first official act of every
British sovereign is to take an oath to maintain 'the government, worship, discipline, rights and privileges' of that
church.

During the eighteenth century Presbyterianism in Scotland underwent a gradual process of far-reaching change, but at the outset the tone and pattern of church life reflected the past as much as they anticipated the future.

The effects of national poverty were everywhere apparent. Churches were unimpressive because dilapidated and unkempt. 'In many parts of Scotland,' remarked a traveller, 'our Lord seems still to be worshipped in a stable – and a very wretched one.' The house where the minister lived was often in keeping with the building in which he officiated. His stipend was small, and the demands of his calling were exacting. He received the respect due both to a man of God and to a person of education, but he was subject to the watchful scrutiny of his kirk-session. And the business of the session absorbed a large proportion of his time. Church discipline was severe and unrelenting. The oversight of the session extended to every part of every person's life. Any rumour of wrongdoing, any suggestion of laxity, was reported to the session and was examined with minute severity. In some areas the elders themselves went forth in search of offenders; every evening they patrolled the streets; they searched the taverns for loiterers; they entered private homes to track down offenders. Had a woman cursed her neighbour during a quarrel? After careful examination she was censured. Had a man carried home a pail of water on the Sabbath day? He must bear his penalty. For serious moral offences, the sinner was condemned to stand in the pillory on Sunday (sometimes for ten or fifteen or even twenty-six weeks) and submit to the admonition of the ministers. This was an ordeal which people dreaded, but it bore unequally on the rich and the poor. The laird's son could avoid punishment by paying a fine; the peasant's daughter had no prospect of escape.

For minister and people alike the Sabbath was a day of high and austere solemnity. All necessary preparations were completed on Saturday night, and on the Sabbath there was no hot meal in Scottish homes until evening. The whole day was so ordered that no secular activity should interfere with

the prescribed routine of reading the Scriptures, repeating
the catechism and participating in public worship. Church
attendance was a privilege, but it was also a duty in which
the faltering will of the people was strengthened by all the
pressures of public opinion. During the hours of service, the
elders patrolled the streets and searched out delinquents in
their homes. Yet the work of making others godly proved
difficult and discouraging. As the century progressed, com-
plaints from presbyteries multiplied: the Sabbath was not
observed with proper strictness.

Services of worship were simple in form, solemn in character, and inordinately long. The metrical psalms held a high
place in the affections of the people. The Scriptures were
read and expounded. Prayers were extempore; a minister
who prepared in advance was considered deficient in faith,
and if he could continue at great length with manifest fervour and without repetition it was regarded as a sign of grace.
It was expected, of course, that the sermon would be prepared with care, but delivered without notes. In 1720, the
General Assembly declared that the reading of sermons was
offensive to God's people and seriously obstructed spiritual
consolation. For the theme of his sermon, the minister
turned to the Word of God, but convention decreed that its
wealth should be displayed within an established pattern.
The 'four-fold state of man' provided the framework within
which the manifold aspects of Christian faith and duty could
most profitably be expounded. Human destiny could best be
understood if man's condition were considered in its original
innocency, in its fallen depravity, under the gospel of grace,
and in the eternal world. It was also expected that at the
second service of the Sabbath day the minister would preach
from his 'ordinary' – a text to which he was committed,
once he had selected it, for many weeks, indeed for many
months. This was a gauge of his ingenuity in finding unexpected truths hidden in familiar places, and its inexorable
compulsion often drove the harassed minister to curious
feats of interpretation.

The tone which pervaded most Scottish preaching was

still stern and unrelenting. Calvinism had hardened into a legalistic temper which distorted the great doctrines of the faith. It is true that the grace of our Lord Jesus Christ was sometimes set forth in all its winning appeal; the promise of pardon was extended, and the assurance of peace was proclaimed, but these were not the themes to which the preachers most commonly gravitated. Hell was a favourite topic. Its terrors were regarded as the most effective deterrents to sin. A great and good man like Ralph Erskine won fame by his vivid descriptions of the agonies of the damned. The penalties heaped upon the reprobate were portrayed with an ingenuity born of fascinated horror. 'God shall not pity them,' said Thomas Boston, 'but laugh at their calamity. The righteous company in heaven shall rejoice in the execution of God's judgement, and shall sing while the smoke riseth up for ever.' This was a terrible theme, even in the hands of a man touched with pity for his fellow-sinners, but with lesser preachers the drama of redemption shrank to 'a mercantile transaction and a vulgar bargain'. They reduced God 'to a sharp, suspicious legal practitioner' and the Cross 'to the proceedings of a sheriff's court'. In the exposition of the Atonement offered by a minister of considerable prestige, we are assured that the Son bore infinite pains 'from the vindictive anger of God ... ; pure wrath, nothing but wrath, the Father loved to see him die.' The very different type of preaching which prevailed later in the century can be understood only against the background of this dark and unrelenting account of the mysteries of grace.

The seriousness and solemnity of Scottish worship culminated in the celebration of the sacrament of the Lord's Supper. So high a festival presupposed the strictest preparation. For weeks in advance, the minister was busy visiting his flock and catechizing his people one by one. The session examined reports of wrongdoing and searched to the bottom every rumour of scandal, and in addition dealt with each of its own members. In his own district each elder was expected to reconcile enemies to one another so that all might come worthily to the table of the Lord. The 'communion season' brought together enormous crowds of worshippers, and the 'great work' lasted for days. On Thursday, Friday, and Saturday there were preaching services (often two or three a day) at which the people were earnestly exhorted to prepare themselves in penitence and with expectation to participate in the 'sacred solemnity'. The churches were far too small to accommodate the throngs which attended, and the services were held in the open air. On Sunday the communion services began at nine o'clock, and often lasted throughout the day. Each successive 'table' – and there might be thirty in all – was admonished by one of the participating ministers, and the penalties of communicating unworthily were graphically described. The 'fencing address' specified the sins (trivial as well as grave) which might disqualify the communicant, and terrible denunciations were levelled against those who drew near without considering what they did. The day ended with a sermon, and on Monday the communion season was brought to a close with a great service of thanksgiving.

Yet the very solemnity of the occasion created serious problems. It was good that the communion should confront men with the extent of their spiritual need and with the greatness of God's mercy in meeting it, but the prevailing atmosphere of the occasion often plunged men's souls into a turmoil of fear and anxiety, while those who were not moved to awe were moved to ridicule. The size of the throngs which gathered was such that a small community could not cope with them. There was no shelter, and bad weather caused great discomfort. Food was often scarce. A poor congregation might be troubled to provide communion wine for so great a throng, and so the communion season would of necessity be postponed, sometimes for months.

During the first half of the eighteenth century the temper of Scottish religious life began to change. The stringencies of the old-fashioned Calvinism were relaxed. The harshness of the dogma so long expounded by the stricter preachers was modified by forces at work in the national life. Belief in devils, witchcraft, and sorcery fell into the background. A new type of Evangelical appeared, earnest and devout yet humane and sympathetic. The terrors of Hell occupied a less prominent place in the thought of ministers and people alike. The relaxing of the old intensities did not necessarily mean the absence of fervour. At Cambuslang and Kilsyth notable and famous revivals took place, and these had far-reaching results.

The new outlook steadily gained ground, and its exponents, the Moderates, finally produced a revolution in Scottish thought. In the first instance, however, they used an instrument which ostensibly bore little relation to intellectual trends, and which had disastrous consequences in Scottish life. Patronage had long been a vexed question in Scotland. More than once it had been both abolished and revived, and under circumstances which identified it with wider issues: the freedom of the church and the authority of the state. In 1712, by action of the parliament at Westminster, it was restored, over the protest of Scotsmen, and against the wishes of the Scottish church. For seventy years patronage was regarded as a major grievance. Every General Assembly instructed its commission to work for its removal. But as the eighteenth century progressed, the Moderates found in patronage an instrument of enlightenment. Through its use it was possible to place ministers in livings even when their theological views were abhorrent to the people. In addition the patronage issue was a means by which the central government of the church could be strengthened and the authority of the General Assembly augmented.

The spirit shown in this matter by the Moderates was not enlightened and awoke violent opposition. It was directly responsible for the emergence of the dissent which was so striking a feature of the eighteenth century. For many years after the Revolution dissenters were a negligible element in Scottish life. The Cameronians were a tiny group of incorrigibles. The Episcopalians were seriously compromised by their Jacobite sympathies; their numbers were small, their congregations weak, their clergy miserably poor. In belief and even in worship they were originally almost indistinguishable from the Church of Scotland. It was patronage which created dissent on an appreciable scale. In 1732 the General Assembly passed an act which strengthened the authority of patrons, and Ebenezer Erskine and four other ministers protested. They were deposed, and promptly formed the Associate Presbytery. In due course, and under similar circumstances, the Relief Church was founded. There was no doubt about the zeal of the seceders. From great distances men and women would gather for worship in a church where they would find pure gospel ministrations, untainted by the contamination of Erastianism. Unfortunately there was also no doubt about the strain of bitterness which they introduced into Scottish life, and its results were evident within their own churches. The Seceders themselves were split by secessions. Burghers and Anti-burghers, Auld Lichts and New Lichts, Lifters and Anti-lifters – so ran the record of division. Nor was the established church any wiser or more charitable than its critics. It ruthlessly pushed through a series of forced settlements, and each resulted in the establishment of a dissenting congregation. The Moderates pressed home their advantage, but the price of victory was high. The church itself came to acquiesce in the patronage it had once denounced, and complacently accepted what their predecessors had bitterly condemned as an indefensible intrusion of the civil power into the life of the church.

Moderatism was primarily an intellectual, not an ecclesiastical, movement. Its greatest victory – also achieved at a heavy cost – was the creation of a new religious temper and a new theological outlook. It could claim a lineage which antedated the intensities of Covenanting days, but its immediate origin can be found in the influence of Shaftesbury's ethics, as mediated through the persuasive teaching of Professor Hutcheson of Glasgow. An optimistic view of human nature replaced the doctrine of total depravity. Reprobation, and even salvation by faith alone, dropped from sight as he expounded an ethic in which man's duty consisted in achieving the beauty of an inner harmony and his happiness in finding himself at one with the vast universe revealed by Newton. The new teaching was infectious. Attempts to check it – notably by heresy trials at Glasgow and St Andrews, failed. Preachers instructed in the new doctrines spoke much of virtue, liberality, and benevolence; they extolled 'the harmony of the passions' and were silent about the great themes of Calvinism. They quoted Plato oftener than Paul, though in passing one might compliment the Apostle by remarking that he 'had a university education, and was instructed in logic by Professor Gamaliel'. These were the 'paganized Christian divines' of whom Erskine complained. It was a leader of the Moderates whom Hume accused of preaching 'heathen morality'. Thomas Chalmers said that the sermons of the Moderates were like a fine winter's day – short, clear, and cold. 'The brevity', he added, 'is good, and the clearness better, but the coldness is fatal. Moonlight preaching ripens no harvest.'

By the middle of the eighteenth century, the triumph of the new school was virtually complete. Its leaders were the ablest and most influential figures in the church, and their influence spread to every area of national life. They promoted trade and fostered improvements in agriculture. They were prominent in the world of letters and in the cultured circles of the capital. They were in the forefront of the intellectual renascence which made Edinburgh one of the most brilliant cities of Europe. During a debate in the General Assembly, Alexander Carlyle extolled the distinction of the ministers of the Church of Scotland. They had written the best histories, ancient and modern; had produced the clearest delineation of the human understanding; had evolved the best system of rhetoric and exemplified it; had composed the best modern tragedy; had produced the most profound mathematical works – and so the catalogue continued. Scotland, after hovering on the very periphery of European culture, now found itself at its centre. It had so completely assimilated the ideas of the French and English Enlightenment that even Voltaire acknowledged that 'it is from Scotland we receive rules of taste in all the arts – from the epic poem to gardening'. And this varied and brilliant life was mainly within the church, not outside it. Hume, indeed, stood apart, and some even attempted to bring him to trial before the General Assembly, but he was on terms of cordial friendship with the leading philosophers of the church. Principal William Robertson, the dominating leader of the church for a generation, was considered one of the great historians of the age. The General Assembly itself gathered together the ablest Scotsmen from every walk of life; in its debates they considered issues of national importance, and the brilliance of its proceedings gained added significance from the fact that it was the only national forum in which important matters were discussed.

These notable gains were offset by serious losses. The clergy had never been so highly respected. They were men of culture and ability, but they had given serious hostages to the state, and the state kept them poor. The lay leaders of the Assembly refused to augment ministerial stipends. 'A poor church', they complacently affirmed, 'is a pure church.' Preaching was simple, direct, and practical, but often it consisted of little more than common sense, decked out as moral counsel. Many of the ministers were faithful and devoted pastors, but when they reveal their inner thoughts and interests (as Alexander Carlyle does in his *Memoirs*) an unrelieved secularism seems to pervade them. The Moderates had drifted far from the doctrines to which they still pledged assent and an uneasy conscience betrays their awareness of the fact. For all its self-confidence, Moderatism lacked both originality and self-propagating power. So it stands condemned in the withering words of that brilliant Scotsman who found its exhortations so unavailing.

> Smith opens out his cauld harangues
>   On practice and on morals,
> And aff the godly pour in thrangs
>   To gie the jars and barrels
>   A lift that day.
>
> What signifies his barren shine
>   Of moral powers and reason?
> His English style and gestures fine
>   Are a' clean out of season.

Like Socrates or Antonine
Or some auld pagan heathen
The moral man he does define
But n'er a work of faith in
What's richt that day.

7

Germany: Orthodoxy, Pietism, and Rationalism

FOR the German principalities the Peace of Westphalia ended an ordeal as severe and prolonged as any which Europe has experienced in modern times. The Thirty Years' War had spread desolation throughout the land. The structure of economic life had been virtually destroyed, culture had ceased to exist, moral standards had collapsed, a war waged on religious pretexts had all but extinguished religious life. The records of the period leave no doubt that for the ordinary man life had become 'poor, nasty, brutish, and short'.

The terms of the peace treaties inevitably represented a compromise. Certain ecclesiastical states were absorbed by their neighbours. Some bishoprics changed hands. The Protestants made gains in the north but suffered losses elsewhere. Three main religions were recognized, Roman Catholic, Lutheran, and Reformed. Each was the established faith in one principality or another; where not the official religion, its status varied considerably from place to place. Minorities were subjected to various kinds of pressure; on occasion these amounted to severe persecution, at other times they assumed more polite but perhaps more insidious forms.

The pattern of organized church life was dictated by the interplay of historic forces and contemporary needs. It had been a tradition in German states that the religion of the prince determined the faith of his people. The principle could no longer be strictly applied. Changes had been so numerous that a simple formula like *cuius regio eius religio* would have aggravated the confusions which it was hoped that the Peace would end. And changes were by no means over. In spite of the exhaustions of war, the proselytizing spirit was active. Various rulers were induced to change their faith. When a Protestant princeling became a Catholic, he could not compel his subjects to follow his example. He could place inducements in their way; he could offer advantages to his co-religionists, and the official faith often possessed powerful attractions. The elector of Saxony espoused Romanism, and was elected King of Poland. In both Hesse and Hanover, the ruling houses flirted with Catholicism, but in the latter case its leading representatives reverted to Lutheranism in time to qualify for the throne of Protestant England. A more tragic example of the tensions between prince and people is provided by the Palatinate. Few states had suffered so grievously during the war; in none were the miseries of conflict protracted so long. In pursuing his expansionist policy, Louis XIV overran the state, and subjected it to terrible devastation. When he withdrew in 1697, he left a Catholic prince in power, with the Jesuits as his ecclesiastical agents. Intense persecution followed. Every effort was made to disrupt Protestantism by exploiting the differences between the Lutherans and Calvinists. The Reformed consistory was corrupted; expedients were devised to degrade the religion of the people; nothing was done to alleviate the misery which Louis had created. The situation became so acute that twice the Protestant powers compelled the emperor to intervene, but the hold of the Jesuits remained unbroken till Napoleon's readjustment of German states. In spite of persecution and emigration the Protestant element never fell below two-thirds of the population, while Catholics remained a minority in spite of all that official encouragement could effect.

The territorial settlement of Germany confirmed the independence of a multitude of principalities, and in each the church was largely dependent on the ruler. Small self-contained establishments were robbed of the invigorating sense of participating in a wider life, and stagnation was an ever present danger. In Protestant states the relations of the ruler with the church were determined by what is called the

'territorial system'. Originally it was a temporary expedient, pending the creation of a National Evangelical
Church. 'Superintendents' were substituted for bishops, but
from the outset it was clear that their powers would be circumscribed by the claims of the prince. As 'high magistrate'
the ruler appointed a supreme ecclesiastical council. A
general superintendent was nominated; the hierarchical
principle was retained to a certain extent, but many administrative functions were transferred to the state. The
prototype of the system was established in Saxony and with
various modifications was adopted in other states. In time
the claims of the princes increased. They were not content
with subservient superintendents; the *jus episcopale*, they insisted, was vested in themselves: by right as well as in fact
they were in effective control of church life. As a result there
were states where no working system of synods existed,
and where those who advocated church courts were branded
as 'crypto-Calvinists', disloyal to an institution characteristic of German life. Provided that the sacraments were
purely administered and the gospel truly taught, Lutheran
thought recognized much variety as permissible in church
order, and was often content with an administration of the
affairs of the church by the state, so long as this made for
good order. Their tradition of thought could appeal with
reason both to Luther and to Melanchthon. Christian
society was conceived as a unity, *unum corpus Christianum*, not
divided into 'spiritual' and 'secular'. In practice these ideas
were much strengthened because the tranquillity of Germany
rested on the peace of Westphalia, which based itself on
the old principle that the prince and the religion of his
state must be in union. When pietism arose with its in-
sistence on the inward and individual character of faith, it
operated in the same direction.

In Prussia the results of this system appeared most clearly,
and from Prussia they spread throughout Germany. It was
a fixed part of the policy of Frederick William I (king
1713–40) to centralize his administration, and part of that
policy established control over the consistories. He set up

(1730) the first ministry for church affairs, with a member of the privy council at its head, who by the end of the reign supervised the consistories both Lutheran and Reformed. This aimed at a modern centralized state which could secure toleration between or union of the Protestant denominations. Thus he tried to dictate the pattern of Lutheran worship and the subject matter of Calvinist sermons, and so tried (without success) to bring the two main Protestant bodies together. Catholics were tolerated; they occupied an inferior position, but were so well treated that the Pope himself was satisfied. The victims of religious persecution (the Protestants ejected from Salzburg and the Huguenots driven from France) were encouraged to immigrate – for a combination of religious, economic, and military reasons.

His son Frederick the Great (king 1740–86) was a different kind of ruler, for he reacted against his father and his father's religion, and privately repudiated Christianity. Nevertheless he pressed the view that the civil ruler has absolute power over all forms of religious activity. The church possessed no independent rights. It had no legal authority and no powers of self-government. Ministers were responsible to the king, not to their congregations; their independence was no greater than, their rights no different from, those of any other servant of the state. Frederick granted equal toleration to all faiths, partly because he regarded all of them as equally spurious, partly because military considerations made it expedient. But toleration did not extend to unlimited attacks on religion; faith might be a delusion but it was still a valuable instrument of social control, and anything that kept the masses quiet was too useful to be discarded. Infidelity was the prerogative of the élite. The restricted freedom which Frederick permitted the church rested on a utilitarian motive; contempt for Christianity as a faith was modified by appreciation of the church as an instrument. The principles underlying this attitude were codified in the Prussian Landrecht of 1791 – a code of law drafted by Frederick's jurists, but issued after his death. The ecclesiastical system under this code granted an appreciable amount of liberty to individuals and congregations. The church was allowed some freedom in calling pastors and judging them, and was permitted to alter its liturgy, but all changes had to be approved by the government. All holders of office were appointed or approved by the state, and property matters were subject to government control. Discipline might be applied, provided it did not infringe a person's honour or property rights. A limited degree of self-government was thus granted the church, but the value of the concession was vitiated by the assumptions which inspired it. The church was not regarded as an institution sustained by a certain faith and expressing that faith in an appropriate corporate life. It was treated as a useful agency of public policy, designed to inculcate such valuable attitudes as integrity, loyalty, submission, and obedience.

What, we may ask, was the character of the church life which such a system encouraged? Laymen had great opportunity to share in church affairs as lawyers, administrators or patrons, but hardly otherwise. Patrons, especially in the earlier part of our period, had the right of presentation to church livings, but they were not always equipped to exercise it wisely. Family influence often played a large part in determining a choice. Occasionally a candidate was forced to accept irrelevant and even humiliating conditions like being driven to marry his predecessor's widow, or even his patron's mistress. As the period advanced, such abuses diminished, and flagrantly unsuitable appointments were rare. The influence of public opinion helped to keep intellectual and moral standards high. By the eighteenth century the level of the Protestant ministry had risen appreciably. Behind the candidate lay a period of study at a university, and often a spell as a teacher or a private tutor. In the universities many of the poorer students were destined for the ministry. Most of them were of humble origin; the sons of more prosperous families chose more lucrative careers. Some scholarships were available for poor students, but they were always insufficient both in number and in amount. Few graduates could expect to receive a congregation at once, and most of them turned temporarily to teaching. Some became tutors and many famous men – e.g., Kant, Hegel, Fichte, Schleiermacher–began their careers in this way.

The standard of living among Protestant pastors was apt to be low. University professors were a favoured group, and were accorded high respect. The ministers in larger towns occupied an intermediate status, though their income was far below that of most government officials. In the country the pastor's lot was often worse than that of a peasant or a successful craftsman. His income usually consisted of tithes, paid with reluctance and collected with difficulty. Necessity compelled him to turn to a variety of expedients to support himself and his family. As the eighteenth century progressed, the state increasingly demanded that the pastors should act as its functionaries. As a result, Protestant ministers acquired an assured position in society, but they lost more of the spiritual independence which they still possessed. The government treated them as useful channels of communication between itself and the people. The pulpit was the most convenient place from which to publish official decrees. As the only educated man in the village, the pastor discharged many duties now performed by civil servants. He provided necessary information, acted as registrar and statistician, assisted in recruiting for the army, appointed midwives, and presided at minor courts. 'A minister', remarked Herder bitterly, 'is only entitled to exist now, under state control and by authority of the prince, as a moral teacher, a farmer, a list-maker, a secret agent of the police.' Certainly he led a varied and busy life. In spite of the difficulties created by his position and the discouragements arising from the temper of the times, he often maintained a worthy, even a high, professional standard. There were hundreds of devout and learned men in the Protestant parsonages of Germany. Herder was one of the few incontestably in the first class as an author, but there were many who made an appreciable contribution to the development of an independent German literature, while the part played by the sons of pastors was notable indeed.

In Roman Catholic principalities the clergy occupied a somewhat higher social position. The members of the hierarchy and the cathedral clergy usually came of good families. In the Rhineland and in the Catholic south, the church provided ecclesiastical princedoms for the younger sons of ruling houses, and in the religious foundations it offered the lesser aristocracy a life of dignified leisure, not unduly restricted by discipline. The latter part of the seventeenth century witnessed considerable missionary activity on the part of the Catholic church. The Counter-Reformation had by no means spent its force. Strenuous efforts were made to convert Protestant princes, and the apostolate to the lapsed was vigorously pressed. The papal nuncios played an important role, and there were a number of conspicuously devoted missionary preachers. In the eighteenth century, the Roman Catholics felt the impact of the various influences at work in German society. The effects of state absolutism were less pronounced than elsewhere but were by no means negligible. Pietism, though Protestant in origin, affected Catholic devotional life, while the challenge of rationalism steadily increased.

Protestant principalities, however, were intellectually more vigorous than the Catholic states; they were therefore the centres of the movements most characteristic of German life during our period. At the outset, the prospects were far from promising. The Thirty Years War left Germany exhausted, and the evidences of an alarming moral collapse were everywhere apparent. The common people were weary of theological controversy, but the church seemed blind to the need for regeneration. The intellect was in the ascendant, and in a particularly arid form, while vast and intricate dogmatic systems fortified the rival positions of Lutheran and Calvinist theologians. There was no perception of the symbolical character of much religious thought. Disputation had become the accepted method by which religious truth was enforced, indeed the prevailing spirit which governed church life. Strict orthodoxy became an obsession. Logic, pedantry, and the parade of learning had sometimes usurped the central place even in worship. A show of learning, appropriate in controversy, was surely out of place in the pulpit. Yet at times the sermon provided a pretext for the parade of abstruse and irrelevant knowledge. The people might be fed on diatribes against Patripassianism and other heresies long dead. 'The sermon', said Grossgebauer, 'is for most preachers an oration or an artificial rhetorical speech pieced together from the Bible.' Though not typical, a sermon of 1605 on 'The very hairs of your head are all numbered' illustrates the arid formalism which did service for Christian truth. The divisions were as follows: (1) the origin, style, form, and natural position of our hair; (2) the correct care of the hair; (3) reminiscences, reminders, warnings, and comfort derived from the hair; (4) how to wear the hair in a good Christian fashion. As the plain English preaching of Tillotson reacted against the subtle style of Andrewes, so German preachers at the end of the seventeenth century sought for plain earnest sense, and distrusted the rhetoric of their predecessors.

Germany was slow to recover from its exhaustion. The universities were still fettered by ancient patterns of thought. Literature was moribund, and science was suspect. The fear of witchcraft still obsessed the minds of the peasants. Anti-semitism was widespread. But elements of promise were not wholly lacking. A more liberal strain of Lutheranism, stemming from Melanchthon's teaching, showed signs of vitality. The University of Helmstedt was relatively free from obscurantism. One of its leading lights, Calixtus (d. 1656), returned to the first five centuries of Christianity and sought there the materials out of which he constructed his theology. Men like Durie, Molanus, and Andreae worked for a peaceful solution of German religious differences. But as the seventeenth century drew toward its close, the aridity of theology and the formalism of church life seemed impervious to attack. Rigidity appeared to be triumphant. 'Every leaf of the tree of life', said Herder, 'was so dissected that the dryads wept for mercy.'

Under such circumstances, Pietism was born. It was the protest of living faith against a lifeless and unbending orthodoxy. Like every revolutionary movement of the spirit, it had its precursors and its pioneers. The hymns of Paul Gerhardt, works of popular devotion like Arndt's *True Christianity*, the graphic and realistic preaching of men like Schupp and Grossgebauer had kept alive a strain of genuine Lutheran piety. The influence of the great German mystics (e.g., Meister Eckhardt and Jacob Boehme) had never been wholly eradicated. The man chiefly responsible for the rise of Pietism was P. J. Spener (d. 1705). In 1675 he published his *Pia desideria*, which combined an attack on existing evils in the church with specific proposals for their reform. He appealed, on the basis of principles which Luther himself had laid down, for a revival of personal religion. He saw that worship had become formal and lifeless; he knew that the church services could recover their power only if they recaptured the freshness and vitality which they had lost. He showed that simplicity and evangelical fervour could make preaching once more relevant to daily needs; he advocated a reform of pastoral methods and of the training of the preachers. Piety and the fear of God should be restored to their rightful and central position, and the clergy should be reminded that their sermons ought to be less disputatious and more devotional in character. The devotional life had grown sluggish and practical charity was neglected; so he established centres of fellowship (his *Collegia pietatis*) which would disseminate the Word of God through all classes of the population. The task of promoting the religious life belonged to the laity as well as to the clergy. Christianity was not an intricate system of abstruse doctrines, but the practice of a transforming way of life. Good works had their legitimate place, because faith must find outward expression, and the two are inseparable: faith is the sun, good works are its rays.

At first his projected reforms aroused hostility. While he was court preacher at Dresden, his relations with the Elector of Saxony were far from easy, but in 1691 he was called to a more influential position in Berlin, and there found encouragement and support. In 1694 the University of Halle was founded to serve as the centre of the new movement. Its influence grew rapidly. At the height of its fame, 1,200 students passed through its theological faculty each year. It also became the training ground for officials of the expanding Prussian state. Nor did the university stand alone. Its work was supplemented by a galaxy of associated institutions – an orphanage, a printing press, a dispensary, a Bible institute, as well as schools of various kinds – and each in its own way served the common end. Under Spener and his colleague and successor, A. H. Francke, the influence of Halle spread far and wide. It stood for a theology less preoccupied with controversy, a church less sunk in apathy and less contaminated by worldliness, a Christian fellowship more deeply conversant with the Bible and more actively participating in every kind of philanthropic enterprise. The Pietists were pioneers in promoting Protestant missionary work. Francke was largely responsible for launching the Halle-Danish mission in South India, and sent Mühlenberg to America to organize the Lutheran Church in the new world. Gradually Pietism spread to all parts of Germany. In the larger centres its impact was very powerful, but it did not always succeed in reaching the smaller parishes. In this respect the work of J. A. Bengel pointed the way to a more effective penetration of the life of the entire church. He was a notable Biblical scholar and a very influential figure in Württemberg. He recognized the limitations from which Pietism had often suffered, and took care to combine emotion and thought, individual conversion and corporate responsibility. To a remarkable degree, Pietism leavened church life in the principality. It assumed the character of a popular movement, and penetrated even to the parish level.

In the later phase of Pietism, the outstanding figure was Count von Zinzendorf. He was a man of ardently emotional temperament. He believed that the mark of true Christianity is a simple and childlike faith: it is enough to believe in the power of the blood of Jesus and to trust wholly in the merits of the Lamb of God. In vivid, almost erotic, imagery he described the relation of the soul to Christ. Love, as a warm emotional glow, lay at the heart of his religious life. In 1722 he offered asylum on his estates to Moravian refugees who had been driven from Hapsburg lands by religious persecution, and the community which they established at Herrnhut became the centre of a new and dynamic phase of the Pietist movement. The distinguishing mark of their life was its combination of intense personal experience with a deep sense of corporate fellowship. At Herrnhut the importance of personal experience was strongly emphasized, but eccentricity was controlled by the disciplines of community life. The Moravian Brethren felt that they were bound together in an indissoluble unity because of the deep personal relationship of each individual to Jesus Christ. In time the fellowship evolved into a separate denomination (the renewed Church of the Brethren) but Zinzendorf, as its bishop, made no attempt to organize schism on an extensive scale. Gradually the more exuberant type of devotional imagery was subdued, and the unhealthy strain of over-intense emotion was brought under control. Herrnhut played a notable part in the expansion of missionary work. It inherited the traditions of earlier Pietism, but it systematized and expanded its efforts. Never has a whole community been so entirely devoted to the spread of the Gospel. Its resources in men and money were limited, but by the end of the eighteenth century the Moravians had established missions in every part of the world. Zinzendorf has been called the greatest German evangelical since Luther, and under his direction Herrnhut made a notable contribution not only to Germany but to the whole of Christendom.

Pietism demonstrated the resilience of German Protestantism; it showed that it had within it immense powers of recuperation and renewal. Scarcely an aspect of church life remained untouched by its influence. It shifted the emphasis from arid controversy to the care of souls; it broke the paralysing hold of Lutheran scholasticism and insisted on the uselessness of dogma when unrelated to life. It stressed the importance of pastoral visitation, and created a new bond between ministers and people. It revived the sense of communal responsibility and of the priestly obligations which all Christians must accept. Unity and corporate fellowship were restored to their proper place in the life of the church. Though its influence was so pervasive, Pietism never lost its sharply defined characteristics as a movement of religious renewal. Regeneration was its dominant theme, and this was defined not as a theological doctrine but as the central and indispensable experience of the Christian. Closely akin to its view of salvation was its emphasis on the power of evil. The soul was the scene of a desperate and decisive encounter. But the way in which the Pietist conceived of sin and of his victory over it meant that religion was largely identified with a certain kind of personal experience. In making Christianity inward, the Pietists often made it subjective. Introspection became a characteristic activity, and sometimes degenerated into a morbid preoccupation with the state of the individual soul. Duttenhofer, a critic who wrote at the end of the eighteenth century, felt that this weakness was due to the lack of a proper sense of proportion. 'By Pietism I understand merely that kind or sort of subjective Christianity which places on devout pious feelings and on external devout forms and customs much more emphasis than they intrinsically deserve.' Emotion played so large a part in the religious life that the role of reason was seriously disparaged. Since the intellect could not fathom the mysteries of human destiny, it was left to feeling and intuition to make good the defect. The attack on reason was directed against two types of opponent: the dogmatic theologian and the rationalist free-thinker. 'He who wishes to comprehend God with his mind becomes an atheist,' wrote Zinzendorf. Pietism failed to keep spiritual vitality and intellectual vigour in proper balance, and this was its most serious defect. It was responsible for the relative sterility of Pietism as a theological force. Pietism was hesitant in its approach to nature and to history, and was suspicious of contemporary movements in science and philosophy. The intellectual timidity of the movement disguised itself in vivid, almost sensuous, forms of expression. Thought might be discouraged, but imagination was allowed free play. At certain points, however, Pietism was responsible for appreciable gains. Christianity and its message ceased to be abstract. The human elements in the Gospel story were rescued from neglect. 'I believe our Saviour himself spoke broad dialect,' said Zinzendorf. And though it stood aloof from the theological debate, Pietism recognized the need for a strong emphasis on the moral responsibilities of the Christian.

In other ways, not always specifically religious in character, Pietism affected German life. It provided a powerful stimulus to education, and the country was indebted to the Pietist leaders for the way in which they devised new theories and experimented with new methods. By stressing the national language as the appropriate medium both for religion and for education they raised its status and thus contributed to the growth of German literature. They resisted the introduction of alien ways of life and of thought. They distrusted French influence, and fearlessly condemned the luxury and extravagance which the German nobility copied from Versailles. They paved the way for a notable increase in the unity and cohesion of the German people. Their influence touched the life of the nation at many points. They did not challenge (or even criticize) class distinctions, but they helped to overcome them. They reached the humblest elements in the population, and brought them into contact with other social groups. The Pietist meetings for fellowship combated the exclusiveness which the church shared with society at large, and fostered active cooperation among the classes. Pietism gave the poor a new self-respect. It was never a revolutionary movement; because it was accused of subversive tendencies, it was careful to affirm its respectability, but unquestionably it helped those who responded to its influence to transcend the class barriers which it did not attack. In denouncing the absolutism of the princes, it was more courageous. In its resistance to the control of religious opinion, Pietism represented an outspoken assertion of individual rights in the face of the entrenched prerogatives of the civil rulers. The creation of German unity had been frustrated as much by religious as by political barriers. As long as the violent polemics of the sixteenth and seventeenth centuries continued, progress was inconceivable; controversy poisoned every phase of life and effectively hindered the creation of a national consciousness. Pietism and rationalism were jointly responsible for creating a more tolerant spirit; of the two, Pietism probably had the more constructive influence. Between them, they undermined the rigid Lutheran orthodoxy which had been the principal bulwark of the particularism of the German principalities. In addition, Pietism fostered the growth of a vigorous patriotism; and in due course this contributed to the development of German nationalism.

At one point after another the subsequent influence of Pietism can be traced in German life. It paved the way for the humanism and the universalism of the Enlightenment. It won for the individual his freedom to develop his capacities in his own way. It was one of the sources of the outpouring of imaginative vitality which made the closing years of the eighteenth century so splendid an era. But as a religious movement its period of full vigour was comparatively brief. Why? Partly because its principles degenerated into prejudices. Its view of doctrine was meagre and utilitarian. It treated the new life as a subjective process and forgot that justification must always be regarded as the act of God. It reduced conversion to a conventional sequence of prescribed experiences. It implied that the way we feel affects our acceptance with God, and this is a sure indication that legalism is beginning to invade the religious life. By restricting its own outlook, Pietism limited its scope.

By the middle of the eighteenth century the vigour of Pietism was clearly on the wane. The response to the simple yet informed ministry of Gerhard Tersteegen (now best remembered for his hymns) proved that the German people were hungry for a more authentic statement of the living Gospel. In Oetinger and Claudius, the strain of Pietist devotion showed powers of adaptation that foreshadowed its revived influence in the nineteenth century.

8

Russia and the Eastern Churches

CHRISTIANITY was by origin an eastern religion. For the first thousand years of its history, the great centres of its life and learning were still in the lands which border the eastern Mediterranean Sea. Gradually the balance shifted westward. The original citadels of the faith were inundated by the tide of the Moslem invasion, while the power and wealth and civilization of the west steadily increased. In the seventeenth century, and even in the eighteenth, it was easy to equate the frontiers of Christendom with those of Western Europe. It is therefore a valuable corrective to remember the ancient churches which maintained a precarious existence in the regions where Christianity began.

Concerning many of them there is little to relate. The conditions which governed their life offered no scope for development; to maintain their character and to perpetuate their life was the measure of their hope. Though they were exposed to common problems they did not share a common life. Many of them traced their separate existence to ancient controversies in the early history of the church. The Nestorians were widely scattered; they could be found in Persia, in South India, and in Turkey. Another group of churches had arisen as a result of the disputes about the one nature (Monophysite) and one will (Monothelite) of our Lord; in Syria there were the Jacobite Christians; in Egypt and Ethiopia, the Copts. These churches were not in communion with the ancient patriarchates of the East (Jerusalem, Antioch, Alexandria, Constantinople), but they had much in common not only with one another but with the Orthodox churches from which they were divided. There were marked similarities in ritual, doctrine, and organization; in general character and even in the atmosphere which pervaded their life they conformed to a common pattern. Most of these churches were small, and had passed through difficult times, often through persecution. Their stubborn tenacity, which was the condition of their survival, was also responsible for an inflexible (almost a fossilized) kind of life.

With the exception of the church in Russia, the Orthodox churches had passed under the sway of Islam. Christians were permitted to exist on sufferance and were condemned to a subordinate and inferior status. Turkish policy organized them into a semi-autonomous community, and made the clergy responsible for the control of the people's life. The price of power was high: the clergy were required to collect the extortionate taxes which the government imposed, and were expected to produce the required tribute of youths to be trained as Turkish troops. The system was nicely calculated to degrade and corrupt the church. The clergy became the agents of oppression; the Greeks of Constantinople became subservient to their Ottoman rulers, and conspired to extend their own influence at the expense of other branches of the church. They secured control of the hierarchies of the Serbian and Bulgarian churches. They gained possession of the patriarchate of Antioch; they did their utmost to seize that of Jerusalem as well. Wherever they were successful they introduced their own liturgy, and substituted Greek for the language of the national church. Steadily they sowed the seeds of animosity among the churches of the Orthodox communion. Apart from a limited measure of power, their gains were small. Worship was permitted, but under precarious conditions. Evangelism (usually the measure of a church's vitality) was forbidden; the penalties for proselytizing were severe, while the advantages of apostasy were ever present. It was inevitable that the monasteries became the real citadels of the church's life. To a more limited extent than in the west, eastern monasticism had been concerned to transform the life of the world around it; of necessity it now became increasingly defensive and self-contained.

*

Only in Russia was the Orthodox church delivered from the incubus of a hostile power, and even in Russia (as events were to prove) it was far from free. Toward the end of the sixteenth century, the Russian church had become national in substance as well as in form. The strong Byzantine tradition assumed that the church would be under the control of the state, but the issues were defined in a way peculiar to Russia. The dukedom of Moscow was invested with a strongly religious significance. The doctrine of the 'third Rome' proclaimed that the Holy Orthodox Tsardom was divinely appointed to preserve the true faith. The second Rome, like the first, had fallen because of apostasy; the third Rome would survive till the Second Coming of Christ. But the faith thus entrusted for safe-keeping was conceived partly in formal and ritualistic terms. This was inevitable under existing circumstances. In many parts of Russia Christianity was still relatively new; it had not been profoundly assimilated by a people until recently still pagan. There was no vigorous theological tradition. The clergy were painfully ill-prepared; indeed, they were often wholly illiterate. Christianity was identified with a certain system of established forms of prayer; and since these were regarded as possessing an almost magical power, the slightest change might rob them of their efficacy. The distinctive task of Russian Orthodoxy was seen as the preservation in perpetuity of the tradition it had received, and in the sixteenth century the authorities of church and state alike had encouraged this devotion to everything that was distinctive of the Russian rite. This had fostered an unquestioning loyalty; it paved the way for a disastrous breach.

The concept of the 'third Rome' had been useful to Moscow in extending its power. In the middle of the seventeenth century an able and aggressive patriarch, Nikon, saw his task as the extending of the Tsar's leadership over all Orthodox people. But this involved the abandonment of the isolation in which the Russians had clung to their distinctive ways. Closer relationships with the five Eastern patriarchs involved a re-examination of the Russian service books.

Hitherto it had been sufficient to abuse the Greeks for their deviations from Russian practice, but careful study showed that at many points the Greeks were right and the Russians wrong. Translations had been faulty, mistakes had crept in through careless copying. Nikon therefore proposed a revision of the Russian forms of worship, but he was not content with merely textual corrections. His ardent temperament drove him to extremes. He borrowed various Greek forms and altered the ceremonies to bring them into conformity with Greek usage.

The result was the Schism of the Old Believers. The immediate pretext might seem trivial. Did a few verbal changes in the ritual really constitute a dangerous revolution? Did it matter profoundly whether the 'Hallelujah' was repeated twice or three times? – or whether the priest, in making the sign of the Cross, used two fingers or three? But details had become of symbolic importance to the common people. They heard little preaching; even among the priests there was the most perfunctory understanding of the creeds, and even of the Ten Commandments and the Lord's Prayer. Religion was equated with the liturgy and faith was sustained by things seen and heard: icons, music, and outward forms. A people of primitive understanding were suddenly required to repudiate things which they had been diligently taught to revere, and they were not prepared for the change. But deeper issues were involved. In a dim and inarticulate way men were wrestling with the question whether Russia was in the true sense an Orthodox kingdom, and whether its people were faithfully fulfilling their messianic vocation. The suspicion was aroused that the 'third Rome' was being impaired and that the true faith had been betrayed. It was believed that Antichrist had taken possession both of the rulers of the state and of the hierarchy of the church, and that the final days were at hand.

Nikon also stood for the independence of the church from state control. In 1658, after quarrelling with the Tsar, he retired to a monastery. A council deposed him in 1666, but the same council condemned his opponents. Until this point the champions of the traditional forms had hoped that their views (because, to them, so manifestly right) would finally prevail. Now the hopelessness of their defence became apparent. Many simply gave up the struggle and lapsed into silence. The contest was not wholly abandoned, and heroic extremists like the Archpriest Avvakum still affirmed the old position. But, on the whole, multitudes of the common people felt that they had been abandoned by their leaders; left to themselves they struggled in the dark. If Antichrist had been released, the end of the world was manifestly at hand, and the strain of the apocalyptic so congenial to the Russian spirit found free expression. The consummation was confidently expected in 1666. The crops were not sown; the people took to the woods, arrayed in white, some laid themselves down in rough coffins to await the end. When the great day tarried, more careful calculations suggested that the correct date was 1699. The return of Peter the Great from abroad seemed to prove that this time there could be no mistake. He moved his capital from Moscow; he abandoned the vestments and the religious habits of the Tsar. He forcibly cut off the beards of the boyars (a matter of concern to Old Believers); by his reform of the Calendar he 'stole eight years from the Lord'; by altering his title to 'emperor' he disguised the fact that the 'number' of his new title was 666 – the number of the 'beast'. Though the coming of Antichrist was so patent a fact, the coming of the millennium was strangely delayed. But a second serious blow had been struck at the old belief in the destiny of the 'third Rome'.

The Old Believers, though subject to severe persecution from the state, were not kept in unity by their sufferings. Two groups appeared among them. The 'priestless' believed that there was no longer any true church on earth; consequently there were no sacraments either, and no means of communication between God and his people except such as were available to all alike. The 'priestists' hesitated to press the idea of Antichrist to so remorseless a conclusion. By various expedients the latter attempted to secure the ministrations of priests untainted by the apostasy of the

national church, and at length were compelled to accept
men of whom nothing more could be said than that they
were content to relinquish their old ties. The 'priestless'
were made of sterner stuff, and from the first adopted an
extremer attitude on every issue. They readily embraced
death; they provoked persecution, and anticipated it by
self-immolation. In 1684, the Tsarevna Sophia issued a
decree which threatened every impenitent follower of the
old faith with the stake, and in the succeeding decade
thousands of men and women rushed to accept the martyr-
dom thus offered. But such extremes could not be sustained,
and the 'priestless' gradually adopted the attitude that persecution should be accepted only when it could not be
avoided. And the regions where it could most consistently
be avoided were in the vast woodlands of the north and
east, along the shores of the White Sea and in Siberia. The
leaders of the sect led the life of nomadic hermits, until Peter
the Great granted them toleration, and they settled down to
a more stable existence. One of their great houses, the
Vygovsky monastery, became a centre of vigorous activity,
economic, intellectual, and artistic.

This in itself indicates that compromises had been made.
At an increasing number of points the stark attitudes of the
earliest schismatics had to undergo modification, and at
each change tension within the ranks of Old Believers became acute. For both wings relations with the state posed
acute dilemmas; so did relations with the world about them.

During the period marked by the Schism, new sects pro-
liferated, partly as a response to foreign influences (especially to contacts with Protestant churches), partly as the
effect of forces indigenous to Russia. The cause was a tem-
peramental reaction in some cases to liturgical worship, in
others to intellectual influences, in still others to mystical
and rationalistic trends. A bewildering variety of patterns appeared among the sects, and here we enter a world which
strikes the Western mind as unfamiliar and bizarre. The
Dukhobors, who arose about the middle of the eighteenth
century, are representative of these 'spiritual' groups,

though they were by no means so extreme as some. There was a strong mystical strain in their doctrine, and their views on pre-existence, on the transmigration of souls, on the dualism of flesh and spirit invited compromises which led to a progressive corruption of their initial witness. In particular their theory of 'Christhood' was a fruitful source of trouble. God dwells, they claimed, in the hearts of all true Christians, but Christ is reincarnate, generation after generation, in the one man of his choice. Hence there arose a dynasty of 'Christs'. The more extreme sects were marked by radical tendencies, both in morals and in social practice, which invited persecution, and severe repression was their lot. The groups which drew their inspiration from the main stream of evangelical Christianity were much more moderate in character.

Within the Established Church, the results of these movements were pronounced. The fall of Nikon and the struggle with the Old Believers weakened the authority of the hierarchy and it was comparatively easy for Peter the Great (1672–1725) to complete the subjection of the church to the state. Like Henry VIII of England, he believed that he could rule the state only if he also ruled the church. The Tsar nominated to the office of patriarch. When the patriarch Adrian died in 1700, Peter refused to nominate a successor, and appointed a bishop to discharge the patriarch's functions as 'administrator'. In 1721, looking westward as usual, Peter established a body rather similar to what the Lutherans called a consistory, and gave it the task of governing the church under the crown. This committee at once declared that the name of synod was essential if they were to command loyalty in the church; and thus they became the Holy Synod which governed the Russian church till 1917. To guide and direct its activities the synod was given a procurator or lay official. At first he was a comparatively unimportant figure; in the nineteenth century he became a powerful instrument of state control.

Peter's aim was to westernize Russia and so carry it forward into the modern age. The first need was to educate a woefully ignorant people. From 1702 onwards an increasing number of schools were founded by church authorities and with church funds. 'The clergy,' Peter told the patriarch in 1700, 'are almost illiterate', and in 1708 he issued a decree compelling ordinands to attend Greek and Latin schools. In 1714 he ordered the church schools also to admit students who were not ordinands, and so to educate the sons of the gentry. Church money not only supported students in the seminaries; it maintained those who attended the navigation schools; it even defrayed the expenses of an encyclopedia. A decree compelled all children of the clergy and of the upper classes to attend school. Peter forbade the promotion of uneducated ecclesiastics over those who had been more adequately trained. The whole process was painfully slow, but by the end of the eighteenth century Russia possessed a class of laymen who could claim some education, however superficial it might be. The priests were also considerably better educated than formerly. By 1800 there were four higher academies and forty-six seminaries. Parishes in the larger centres were now likely to have priests with some measure of education. But unfortunately the gap between the village priest and his squire had not diminished. If anything it had widened. Village priests were almost as dependent upon the landowner as the peasants; and the rites of the countryside contrasted strangely with the superficial deism which was increasingly characteristic of the educated laymen. These were the people who spoke with derision of 'ploughmen in cassocks'.

The church encountered its gravest difficulties during the reign of the Empress Anne (1730–40). She openly despised the Orthodox, and treated the clergy with more contempt than any Tsar before or since. The Empress Catherine the Great (1762–96) also had little genuine sympathy with the Russian church. She was a German deist, far removed in spirit from Orthodoxy and with no understanding of its distinctive genius. But at least she was tactful and was willing to conform. Her guiding principle was epitomized in her motto: 'Respect the church, but let it have no influence in the state.' Under her patronizing but contemptuous despotism, the church even began to show signs of renewed vigour. The previous half century had seen a spectacular fall in the number of religious houses. In 1701 there had been 965 monasteries and 236 nunneries; by 1764 the figures had dropped to 319 and 68 respectively. Now there were clear indications that a revival was under way But difficulties of a new kind appeared. In 1764 Catherine carried through a sweeping secularization of monastic estates. Admittedly these vast lands had often been very inefficiently administered, and the income had not always been wisely used. The lot of the serfs had not been easy under the church; under the state it was to be even worse (cf. p. 227). Catherine assigned a part of the revenues of the monastic estates for the support of the clergy, but two-thirds (eventually seven-eighths) of the funds were diverted to the use of the state.

*

In the eighteenth century Western Europe experienced an intellectual ferment which called in question many traditional beliefs. The Orthodox world could point to little corresponding activity. In part this was due to the accepted pattern of eastern thought. The development of dogma was regarded as complete; since John of Damascus (*c*. 750) little had been added to the accepted definitions of belief, and it was assumed that nothing remained unsaid. Moreover, conditions were unfavourable to thought. The ancient centres of Orthodoxy were under the yoke of Islam, while in Russia the backwardness of the people, the primitive character of their life, and the illiteracy prevalent even among the priests discouraged scholarship and speculation. Yet this period was not wholly sterile. Kiev was a centre of learning, and a confession prepared by its metropolitan was accepted by the eastern patriarchates and by the Council of Jerusalem (1672) as defining the beliefs of the Orthodox world. This council is one of the most important in modern Orthodox history, and its confession ranks (with that of Kiev) as the most definitive attempt to supplement the only authoritative statements accepted by the Eastern Church – viz., the canons of the Ecumenical Councils.

Nor must the Russian reaction to western influences be ignored. There was little independent theological thought, but the arguments of Calvinist, Lutheran, and Roman Catholic writers were studied. Debate tended to be unduly governed by scholastic presuppositions, nor was it wholly free. Anna, Catherine II, and Alexander I tended to throw their influence on the Protestant side; its advocates had shown greater skill in reconciling appeals for freedom of thought with an attitude which left the church in subjection to the state.

9

The Hanoverian Age in England

THE Church of England in the Hanoverian period had solid merits and undoubted faults. Posterity has chiefly remembered the faults, and the character of many eighteenth-century churchmen gives this selective view a certain plausibility. They were robust in thought and vigorous in expression, but the range of their sympathies was circumscribed. They equated what was reasonable with what commended itself to common sense. Emotion was suspect and 'enthusiasm' anathema. They were often truculent in controversy, though their ideal was a studied moderation. Their sermons were rational rather than mystical in tone, ethical rather than dogmatic in content. Nevertheless they recognized that a licentious age had to be confronted with the claims of morality, and they pressed its demands upon a generation none too ready to listen. They set too high a value on sedate propriety, but preserved in an intensely secular age a genuine feeling for the church. The massive quality of their thought and learning is highly impressive. They met and overcame a threat to the Christian faith, and the vigour of their reaction stands in marked contrast with the inept apologetic of their counterparts in France.

The limited nature of their achievement was due in part to the heavy demands of the state, in part to the effects of the spirit of the age. The church was inevitably affected by the unadventurous temper which pervaded society. The prevailing attitude was in large measure the product of influences which had originated in the preceding period. For a century and a half English life had been embroiled in ceaseless controversy. The prevailing exhaustion demanded an interval of peace, and the eighteenth century provided it. The Hanoverian age was content with an unheroic temper.

Its predominant interests were commercial; its most serious crisis was caused by speculation in stocks; its main disputes concerned currency and excise; its chief victories were the conquest of new markets. Its rulers were opportunists, adept at manipulation and intrigue, and with standards usually adaptable and often low. Though England prospered, the counterpart of material gain was spiritual loss. The task of the church was gravely complicated by prevailing standards, and any fair judgement must make allowance for this fact.

The spirit of the new age was most clearly exemplified by its leading politician. Walpole usually subordinated his personal convictions to political necessities. His attitude to relief for nonconformists provides an excellent example of his approach to religious issues. He favoured a policy of good-natured toleration – so far as it could conveniently be applied. The nonconformists felt that their support of the House of Hanover, reinforced by their loyalty during the rebellion of 1715, entitled them to generous treatment. In 1718, the Occasional Conformity and Schism Acts were repealed. By the Act for Quieting and Establishing Corporations the dissenters were allowed to hold certain offices, subject to specified conditions. From 1727 onward the annual Indemnity Acts relieved them of the disabilities imposed by past legislation, but beyond this Walpole refused to go. His zeal for toleration was practical, not theoretical. He knew that the Anglican Church would oppose any further concessions, and declined to risk his political position by advocating full legal toleration in a House of Commons composed of country squires.

Walpole, with his dislike of adventurous policies, was content to see the church reduced to quiescence. The Sacheverell controversy had taught him the explosive potentialities of church feuds, and he had no wish to see such conflicts revived. The Jacobite party was closely watched; when opportunity served, Bishop Atterbury, the leader of the extreme wing of the High Church Tories, was banished. Convocation had been in turmoil for some years; it was silenced.

Walpole's reaction to Berkeley's proposed college in Bermuda is particularly revealing. Berkeley believed that his institution would help to evangelize the new world; he even hoped that it might stir the conscience of an old world increasingly smothered by mercantile preoccupations. Walpole yielded to Berkeley's persuasive advocacy so far as to promise subsidies for the college, but he was careful never to pay them, and his procrastination was fatal to the project. To a genial materialist like Walpole, Berkeley's disinterested zeal was suspect. So was Oglethorpe's enthusiasm for his new colony in Georgia. Such schemes neither brought immediate economic benefit to the state, nor offered political advantage to the government.

The domestic affairs of the Church of England, however, were in a different category. Walpole realized that the Whigs could not neglect the church, lest its control should slip into hostile hands. He must prove that Anglicanism had no more to fear from the Whigs than from the Tories, but it was not easy to create the desired impression. There were strong anti-clerical prejudices in certain sections of his party. Walpole found that when church affairs were debated in parliament, some of his supporters claimed the right to give 'the bishops and parsons very hard as well as very popular slaps'. Many took the attitude that 'if they went uniformly with the court in matters relating to the state, they were at liberty to do what they pleased' in matters relating to the church. Party journalists were loath to forgo attacks on the establishment, and adopted the new attitude with some reluctance. The *London Journal* conceded that a Latitudinarian bishop like Hoadly might be a valuable asset as 'the great apostle and converter of the clergy to the principles of the Revolution and the sentiments of liberty'. The *Independent Whig* contrasted 'proud, persecuting, covetous, rebellious, perjured priests' (it specified Sacheverell and Atterbury) with 'loyal, moderate men; men of conscience and moderation', and grudgingly admitted that a church guided by such leaders might be a useful (though perhaps not a divine) institution. This was guarded enthusiasm, but it was a step towards a view that increasingly prevailed: the church was regarded as the ecclesiastical arm of the Whig administration. If Walpole was sometimes embarrassed by his followers, his position was easy compared with that of Bishop Gibson of London, his great ally in the management of church affairs. Gibson was both a staunch churchman and a convinced Whig. His difficulties stemmed from the intermediate position in which his party still found itself. The Whigs were traditionally the defenders of dissenters and the champions of a free press. They believed in toleration and so were lenient towards unorthodoxy. But the Whig churchmen themselves regarded the church as a part of the constitutional settlement, as a body of immense political importance whose support must be won for the Hanoverian regime. Few developments in the first half of the eighteenth century were so important as the conversion of the Whig party to the support of the Establishment. The church became a prize for which politicians contended, not an issue on which they were divided.

Many of the pronounced characteristics of the Hanoverian church are directly due to its entanglement in the partisan politics of the period. The House of Lords, a relatively small body, still wielded effective power. The bishops formed an important element in it, and in the fierce struggles of the time their votes could easily prove decisive. In 1733 the support of the episcopal bench saved Walpole from defeat, and no politician could overlook so striking a lesson. The appointment of bishops was one of the few ways in which the balance of power could be affected, and it became a matter of prime concern to select men of proven party loyalty. In making appointments, political considerations outweighed all others. A court chaplain of the period remarked that when a bishop 'rose by the weight of his character', it was 'against all rules of gravity and experience'. Even a scholar of towering reputation, like William Warburton, could not gain promotion without the aid of powerful sponsors. An aspiring churchman needed influential friends, and had to choose them with care. To hitch your wagon to a falling star was fatal: when a patron lost power, his clients forfeited their prospects. Such a system made churchmen party politicians. Some, indeed, resented the position in which they were placed. Laurence Sterne, the author of *Tristram Shandy*, remarked that his uncle (a prebendary of York) was 'a party-man', and added, 'I was not, and detested such dirty work, thinking it beneath me.' Few could afford the luxury of such an attitude. The clerical profession was overcrowded, and indifference to advancement spelt poverty. So the clergy courted the great, and lived in patient hope of future favours. Even the prospect of a desirable vacancy precipitated an indecent scramble for the place. Before a man was dead, contenders were posting to press their claims upon patrons. 'I think it my duty to acquaint your Grace,' wrote Thomas Newton to the Duke of Newcastle, 'that the Archbishop of York lies a-dying, and, as all here think, cannot possibly live beyond tomorrow morning, if so long; upon this occasion of two vacancies, I beg, I hope, I trust your Grace's kindness and goodness will be shown to one who has long solicited your favour.' Newcastle raised the use of patronage from the level of a sordid abuse to the status of a complex political art. No benefice was too small to have a place in his intricate manipulations. He nominated bishops, and some of them seem to have yielded to him the filling of the livings in their gift. Though he excelled at this inglorious game, many others played it with equal zest. In pressing the claims of a protégé, Lord Middleton warned his Grace that if his candidate 'was not well preferred he would make the Nottinghamshire election cost more than a little'. A vacant deanery could precipitate not merely feverish solicitation from aspirants but bitter competition among patrons.

Though success might bring the rising churchman gain and gratification, it certainly brought him no emancipation. Even a bishop was still in the power of political chieftains. The value of the different sees varied enormously. Canterbury was worth £7,000 per annum, Durham £6,000, Winchester, £5,000; but at Rochester the income was only £600, at Oxford £500, at Bristol £450. Yet in the poorer sees, a bishop's expenses were little less than those of his more favoured brethren. Normally a man was elevated first to a poor bishopric. He acquired prestige, but poverty was entailed upon him until the government saw fit to translate him to a more lucrative position. Such promotion had to be deserved, and it was earned by faithful political service. For a considerable part of each year the bishop was expected to take his place in the House of Lords. If he had the gift of oratory, he would use it to support the party that had appointed him, but at least the way he used his vote would be carefully observed. Independence was not merely discouraged, it was severely penalized. An indiscreet bishop would be left in his poor see till he had digested the bitter fruits of insubordination. Richard Watson, a sturdy independent, was left at Llandaff (£550) for life.

Nor did the end of the parliamentary session bring relief. In his own diocese, the bishop was expected to promote his party's cause. He was an important local magnate; it was his duty to confirm the gentry in their loyalty, and to win over the waverers. He was to report to London any significant movements of opinion, either through the Archbishop of Canterbury, or directly to the minister himself. Lavish hospitality was an obligation, not because it was an apostolic virtue, but because it was of political advantage. At election times, the bishop was expected to remind his clergy of their duty, and to see that they encouraged the freeholders to use their votes in the desired way. Such tasks were usually discharged without demur. To take a single example, Bishop Hare of Chichester supported the Duke of Newcastle with a loyalty that was happily untainted by servility.

Even in the eighteenth century no one pretended that a bishop was primarily a politician. His place in public life enormously complicated his real task, but it did not exonerate him from attempting to perform it. As far as conscientious effort is concerned, the episcopate of the period has received less credit than it deserves. Apart from the interruptions caused by parliamentary attendance, the bishops faced almost insuperable difficulties. Their dioceses were enormous, and the means of communication were primitive. It was hard to arrange confirmation itineraries, and harder still to fulfil them. There is abundant evidence that many bishops seriously tried to do their best. Wake and Gibson at Lincoln in the first half of the century, Keppel and Ross at Exeter in the second half, made valiant efforts to cover the parishes under their care. In 1764, Bishop Keppel confirmed more than forty thousand persons in the course of his confirmation tour. Bishop Hurd's record at Worcester suggests that episcopal standards were as high as they had ever been.

Non-residence is a charge often brought against the bishops of the period, but it is usually founded on extreme cases. Bishop Hoadly was a notorious offender, and those who dislike his theology have magnified his faults. During his six years as Bishop of Bangor he never set foot within his diocese – an even worse record than Laud's at St David's – but Hoadly was a cripple, who should never have accepted a bishopric; since that presupposes a degree of self-denial that few clerics of the age could have comprehended, the position should never have been offered to him. That it was, and that it was accepted, illustrates a different fault: the episcopate was regarded primarily as a reward for political services, not as a field for pastoral oversight. The fact that Hoadly could always persuade his fellow bishops (all of them busy men) to undertake the duties which he could not discharge, illustrates one of the more amiable traits of the period.

Candidates for ordination presented themselves to their bishop if and when they could find him. His absence in London often made this difficult, and a trip to the capital might prove necessary. When a bishop did not intend to hold an ordination, he issued letters dimissory to be presented to a brother bishop. But there was no satisfactory check on the character or the qualifications of candidates. A man who had taken a degree might never have read theology. If men were inadequately prepared before ordination, they were inadequately supervised after it. This was one of the gravest weaknesses in the Hanoverian Church. James Woodforde's racy

and informative *Diary of a Country Parson* shows that his contacts with his bishop were few and formal. It could hardly
be otherwise in view of the magnitude of the bishop's task
and the number of distractions which interfered with his
discharge of it, but the clergy were left largely to their own
devices. A man like Woodforde managed very well; he had
a good living, was reasonably faithful in fulfilling his duties,
and was happy among his neighbours. The same could not
be said of all his brethren, and the lack of oversight accounts
in part for the existence of a vagrant throng of unbeneficed
clergy who brought discredit on their order.

The few who were favoured were divided from the many
who were not. High positions could be a stepping-stone to
wealth, and some bishops amassed fortunes. When Archbishop Hutton died, a candid observer reported that 'he
left £50,000 which he has saved out of the Church in
twelve years, and not one penny to any good use or public
charity'. This was not a unique case, and public opinion was
not unduly critical of bishops who grasped at advancement.
When Dr Pyle went to live with Bishop Hoadly he remarked
that the one danger he feared was 'from the table, which is
both plentiful and elegant', and he contrasted the lavish
spread with the simpler fare with which most clergymen
were perforce content. Some of the clergy cultivated extravagant tastes, others were born to them. As the eighteenth
century progressed, an increasing number of well-born men
appeared in the ranks of the clergy, giving cause for a
measure of gratification, touched with relief, inasmuch as
the scandal that 'not many noble are called' was now
providentially being removed. The younger sons of the
nobility were candidates for bishoprics and deaneries, those
of the gentry for prebends and the richer benefices. As a
result the higher clergy were often related by kinship as well
as by interest to the leaders of the political parties. The need
for an income appropriate to a noble cleric made the practice
of accumulating preferments even commoner than before.

Pluralism was not an abuse which originated in the eighteenth century. It had been accepted practice among the

Caroline divines, and was inseparable from the life of a church which was imperfectly reformed. The habits and standards of Hanoverian clerics meant that they developed with unabashed enthusiasm a pattern that they had inherited from the past. Pluralism was the only way of dealing with extreme and arbitrary variations in the emoluments of particular offices. We have already noted that episcopal incomes differed enormously. Politicians had no desire to reform a system which placed in their hands useful disciplinary powers, but they were willing to allow certain mitigations. Valuable deaneries (St Paul's, Westminster, Christ Church) were usually held by the bishops appointed to poorer sees (Bristol, Rochester, Oxford). A new bishop expected to retain some of his more remunerative livings till he had had a chance to pay his heavy initial expenses. A statute of Henry VIII extended the right of holding pluralities to certain classes of the clergy (chaplains of peers and others), and thus the door was opened wide to abuses. The system became so complicated that the archbishops despaired of correcting the practice and at best hoped to keep a dangerous privilege within constitutional bounds. Ambitious men were free to accumulate preferments as fast as good fortune would permit, and only the disappointed were apt to protest. The progress of a young man with useful connexions is illustrated by the career of John Hoadly, son of the famous bishop. In rapid succession he received the chancellorship of the diocese of Winchester, a prebendal stall in the cathedral, the mastership of the Hospital of St Cross, and six livings, and retained most of them till his death. Such a record occasioned envious comment, but the eighteenth century set high store by worldly advancement, and the clerical 'success story' was part of the accepted pattern. The age was usually harsher in its ridicule of those who failed than in its criticism of those who succeeded.

Under prevailing conditions, a certain degree of pluralism was inevitable. The income of many livings was patently insufficient to support the incumbents. At the beginning of the eighteenth century over 5,500 livings (more than half the total) were worth less than £50 a year, over 2,100 less than £30, over 1200 less than £20. In Lincolnshire there were many small benefices which paid from £5 to £20. In important market towns, the stipend was often purely nominal; in Colchester there were two churches that paid respectively £3 and £1 1s. a year. Under such circumstances, pluralism was the only alternative to drastic reform. The abuse lay, not in the fact that one man held more than one living, but in the extreme inequalities which the system permitted. A few men grew rich; the rest were condemned to hopeless poverty.

Because pluralism meant non-residence, many churches were served by curates. The plight of these men was proverbial. 'A journeyman in almost any trade or business,' wrote William Jones in his *Diary*, 'even a bricklayer's labourer or the turner of a razor-grinder's wheel, all circumstances considered, is generally better paid than a stipendiary curate.' William Law, in his ironical sketch of a complacent clergyman, remarks that 'he makes it a matter of conscience to keep a sober curate on one of [his livings], whom he hires to take care of all the souls in the parish at as cheap a rate as a sober man can be procured'. That rate was about £20 to £30 a year. Some were more fortunate, but not all. In 1713, Archbishop Tenison spoke of curates who received only £5–6; 'having no fixed place of abode, and but a poor and precarious maintenance, [they] are powerfully tempted to a kind of vagrant and dishonourable life, wandering for better subsistence from parish to parish'. The glaring contrast between the curate's plight and the good fortune of his richer brethren created bitterness. 'There the old rascal goes,' cried Smollett's curate after meeting his vicar at the inn, 'and the d—l go with him. You see how the world wags, gentlemen. By Gad, this rogue of a vicar does not deserve to live; and yet he has two livings worth £400 per annum, while poor I am fain to do all his drudgery . . .; for what? why, truly, for £20 a year' (*Roderick Random*).

The problem was aggravated by the fact that the supply of clergymen exceeded the demand. Addison claimed that all the learned professions were overcrowded, and this was especially true of the ministry. Richard Bentley, the famous master of Trinity, marvelled that so many men pressed into a calling where the prospects for most of them were so bleak; the answer, he suggested, might be supplied by the analogy of a lottery, in which a few glittering prizes blinded people to the enormous number of blanks. Many of the abuses which enervated church life were of long standing; some dated from the Middle Ages. The disconcerting thing is not that they existed, but that they aroused so little protest. It was too readily assumed that glaring anomalies were rooted in the nature of things, and must therefore be accepted without demur.

The wide range of fortune which prevailed among the clergy makes it difficult to generalize about the place which they occupied in society. There is little doubt that they were unpopular. Neither before nor since has the clerical order been exposed to such general attack. In plays and in novels they were the victims of savage ridicule. For much of this contempt they themselves were responsible. In the early years of the century they had created a tradition which lingered in the popular mind. The violent partisanship of party struggles, the bitterness of the convocation controversies, the advocacy of persecution, the championship of extreme views – all had fostered the impression that as a class the clergy were quarrelsome and intemperate men. The prevalence of the resultant attitude explains the vein of pessimism which runs through the work of many of the most distinguished churchmen of the age. Both in Bishop Butler's preface to *The Analogy* and in his Charge to the clergy of Durham, he took the gloomiest view of the prospects of religion. Thomas Secker, subsequently Archbishop of Canterbury, struck an equally sombre note. 'Christianity is now railed at and ridiculed with very little reserve, and its teachers without any at all. Against us our adversaries appear to have set themselves to be as bitter as they can, not only beyond all truth, but beyond all probability, exaggerating without mercy.'

Unquestionably there were worthless and dissolute parish priests, and the satirists made the most of the fact. But there was another side to the picture, as even the novels of the period remind us. Though we have Fielding's Supple and Thwackum, we also have Parson Adams and the Vicar of Wakefield. The correspondence of the S.P.C.K. and the returns to the questionnaires sent out by diocesans and archdeacons show that many of the clergy were earnest men with a high sense of duty. In remote country livings much faithful work was quietly done. The heroic virtues, it is true, were seldom cultivated; most men were content with those that called for little sacrifice. An almost pathological dread of fanaticism placed an undue value on moderation and easily encouraged complacency. But at many points the church of the eighteenth century was in intimate touch with contemporary life. Of Dr Taylor of Ashbourne, Boswell remarked approvingly that 'his size and figure and coun- tenance and manner were that of a hearty English squire, with the parson superimposed'. Some of the clergy, as Crabbe observed, were sportsmen first and foremost, but they were not divorced from the interests of their people. Paley contended that the country rector who reconciled him- self to a simple life among his neighbours would derive from it deep and genuine satisfactions, and the truth of his remark was often verified. This situation had its drawbacks; the relationship was close because the standards of the clergy were not conspicuously higher than those of their society. They had a leavening, not a transforming effect, but at least the Church did not stand aloof from the life of the age.

The measure of influence which the church exerted is difficult to gauge. In some quarters it was considerable, and appears to greatest advantage in the lives of some of the leading laymen of the period. Men in responsible positions were often deeply devout. Those who regard the Duke of Newcastle as a supreme exponent of the arts of political patronage are surprised to find in his correspondence signs of a genuine spiritual concern. Even the thought of casually claiming the privileges of a communicant was abhorrent to him, and he prepared himself for the sacrament with scrupulous care. Perhaps his concern should have extended more widely than it did, but it was genuine as far as it went. Viscount Percival was another highly placed churchman whose papers reflect the restrained piety of the eighteenth century in its most authentic form. Dr Samuel Johnson, in some ways the most representative figure of his age, was a man of sincere and unaffected piety, whose prayers have permanently enriched English devotional literature. William Cowper, whose diffident outlook was far removed from the robust common sense of Johnson, was deeply influenced by the evangelical movement and his Olney hymns are still gratefully used.

Such men, though conspicuous, were not exceptional, but church leaders tended to be more conscious of their foes than of their friends. Bishop Gibson was appalled at the wickedness rampant in both the highest and the lowest strata of society. Bishop Secker believed that 'the distinguishing mark of the present age' was 'an open and professed disregard of religion', reflected in 'dissoluteness and contempt of principle in the higher part of the world' and in 'profligate intemperance and fearlessness of committing crimes in the lower'. This was the society which Hogarth painted with such candour and power. Immorality was prevalent, but it did not pass unreproved. The bishops repeatedly protested against the demoralizing masquerades held at court. They supported proposals to check the traffic in gin which was causing such havoc among the poor. In the earlier years of the century the Societies for the Reformation of Manners vigorously prosecuted immorality, and by 1736 they had initiated more than 100,000 actions. Their methods, however, made them extremely unpopular.

Moralists found the upper classes cynical and sophisticated, the lower classes brutalized and debauched, but from the middle classes they received a ready response. The eighteenth century was the golden age of philanthropy. The need was great; men and women pressed forward to meet it, and in doing so they were prompted by a variety of motives.

A contributor to the *Gentleman's Magazine* pointed out that 'benevolence is the most lasting, valuable, and exquisite pleasure'. 'Goodness and charity', said a popular preacher, 'keep the mind always in a comfortable, happy frame.' Those who were indifferent to such sentimental appeals often responded to the argument that philanthropy was the great bulwark against social unrest. 'If compassion cannot move you,' said the Rev. William Sharp in 1755, 'let considerations of interest prevail with you', and he reminded his hearers that the poor, if neglected, would prove a menace, but if encouraged might well become 'honest, laborious, ingenious artisans'. Religious motives, however, were the most general and the most effective. 'Whatever is laid out in charity', said Bishop Gibson, 'God accounts an offering and loan to himself; and accordingly he will repay it.' The reward might be deferred till the next world, but it was certain.

Such appeals were necessary because of the prevalent attitude towards poverty. Defoe spoke for many of his contemporaries when he claimed that unemployment was due to laziness: the poor would not work because it was more profitable to beg. The eighteenth century refused to believe that poverty might reflect maladjustments in society. Even zealous reformers adopted a patronizing attitude to the poor. When a new enterprise was launched at Brentford, one of the ladies of the parish went to the homes of the needy and urged them 'to avail themselves of this opportunity of conciliating the favour of their superiors, by accepting with humility and gratitude an offer which was made with a view of promoting the present and future welfare of themselves and families'. It was always necessary to defend charitable projects against the criticism that they would raise the poor above their rightful status in society. Educational enthusiasts in particular had to insist that their schemes would neither disqualify children for the menial tasks they were intended to perform, nor sow the seeds of insubordination in their minds. Even so gentle and humane a spirit as Isaac Watts perfectly epitomized the prevailing attitude:

What though I be low and mean,
   I'll engage the rich to love me,
While I'm modest, neat and clean,
   And submit when they reprove me.

The charity schools encountered a good deal of opposition and in spite of it performed a very valuable service. Churchmen and dissenters combined to provide a rudimentary education (with various social service benefits added) for the children of the poor. It was generally conceded that unless these children could be trained as useful members of society a life of debauchery would inevitably engulf them. The charity schools were established to rescue such children from the fate that otherwise awaited them. The formal teaching which was provided was elementary in its scope, but was supplemented by training in various practical skills. The problems – financial, administrative, educational – were very great, but the schools met an urgent need, and they laid the foundations of a more adequate system of general education. Similar in purpose, but slightly different in character, were the schools of industry which Mrs Trimmer organized. 'It is a disgrace to any parish', she said, 'to see the children of the poor, who are old enough to do any kind of work, running about the streets ragged and dirty.' If they could master a craft, they would not only be qualified for a useful life but would be able to support themselves while they were being trained. Experience, however, showed that the practical difficulties were insuperable. Young beginners inevitably spoiled good material, and many of the articles produced proved unfit for sale. Capable teachers were hard to find; the assumptions on which the scheme rested proved unsound, and most of the schools soon collapsed.

In the later part of the century, the most important venture in popular education was the Sunday School movement. Tentative experiments were made in various places, but it was Robert Raikes of Gloucester who organized the movement on a national scale. He was the publisher of a well-known provincial paper; he could therefore use the press to

disseminate his ideas, and they spread widely and rapidly.
He began with modest expectations: if his Sunday School
achieved nothing else, it would at least 'check the deplorable
profanation of the Sabbath'. His success was remarkable,
especially in view of the rigorous routine which he insti-
tuted. The regular sessions of the school ran from eight
o'clock in the morning till eight o'clock at night, with suitable breaks for church attendance. These children, it should
be added, were accustomed to long hours, working at the
Gloucester pin factories· throughout the week. Eighteenth-
century philanthropists were suspicious of play, and pleased
when there were few opportunities for it. The regulations
for the school established at Stroud indicate the nature of
the programme and reflect the spirit which inspired it. 'The
children are to be taught to read, and to be instructed in the
plain duties of the Christian religion, with a particular view
to their good and industrious behaviour in their future
character of labourers and servants.' In the eighteenth century, schools for the poor, no matter what their pattern,
were regarded with suspicion; the Sunday Schools were no
exception. Education, it was claimed, bred unrest, and in
self-defence the organizers of the schools felt bound to emphasize due subordination to authority. This, of course, was
in full conformity with the principles which governed a great
deal of eighteenth-century philanthropy. But the schools had
their champions as well as their critics. In 1788, John Wesley visited the Sunday School at Bolton, and wrote enthusiastically about the neat and clean appearance of the children. Their conduct, he felt, was entirely exemplary. 'All
were serious and well-behaved. They are a pattern to all the
town. Their usual diversion is to visit the poor that are
sick . . . to exhort, comfort, and pray with them.'

The needs of the helpless and the unfortunate were not
forgotten. Captain Coram was horrified at the number of
infants who were abandoned by their parents and left to
die. Children who were committed to workhouses had little
better chance of survival; in a typical institution of this kind
the mortality rate, over a period of seven years, was one

hundred per cent. To remedy this situation, Coram helped to establish the Foundling Hospital, which rapidly became a fashionable charity. Jonas Hanway, one of the partners in this enterprise, was disturbed at the plight of prostitutes and for them founded the Magdalen Hospital. Hanway's sympathy also extended to chimney-sweeps, and he campaigned for some regulation of the conditions under which these waifs were compelled to work. During this period, hospitals for the sick were established in large numbers, and many of the most famous institutions in England had their origin in the philanthropic concern of the eighteenth century. Nor should we forget John Howard's unwearied efforts to expose the appalling conditions which prevailed in most prisons. Much of this concern was sustained by a widely accepted belief in divine benevolence. At the parish level, this doctrine inspired the varied charitable activities which are so carefully recorded in Parson Woodforde's *Diary* – the provision of food and drink for the ill or the aged, and of assistance to the infirm and the unfortunate.

Meanwhile church life in the parishes maintained its uneventful course. It was sometimes formal but seldom dead. Worship was pedestrian and preaching was prosaic. But sermons were appreciated; when they were not provided, the people would not attend. Frequent communion was the exception rather than the rule. In country parishes the sacrament was usually administered four times a year; in London monthly celebrations were more general. Few new churches were built and existing ones were carelessly maintained. 'In the present turn of the age,' said Bishop Butler, 'one may observe a wonderful frugality in everything which has respect to religion, and extravagance in everything else.'

For the nonconformists, the eighteenth century was a placid and unheroic age. Their forefathers had arisen in their wrath to bring down king and bishops, but scarcely an echo of the old zeal survived. The dissenters were consigned to a backwater of the national life, and their efforts to improve their status achieved few results. They were active in business, and many of them prospered. The Quakers became men of substance, and to Quaker enterprise some of the great banking houses of England owe their origin. In science and invention the nonconformists also played an important part, but on the whole they were inconspicuous people, living inoffensive lives. As the century progressed their vitality perceptibly waned. Available statistics (which are few and unreliable) suggest that during the first quarter of the century the dissenters may have numbered from 250,000 to 300,000; thereafter they steadily declined. Edmund Calamy, the historian of the Great Ejection and one of the leaders of nonconformity in the early part of the Hanoverian age, reports that there was general concern 'about the decay of the Dissenting interest and the occasion of it', and this anxiety prompted an animated pamphlet debate on the subject.

Locally the position of the nonconformists remained essentially unchanged. The Act of Toleration acknowledged their right to exist and to worship as they wished, even gave them an official claim to a second-class status. After the accession of George I, the vindictive laws passed in Anne's reign were repealed, but otherwise nonconformist disabilities remained untouched. This was a severe disappointment. The dissenters had hoped for more cooperation from the Whigs than was forthcoming. Yet the Anglican leaders were not solidly opposed to concessions. Some bishops believed that the Act of Toleration presupposed further concessions, and there were sporadic movements in favour of comprehension. These negotiations involved some of the most respected figures on both sides, and it is possible that a little more resolution might have brought a considerable proportion of nonconformity into the Church of England. At the outset, Anglican hesitancy was due as much to fear of popery as to distrust of dissent. Gibson, for example, believed that the enemies of the church were so many and so strong that it was dangerous to tamper with the legal bulwarks of the establishment. The Test and Corporation Acts might be offensive, but they were laws and should not be rescinded. So the efforts to procure their abolition were doomed to failure. Gibson (for conscientious reasons) and Walpole (for political ones) refused to yield; in 1732, 1734, 1736, and 1739 the story was the same. In some respects the position of the dissenters actually deteriorated. Lord Hardwicke's Marriage Act of 1753 (aimed at clandestine weddings performed by vagrant Anglican clergymen) had the effect of banning nonconformist marriages. In many remote communities funerals also presented a problem. If the dissenters did not own a burial ground, the rector might refuse to bury their dead, on the ground that only baptized persons were eligible and those baptized elsewhere than in the parish church were not baptized at all. In meeting difficulties of this kind the nonconformists relied on two voluntary bodies recruited from the stronger and wealthier congregations in or near the capital. 'The ministers of the three denominations', formed in 1727, were available for counsel and advice. 'The deputies of the Protestant Dissenters', organized five years later, played an important role in protecting the legal rights of nonconformists against invasion.

The meeting house was the focus of nonconformist life. It was usually an austere rectangular building, marked by the simplicity and good taste which the eighteenth century so consistently achieved. On the long side, facing the entrance, was the high pulpit, often surmounted by a sounding board and decked with a pulpit cushion – the only touch of colour in the building and one of the few luxuries in which the congregation indulged. Worship followed the pattern inherited from the past and bequeathed to the future. Prayers, hymns, the reading of Scripture, and the preaching of the Word were the essential and invariable ingredients. Services were long. Differences among the various nonconformist bodies were not pronounced. The 'three denominations' were the Presbyterians, the Independents (Congregationalists), and the Baptists. The Quakers were far more subdued than in their earlier days, and had abandoned the vigorous witness which once proved so disturbing to other bodies. Most of the small sects which had flourished in the seventeenth century had disappeared. In most respects the

Presbyterians were indistinguishable from the Independents. They believed in a national system of representative 'church courts', but they never succeeded in establishing it. The church meeting, which played so important a part in Independent congregations, was usually less effective (or wholly absent) among the Presbyterians, because its functions were theoretically discharged by a higher court – which did not exist. Presbyterians paid less attention to the church roll and to the profession of faith which new members accepted. Often their congregations were ruled by small oligarchies of pew holders and subscribers, and the decisive authority passed into the hands of trustees. These developments undoubtedly facilitated the trend which ultimately swept most of the Presbyterian congregations into Unitarianism. In all the dissenting bodies there was a conspicuous lack of any sense of denominational unity on a national scale.

In higher education, the dissenters made a genuine contribution to national life. Oxford and Cambridge excluded all save Anglicans, and though this was not a serious deprivation in the eighteenth century, it required the provision of alternative facilities. The dissenting academies probably provided the best education available in England. The curriculum was flexible, and included subjects elsewhere neglected, such as science, geography, and modern languages. Numbers were small, oversight was close, and fellowship between staff and students was intimate. Many of the academies were closely related to a particular minister; when he moved to a different congregation, the institution migrated with him; when he died, it often collapsed. Philip Doddridge, who ministered to a church in Northampton, was a celebrated tutor, and the excellence of his teaching is shown by the comprehensive lecture courses which were published after his death. Joseph Priestley, who could speak from experience both as a student and as a tutor, gives us some interesting glimpses of the academies, and also indicates why they sometimes contributed to the doctrinal change which was taking place within nonconformity.

Theology, indeed, posed the crucial issue of the century:

could credal positions be modified without endangering the faith? Soon after the Act of Toleration, 'the Happy Union' – an amalgamation of Presbyterians and Independents – disintegrated because of differences in doctrine. Early in the new century, the nonconformists were affected by the influences which precipitated the Trinitarian controversy in the Church of England: the character of Christ's divinity was earnestly canvassed, and in 1718–19 a crisis developed. At Exeter the views of James Peirce had been causing considerable concern, and the whole question was referred to the nonconformist leaders in London. Those fearful of theological innovation urged that all ministers should be asked to subscribe to a doctrinal formula phrased in traditional Calvinistic terms. Those with Arian leanings opposed the proposal; they claimed that statements of belief should be couched in biblical language. At a conference held at Salter's Hall the issue was hotly debated, and those present divided into 'subscribers' and 'non-subscribers'. The lines were not drawn strictly along denominational lines, but Presbyterians and General Baptists were apt to be in the 'non-subscribing' majority. The conference discredited this particular method of settling doctrinal disputes, and throughout the remainder of the eighteenth century issues of this kind were left to congregational decision.

In the upshot, the Presbyterians increasingly veered toward Unitarianism, while the Independents for the most part remained loyal to Calvinism. Various explanations can be offered for the stauncher orthodoxy of the Independents. The importance of the church fellowship, the responsibility of the whole congregation for calling a minister, the intimate contact between pastors and people, the significance attached to the profession of faith which each member made on reception into the congregation – these all tended to preserve intact the accepted pattern of belief. Hymns, which occupied an important place in worship, produced a similar result. The metrical psalms and paraphrases were an effective teaching medium. Isaac Watts and Philip Doddridge immensely enriched the resources of congregational praise;

their hymns insensibly but powerfully confirmed the faith of those who sang them. Calvinistic theology sometimes seemed to harden into conventional and sterile formalism, but it preserved a deposit of the historic faith. When the evangelical revival came, the Independents were able to respond. Calvinism proved to be an excellent preparation for the new vitality which swept orthodox nonconformity forward to its vigorous expansion in the nineteenth century. One of the signs that a new day was dawning was the founding of the London Missionary Society in 1795. Nor was this the only indication of an awakening concern for the evangelization of the world. Three years previously the Baptist Missionary Society had started on its career of distinguished service, and in 1793, when William Carey set sail for India, one of the notable epics of modern Christianity began.

Throughout the eighteenth century the Roman Catholics in England were a small and dispirited minority. With the overthrow of James II they had forfeited all power to influence national affairs, while they retained to the full their capacity to awaken fear. As long as Jacobitism remained a threat, they were regarded with suspicion. The fear was natural, since the Stuart Pretenders were champions of the Catholic cause; it was unfounded, because few English Catholics supported either of the rebellions. A sober churchman like Gibson regarded with alarm even the suggestion of the slightest concessions, though there is no doubt that early in the century the fortunes of Catholicism reached their lowest ebb. Its representatives were socially isolated and politically impotent. For the most part they were left in peace; the Hanoverian age had little persecuting zeal, and the penal laws were seldom enforced. In a modest way the Catholics began to rally. In due course the needs of the industrial age brought Irish immigration, and with it greater numerical strength. Some of the problems which beset the Catholics were of their own devising. Bitter rivalry divided the Jesuits and the 'secular clergy', and this domestic cleavage weakened the cause as a whole and complicated the work of the vicars apostolic – the bishops charged with the oversight of English Catholics. One of them, Richard Challoner, was a leader who brought to his difficult task genuine piety and a strong pastoral concern, and in his *Garden of the Soul* he bequeathed to his fellow-Catholics a minor devotional classic. But the Catholic position remained insecure. Popular fanaticism was easily inflamed, and the Relief Acts of 1778 and 1779 precipitated riots in Edinburgh and London (the Gordon Riots, 1780). By 1791 it was considered safe to grant further respite; Catholics who took the oath of allegiance were freed from disabilities relating to education, property, and the practice of the law. Catholic peers were given the right of access to the king; they were permitted attendance at religious services and were allowed to enter religious orders. These benefits were extended to Scottish and Irish Catholics.

In Ireland, Catholic grievances were more serious than in England because the religion of the majority was proscribed. In the early part of the eighteenth century, the official attitude was not sufficiently severe to eradicate Catholicism, but it was harsh enough to intensify the bitterness bequeathed by previous generations. In Ireland, as elsewhere, the characteristic temper of the age of reason had its influence, and the position of the Catholics steadily improved. In the second half of the century there were few signs of religious intolerance, and the religious provisions of the Penal Code largely fell into abeyance. Some Catholics, attracted by the material advantages of conformity, forsook their faith, and John Wesley – always a keen observer – remarked on the spirit of indifference toward religion which seemed to prevail everywhere in Ireland. In the face of many discouragements, the Catholic priests faithfully shepherded their people, and they were ably assisted by the hedgerow schools – a picturesque and surprisingly effective system of popular education.

*

The eighteenth century was a relatively static age, yet as it progressed its character imperceptibly altered. Moral standards rose. Signs of spiritual vitality appeared. Churchmanship began to respond to new influences, though in its fundamental character it remained unchanged. It was compounded in almost equal measure of elements of weakness and of strength. It was not inspiring but it was certainly not contemptible. In outlook it was neither mystical nor otherworldly. It set exaggerated store by moderation, and the qualities it esteemed most highly were temperance, restraint, and reasonableness. It had little sympathy with the more austere virtues and studiously ignored the claims of self-denial. It adapted itself all too readily to the tastes of an age which exalted common sense and pursued material prosperity, yet it stoutly resisted the rampant immorality and the rationalist disbelief of a hard-bitten society. Even in its worthiest representatives it lacked originality, poetic sensibility, and prophetic insight; in justice we must concede that it possessed solid scholarship, unwearied industry, practical sagacity, and sober piety.

10

Methodism and the Evangelical Revival

THE Hanoverian Church of England, despite its redeeming qualities, stood sorely in need of reform. The age of reason had forgotten certain fundamental human needs; natural religion might satisfy the minds of some, but the hearts of multitudes were hungry. The weaknesses of the established church – its failure to provide adequate care, the inflexibility of its parish system, its neglect of the new towns – left a vast and needy population waiting to be touched by a new word of power. 'Just at this time, when we wanted little of "filling up the measure of our iniquities", two or three clergymen of the Church of England began vehemently to "call sinners to repentance". In two or three years they had sounded the alarm to the utmost borders of the land. Many thousands gathered to hear them; and in every place where they came, many began to show such a concern for religion as they never had done before.' This is Wesley's own account of the beginnings of the Methodist revival.

John Wesley was born in 1703 in the Lincolnshire rectory of Epworth. His father was a man of ability – ardent, opinionated, impractical; a poet as well as an irrepressible controversialist, an unbending churchman, and an unyielding Tory. His mother was a remarkable woman by any standard. To great natural ability she united a strong sense of duty and of her responsibility as the mother of a large family. Her system of child training was stern in its simplicity. The first essential was to break the unregenerate will of a child; the second, to guide him by strict discipline in the way in which he ought to go. The system is theoretically defective; it produced John and Charles Wesley.

John went to Christ Church, Oxford, and in due course became a fellow of Lincoln College. Charles followed him to Christ Church, and was responsible for assembling the little

band of seekers known as the 'Holy Club'. Its members met
regularly for fellowship, for Bible study, and for prayer. They
were faithful in attendance at the ordinances of the church,
and pledged themselves to assist the needy and the destitute.
Oxford was predominantly a clerical community; that such
a programme should have provoked ridicule is a revealing
commentary on the condition of the Hanoverian church.

The members of the Holy Club were ardent and unsatis-
fied. In search of more exacting service, the Wesleys set sail
for Oglethorpe's new colony of Georgia. At this stage, John
Wesley was an unyielding rigorist. He had no mercy on himself, nor on others. He had not found peace within, he
created enmity about him, and was virtually driven from
the colony. He brought back to England his sense of insufficiency, now fortified by the knowledge that he had miserably
failed. For some time he floundered about in search of light.
Both on shipboard and in Georgia he had met, and been
profoundly impressed by, the Moravians. In London, one
of their number continued the work already begun, and at
length, on 24 May 1738, the light broke in upon John
Wesley's soul. 'In the evening', he wrote, 'I went very un-
willingly to a society in Aldersgate Street, where one was
reading Luther's preface to the *Epistle to the Romans*. About
a quarter to nine, while he was describing the change which
God works in the heart through faith in Christ, I felt my
heart strangely warmed. I felt that I did trust in Christ,
Christ alone, for salvation; and an assurance was given me
that he had taken away *my* sins, even *mine*, and saved me
from the law of sin and death.'

In Wesley's *Journal* there immediately follows this comment: 'I then testified openly to all there what I now first
felt in my heart.' He had found his message. He had not yet
found his method. With monotonous regularity he discovered
that the doors of the parish churches were closed against
him. Wherever he preached, he was informed that he need
not return. His orbit seemed to be steadily contracting. It
was George Whitefield, a friend of the Holy Club days, who
showed him the way ahead and helped him to find a new

and marvellous medium. If he could not preach in the churches, why not preach in the fields? 'At four in the afternoon,' Wesley records in his *Journal* on 2 April 1739, 'I submitted to be more vile, and proclaimed in the highways the glad tidings of salvation, speaking from a little eminence . . . to about three thousand people. The scripture from which I spoke was this . . . "The Spirit of the Lord is upon me, because he hath anointed me to preach the Gospel to the poor. He hath sent me to heal the broken-hearted; to preach deliverance to the captives, and recovery of sight to the blind; to set at liberty them that are bruised, to proclaim the acceptable year of the Lord." '

Thus begins one of the most remarkable episodes in the history of the church. Page after page, the sober prose of the *Journal* unfolds the marvellous story. John Wesley set out to carry the Gospel to people wherever they were willing to listen, and experience showed that throughout the length and breadth of the land they were waiting for such a preacher. 'In journeyings oft . . .', said the Apostle, and Wesley might have echoed his words. A conservative calculation suggests that he covered a quarter of a million miles in days when travelling was both difficult and dangerous. He preached to unnumbered multitudes. Two, three, five, ten thousand – these were by no means exceptional congregations; sometimes the figures rose to twenty and even thirty thousand. He preached in the streets or in the churchyards, in the fields or on the moors. He could always gather an audience, but he could not always gain a hearing. Crowds were often hostile, sometimes dangerous. Rocks and stones or other missiles would come flying at the preacher; sometimes he was mobbed and beaten. There was much misery and distress in the second half of the eighteenth century. Food was scarce, prices were high, and often the prevalent discontent vented itself on the Methodist preachers. Sometimes it was incited against them by hostile squires or parsons. But Wesley feared not the face of man. By a strange personal magnetism he awed the turbulent crowds and constrained them to silence. Even when driven out, he never hesitated to return. As a record of indomitable courage there are few narratives that can match it.

Both Wesley and Whitefield were preachers of extraordinary power. In his ability to sway an audience, Whitefield was supreme. He won the admiration of David Garrick, perhaps the ablest exponent of the art of rhetoric in an age of magnificent orators. He commanded the attention, if not the assent, of worldlings as hardened as the cynical Earl of Chesterfield. Wesley's power is more difficult to understand. His sermons, so closely reasoned, so massive in their doctrinal structure, bear little resemblance to what our age would consider popular preaching. Yet he could collect a congregation at any hour of the day. By preference he preached at five o'clock in the morning, but at night – even amid the violence of a thunderstorm – his hearers hung upon his words with absorbed attention. The preaching of both leaders produced the most dramatic results. As emotion swept the crowd, some confessed themselves sinners; some shouted that they were kings; some broke into songs of thanksgiving; some were seized with convulsions. 'While I was preaching,' records Wesley, 'one before me dropped down as dead, and presently a second or a third. Five others sank down in half an hour, most of whom were in violent agonies. We called upon the Lord and he gave us an answer of peace.' A brutalized age, long deprived of any outlet for religious emotions, reacted strongly to the new preaching, and it is not surprising that Hanoverian clerics looked askance at such manifestations of the Spirit.

In the early days of the revival, Wesley and Whitefield were joint leaders in a common task. They had had the same experience, they shared the same enthusiasm, they used the same methods. But they did not hold the same beliefs. Whitefield was a Calvinist, Wesley was not. Calvinism, which exalts the absolute sovereignty of God, claims that in his inscrutable wisdom he has ordained to salvation only those whom he selects. Arminianism, on the other hand, leaves far greater scope for man's free will. Wesley was a convinced Arminian. He held firmly to the belief that 'God

willeth all men to be saved'. Whitefield viewed such beliefs
with dismay. In *A Letter to the Rev. Mr John Wesley* (1752),
he claimed that because Wesley had misunderstood the
doctrine of election he had fallen into the heresy of universal
redemption. To Whitefield it was clear that Arminianism
dulled the all-important sense of sin; it made men complacent, whereas election tended to 'rouse the soul out its
carnal security'. Was Wesley right, he asked, in holding
that Calvinism killed all hope and led to indifference? Did
not the contrary view surrender the vital concept of an
almighty God? This was a debate between great men, both
deeply concerned about great issues. In his blunt way,
Wesley once told his friend that 'your God is my devil'.
Because they were great men, they parted in charity, but the
debate was continued by lesser men in a more vindictive
spirit, and had lasting results on the course of the evangelical
revival.

Wesley differed from Whitefield in doctrine and was distinctly his inferior in the arts of pure oratory, but as an
organizer he was supreme. In this area his gifts were transcendent, and lifted him into that select company to whom
the over-worked term 'genius' can properly be applied.
Wherever Whitefield went he left an overwhelming impression of impassioned eloquence; wherever Wesley went he
left a company of men and women closely knit together in
a common life. At an early stage he realized the importance
of organization. Even in Georgia, he recommended his more
earnest hearers 'to form themselves into a sort of little
society, to meet once or twice in a week, in order to reprove,
instruct, and exhort one another'. This method was
promptly applied to his expanding work in England. In
Bristol, in 1742, the members of the Society decided to
divide themselves into classes of about twelve each and to
appoint leaders to be responsible for oversight and for the
receipt of 'class money' (a penny a week). The pattern thus
established was adopted wherever Methodism spread. In
the following year, Wesley set forth a code of rules for his
followers, which laid on each of them the duty of resisting

evil, of doing good wherever possible, and of attending the ordinances, and he 'desired everyone seriously to consider whether he was willing to conform thereto or no'. Here was the basis for the discipline which became so characteristic of the movement. A year later, we have the genesis of the Conference – originally a consultation about increasing problems and responsibilities, soon a powerful part of the system of government. In 1746 a further step was taken, and neighbouring societies were formed into 'circuits or rounds'. Quarterly meetings were added in due course, and when Districts were set up the system was complete.

A closely knit organization and a strong central government were thus characteristic of Methodism from the beginning. The measure of personal authority wielded by Wesley himself was immense, but perhaps the notable feature of the system was the degree to which it developed lay leadership. The class leaders, stewards, trustees, and local preachers gained experience of administration and grew in stature. The qualifications for office did not put responsibility beyond the reach of humble folk, and gave the movement a firm foundation in popular support. Regular business meetings at every level of activity unified 'the connexion', and simplified the task of supervision. Every member was drawn into a corporate life whose extension depended upon his regular financial support.

Methodism had embarked upon a bold experiment. Necessity, reinforced by conviction, made Wesley rely increasingly on the gifts and capacities lying dormant in the average man. But this meant that he had to train his people, and often they had to be taught the simplest duties of the Christian life. This accounts for the strict discipline, corporate as well as personal, which Wesley enforced. In his private life, each member had to conform to an exacting standard. He was pledged to various forms of religious activity – regular reading of the Bible, the practice of public and private prayer, full participation in the varied activities of the society, and the conversion of others to his way of life. He was given direction concerning food and drink, clothing and ornaments, forms of self-indulgence, the use of money, buying and selling, the observance of the Sabbath, and attendance at church. The conscience of the individual was reinforced by the concern of the class meeting. Each member was expected to report his victories or defeats, and his way of life was subjected to searching scrutiny. As he advanced in responsibility he was expected to submit to an increasingly stringent discipline. The penalty for failure was expulsion, and this was no empty threat. At Newcastle, in 1743, Wesley read the rules, and proceeded to exclude sixty-four members, guilty of cursing, swearing, Sabbath-breaking, drunkenness, quarrelling and brawling, wife-beating, lying, railing, idleness and laziness, lightness and carelessness. Rigorous discipline was the counterpart of the human material which Wesley was trying to reform. He himself never questioned either the necessity of the method or the benefits which it produced. Wherever discipline was enforced, numbers rose and spiritual vitality increased.

The nature of his constituency determined the character of his programme. He went by choice to the needy and neglected. Beyond any of his contemporaries, he knew the poor and loved them. He spoke with withering scorn of the selfish ostentation of the rich, but 'I love the poor,' he said; 'in many of them I find pure genuine grace, unmixed with paint, folly, and affectation.' Many of his enterprises were inspired by their needs. 'All my leisure hours this week,' he records in 1783, 'I am employed in visiting the . . . poor and in begging for them.' He raised considerable sums of money in order to buy necessities, which he often distributed in person. When well past eighty, he spent four days on such a mission, trudging through streets 'filled with melting snow, which often lay ankle deep, so that my feet were steeped in snow water . . . from morning till evening'. He opened a dispensary 'for many of the poor that were sick'. He started a loan society to tide needy people over temporary distress or to launch them on some enterprise that promised a better way of life. He founded a home for widows and a school for poor children. He even recognized that poverty was not

merely 'a sore evil', but a social problem with which the
government ought to be concerned, and in his *Thoughts on
the Present Scarcity of Provisions* (1773), he suggested practical
measures which it might adopt.

Lack of money was the problem of some; the possession
of it was the problem of others, and Wesley gave much
thought to the subject of wealth and its proper use. Because
Methodism converted men to lives of sobriety and industry,
the members of the society prospered. Wesley did not regard
the acquisition of wealth as wrong, especially when it was
the result of honest industry. He certainly regarded it as
dangerous, and he viewed with concern the growing prosperity of his people. 'I went on to Macclesfield,' he writes,
'and found a people still alive to God, in spite of swiftly
increasing riches. If they continue so, it will be the first
instance I have known in above half a century. I warned
them in the strongest terms I could . . .' His own practice
was strict. 'For upward of eighty-six years I have kept my
accounts exactly. I will not attempt it any longer, being
satisfied . . . that I save all I can, and give all I can – that is,
all I have.'

In politics Wesley was a Tory, a loyal subject of the
Hanoverian kings, and a firm believer in the system of
government inaugurated by the Revolution of 1688. Much
has been written of his part in saving England from the kind
of upheaval which convulsed France at the close of the
century. But there was no close parallel between conditions
on the two sides of the Channel. England had had a constitutional revolution, and the economic life of the country
was already being transformed. This does not depreciate the
role Wesley played in reaching the poor of England. 'There
were thousands of men and women in Manchester and
Leeds', wrote the Hammonds, 'who found self-respect and
contentment in the duties and dreams of their religion.' The
loyalty which Wesley inculcated in his members gave them
a solidity which was of some significance in a disturbed
period, and which predisposed them to support the more
gradual processes of reform which in the next century

transformed English public life. And when preaching the
duties of good citizenship, Wesley was resolute in attacking the
abuses which he recognized in public life. With every means
at his disposal he opposed bribery and corruption in politics. He campaigned ceaselessly against the press gang, and
insisted that no Methodist should have any part in smug-
gling or in the plundering of wrecked vessels. Nor should his
unflinching stand against slavery be overlooked.

In certain directions his influence was used to more
dubious effect. His views on toleration were restricted by his
dislike of popery and his fear of its influence. In this he shared
the attitude of a generation which clung too tenaciously to
the fears rekindled by James II, and on this question his
views were those of his great contemporary, the Earl of
Chatham. In education his lack of imagination gave him
little understanding of the young. In his school at Kings-
wood, the pupils' day began at 4 a.m., but in a curriculum
crammed with every conceivable subject, he allowed no
time at all for play. Here again Wesley shared the limitations of his age, and it is not fair to judge Hanoverian practices by modern theories. It is only right to remember that
few men in his period did more to promote the cause of
education – and to add that his practice was better than his
principles. On one point contemporary accounts agree: his
great love of little children and his power to attract them.
Methodism began among poor people; its advance was built
upon the pennies they contributed. This accounts for its
indifference to art, to music, and to literature. In these
areas it was almost wholly sterile, with one very notable
exception. The hymns of the movement were its greatest
glory. They explain the power of its appeal, and constitute
its most revealing record. Charles Wesley left an imperish-
able legacy not only to Methodism but to the whole Christian world.

Methodism sprang up within the Church of England, and
Wesley was determined that it should never separate from
it. Early in his ministry, when 'a serious clergyman' asked
'in what points' the Methodists differed from the Church,

Wesley answered, 'In none.' 'The doctrines we preach', he added, 'are the doctrines of the Church of England; indeed, the fundamental doctrines of the church, laid down in her prayers, articles, and homilies.' 'I live and die a member of the Church of England,' he said. 'None who regard my judgement or advice will ever separate from it.' Nor were these isolated statements; they can be multiplied times without number, and resolutions of the conference reinforced them. There is a deep pathos but a certain inevitability about the final breach. The Hanoverian Church was ill equipped to deal with such a phenomenon as Methodism. The reaction of the bishops was varied. Gibson was cautious, aware of difficulties, but anxious not to condemn. Archbishop Potter was cordial. 'Mr Wesley,' said Bishop Lowth, 'may I be found sitting at your feet in another world.' Many of the bishops were outspoken in their opposition. Warburton wrote a strong attack on the Methodist doctrine of grace, and on Wesley as the ablest proponent of the dangerous new trend in religion. Bishop Butler was also hostile; his famous rebuke ('Sir, the pretending to extraordinary revelations and gifts of the Holy Ghost is a horrid thing – a very horrid thing') shows how far removed in spirit a great Hanoverian churchman could be from the new movement. There was no unanimity among the bishops because there was no concerted policy in the church. Convocation was in abeyance, and consequently none could be framed. In any case, attention was concentrated on other things; many highly placed ecclesiastics were absorbed in the intricacies of place-hunting, and they did not see that Methodism was a challenge to the church. As the new societies expanded, they developed the characteristics of congregations. Many of their members, snatched from indifference and irreligion, had no attachment to the established church, and desired none. The developing life of the movement became less and less dependent on the church; in spite of everything that Wesley said, many of his followers were content that it should be so. The severance of Methodism from the church was the consequence of Wesley's acceptance of an apostolate to the growing industrial population which was virtually untouched by Anglican ministrations. But the church could not overlook Wesley's claim to disregard parish boundaries; still less could it admit his right to ordain. Wesley had become increasingly perturbed at the failure of the church to provide adequate ministrations in the colonies; study and reflection persuaded him that presbyters could legitimately ordain. Consequently he embarked on a course that his own church could not countenance. The separation between Anglicanism and Methodism may have been inevitable; it is impossible not to regard it with profound regret.

Many features of the Methodist revival can be explained in terms of the needs of the time and the gifts of the man who was raised up to meet them. In both social and religious matters England was ready to listen to Wesley's message. He came with the assurance that God's forgiveness was available to all: the power of a new life could be had for the asking. The flexibility of his method and the novelty of preaching in the open air gave the widest currency to the good news he brought, while his superb gifts of organization conserved the results which he achieved. But to Wesley himself such explanations would have seemed irrelevant. In his eightieth year he himself found the secret of his ministry chiefly in 'the power of God, fitting me for what he calls me to'. He was persuaded that his whole life and every detail of it were under the immediate direction of God. And in the response of the people he found confirmation of this same power. 'The drunkard', wrote Wesley, 'commenced sober and temperate; the whore-monger abstained from adultery and fornication, the unjust from oppression and wrong. He that had been accustomed to curse and swear for many years, now swore no more. The sluggard began to work with his hands, that he might eat his own bread. The miser learned to deal his bread to the hungry, and to cover the naked with a garment. Indeed, the whole of their life was changed: they had left off doing evil and learned to do well.' A Methodist, said Wesley, is 'happy in God, yea, always happy'; a quality which survives in the songs of the movement was first expressed in the lives of its members. One of the most satisfactory accounts of the dynamic quality of Methodism is Wesley's description of the Yorkshire societies in 1751. 'I found them all alive, strong, vigorous of soul, blessing, loving and praising God their Saviour. . . . From the beginning they had been taught both the law and the gospel. "God loves *you*: therefore love and obey *Him*. Christ died for *you*: therefore die to sin. Christ is risen: therefore rise in the image of God. Christ liveth evermore: therefore live to God, till you live with him in glory." So *we* preached; and so *you* believed. This is the scriptural way, the *Methodist* way, the true way. God grant we may never turn from it, to the right hand or to the left.'

The evangelical revival cannot be equated with the Methodist movement, still less with the life of the Wesleyan societies. Whitefield, after parting company with Wesley on doctrine, continued to work along parallel lines, though with more ephemeral results. After his comparatively early death, Calvinistic Methodism was most prominently represented by the Countess of Huntingdon. She undertook to commend Methodism to the upper classes; in addition she claimed the right as a peeress to appoint as her chaplains clergymen willing to work on behalf of Methodism. These men, were, of course, predominantly priests of the Church of England, since Methodism was still a movement, not a denomination. But the Countess also had close relations with nonconformity. Her theological college at Trevecca trained clergy both for the church and for the dissenting bodies. Her chaplains exerted a wider influence than their numbers would have suggested, and her practices were challenged. In 1779 the consistory court of London disallowed her claim that she could appoint to the rank of chaplain, and use in public ministrations, as many Anglican priests as she desired. She thereupon registered her chapels as dissenting meeting houses, and 'the Countess of Huntingdon's Connexion' became a nonconformist body. In one more respect the ties between Anglicanism and Methodism were severed.

Methodism began within the established church. White-field and Wesley were Anglican priests, and their aim was to revitalize the church. Many clergymen who were influenced by their example did not identify themselves with their movement. Samuel Walker of Truro, who was largely responsible for a notable revival in western Cornwall, gathered his converts into societies similar to those of Wesley. Grimshaw of Haworth and Berridge of Everton were itinerant evangelists as well as parish priests. Like the Methodists, they emphasized the need for a vital spiritual religion. They believed that the immediate action of the Holy Spirit leads men through conversion to a holy life. Their theological affinities were with Whitefield rather than with Wesley. Toplady (author of *Rock of Ages*, and of many vigorous polemical works) was a vehement Calvinist. The Evangelicals accepted the total depravity of man: of his own will, he cannot turn to God, and restoration to divine favour can be effected by Christ alone. They were opposed both to the meagre theology of their age and to the unabashed world-liness of the Hanoverian Church. Bluntly and without quali-fication they proclaimed the great evangelical doctrines.

These men were in conscious revolt against many of the characteristic aspects of their age. Their protest against its frivolity intensified the puritanical strain so congenial to their Calvinistic outlook. They condemned cards, theatres, dancing, and all amusements that savoured of dissipation. They kept steadily in the forefront of their thought the high seriousness of life and the dread solemnity of death, and they insisted that the demands both of time and of eternity can be met victoriously only by those who rely completely upon divine aid.

They combined this strength with some less admirable elements. They developed an almost morbid preoccupation with death. In their reaction against rationalism they allowed unfettered scope to the emotions. Because the prevalent theology had developed Latitudinarian, even Socinian, tendencies, they deprecated intellectual pursuits and relied on an uncritical Biblical literalism. As a result, the evangelical movement proved comparatively sterile as a theological force. Stock phrases supplanted reasoned arguments, and a distinctive idiom became the badge of piety.

In the closing years of the eighteenth century, the Evangelicals made rapid headway. John Newton, William Romaine, and Thomas Scott were active in London; so were Richard Cecil and Basil Wood. Bishop Beilby Porteus encouraged them, and in increasing numbers the clergy of the capital associated themselves with the movement. At Oxford they were weak, at Cambridge strong. Isaac Milner, the President of Queens', was a notable figure both in the university and beyond it. Charles Simeon, a fellow of King's, exercised a highly influential ministry at Holy Trinity Church. At Cambridge, and increasingly throughout the Church of England, religious earnestness found a congenial home in the Evangelical party. Not many of its members were in positions of power, but by the end of the century it had established itself as the most active and aggressive group in the church.

The Evangelicals, unlike the Methodists, remained within the church, but they emphasized only one aspect of its teaching, and attached little value to methods on which it had always relied. In their intense preoccupation with the salvation of the individual, they minimized the corporate life of the church. But they proved that men and women can be converted to a new life and can be sustained in true godliness. Nor was their influence a doctrinaire and other-worldly force. They were devoted to good works, and showed that the Gospel which transformed individuals can profoundly affect society as well.

This growing awareness of Christian responsibility for the weak and the destitute inspired some of the notable movements which flourished during the closing years of our period. The crusade against the slave trade represents perhaps the greatest victory of the awakened Christian conscience over a strongly entrenched evil. In the long, slow process of exposing the traffic in human lives the Quakers played a distinguished part, but the contribution of the

'Clapham Sect' (a group of earnest and influential Evangelicals) was decisive. The slave trade was firmly established
and powerfully supported. It had been an axiom of British
policy that the prosperity of the country – the expansion of
its manufacturing, shipping, and colonial trade – required
active participation in this traffic. The trade in slaves had
been sanctioned by three seventeenth-century charters; it
had been legalized by an Act of Parliament in 1698;
Britain's share had been augmented by treaties in 1713,
1725, and 1748. The African Company was described as 'the
most beneficial to this island of all the companies that ever
were formed by our merchants'. The trade had been pushed
with considerable success. During the century before 1786,
the British alone transported at least 2,000,000 negroes to
the new world. All the other maritime nations – the French,
the Portuguese, the Dutch, the Danes, and the New
Englanders – had a share in the traffic. But finally an age
not unduly sensitive to human suffering was shocked by the
horrors of 'the middle passage' and by the rigours of the
plantation system. The rising tide of humanitarian feeling
began to protest. Some of the most distinguished men of the
day challenged the commercial interests involved. In 1787
the Committee for the Abolition of the Slave Trade was
formed, and Grenville Sharp, Clarkson, Zachary Macaulay,
and William Wilberforce were prominent members. A committee of the Privy Council collected a great deal of information about the traffic, and in 1788 William Pitt, in Wilberforce's absence through illness, raised the subject in the
House of Commons. Repeal was delayed by the preoccupations of war as well as by fear that unilateral action would
merely benefit England's rivals. Victory tarried; the persistence of Wilberforce and his associates guaranteed ultimate
success. This was a notable triumph of the Christian conscience, and its origins, as well as the spirit which sustained
the long endeavour, are revealed in Wilberforce's famous
work, *A Practical View of the Prevailing Religious Systems*. This
popular book was the most influential manifesto of the
Evangelical party.

The work of Hannah More illustrates another aspect of Evangelical zeal. Before her conversion, this able woman had been a prominent literary and social figure. Her growing interest in 'serious Christianity' found expression in *Thoughts on the Importance of the Manners of the Great to General Society* (1788), a courageous work which had an appreciable effect on social customs. Wilberforce directed her attention to the conditions which prevailed in the villages of the Mendip Hills. The labourers were ignorant and poverty-stricken; the more substantial farmers were despotic and overbearing; the clergy were indifferent and indolent. In thirteen adjoining communities there was not a single resident clergyman of any kind. To combat the prevailing ignorance and vice, Hannah More and her sister established schools, first for the children, then for the adults. At every turn they encountered an opposition bred of superstition and fear. The courage of these women, as well as their enlightened and disinterested enthusiasm, reflected the evangelical spirit in its most attractive guise.

In many other areas the Evangelicals were active. They helped to establish the Church Missionary Society, the Religious Tract Society, and the British and Foreign Bible Society. Their spirit was sometimes narrow and their sympathies circumscribed, but at one point after another their influence stimulated and guided the Christian conscience.

11

England: The Rise and Fall of the Cult of Reason

In the early part of the eighteenth century, the prestige of English thought stood very high. This was largely due to the immense authority of two men: Isaac Newton, who had unlocked the secrets of the physical universe, and John Locke, who had laid bare the inner nature of man. English ideas, when transplanted to continental countries, often proved revolutionary in their implications.

In England itself the conflict of ideas was intense but seldom turbulent. Though the contestants differed about great essentials, they shared certain fundamental assumptions. The new science disposed men to regard the universe as an orderly system, guided by a purpose in which man can participate and governed by laws which human intelligence can grasp. The new philosophy had opened the way to a deeper understanding of human nature and particularly to a new appreciation of the workings of the human mind. As the eighteenth century began, there was a widespread assumption that the truths of Christianity could and should be made attractive to men of calm and dispassionate judgement. The recent past had been disfigured by violent and apparently unprofitable controversies; therefore faith seemed most attractive when presented in its most reasonable light. This reaction against the factiousness of theological disputes showed itself in two forms: positively, in the wide diffusion of Latitudinarian views; negatively, in the challenge of Deism.

Latitudinarianism seems such a dull and meagre form of faith that it is easy to dismiss it with impatience. In an earlier chapter we have noted its rise. In a slightly modified form it persisted throughout most of the eighteenth century, and represents one of the most significant movements of religious thought since the Reformation. Its objectives were more important than its achievements. It had a sure instinct for the issues that would be of lasting interest, and many of them have reappeared in a fresh guise in each subsequent century. The Latitudinarians undertook the task of reconciling the church to the changes which a new intellectual environment demanded. They believed that the essentials of the faith could be expressed in simple, non-technical terms that paid little attention to traditional formulations. Perhaps the greatest exponent of this point of view was Dr Samuel Clarke, whose Boyle Lectures on *The Being and Attributes of God* impressed his contemporaries as a miracle of lucid and reasonable exposition. The harmony and order of the universe pointed to a Creator who is as beneficent as he is wise. The fatherly rule of God demanded of his children a benevolence like his own, and these elementary truths – the fatherhood of God and our duty to show a good will comparable with his – were the essential ingredients in their teaching. Important consequences followed from this simple pattern of belief. In a universe of order and beauty man was freed from all dark, foreboding fears; if the galaxies of heaven were fashioned for his delight, how great must be his native dignity! How appropriate to ponder the mysteries of his own nature! Man subtly became the centre of his own delighted scrutiny, and he felt that this preoccupation with himself was right. Pope, with his genius for giving memorable form to popular convictions, perfectly expressed the outlook of his age:

> Know then thyself, presume not God to scan,
> The proper study of mankind is man.

Having minimized the speculative element in religion, the Latitudinarians were free to emphasize its practical implications. In stressing our moral duty, they fortified man's faltering purposes by reminding him of the consequences of good works. It was wise to be sober and pious, because virtue brings its own reward. This is true in this world, and immediate advantage is reinforced by the assured prospect of eternal bliss. Tillotson was dead, but his sermons were the ethical handbook of the new age, and on this point he was perfectly explicit. 'Now these two things', he wrote, 'must needs make our duty very easy: a considerable reward in hand, and not only the hopes but the assurance of a far greater recompense hereafter.'

It is dangerous, however, to quote from the Latitudinarians: their own words so easily appear a caricature of their position. For all their faults, they had very considerable virtues. They showed a robust common sense, a vigorous though unimaginative learning, and a strong persuasion of the relevance of religion to their age. Controversy brought out their latent strength, and they bore an important part in the great struggle that marked the first half of the eighteenth century. Everyone conceded that belief stands or falls as it commends itself to human intelligence. In this respect the defenders of Christianity met its foes at least halfway. They were willing to put orthodoxy on trial at the bar of reason, and were satisfied that it would emerge triumphant from the test. God himself was expected to produce credentials satisfactory to reason. Christianity *is* the religion of reason; the Christian God *is* the God of Nature. The title of Locke's work, *The Reasonableness of Christianity*, epitomizes the basic conviction of the age. In this sense, rationalism was an assumption common to all the disputants; it was not a doctrine about religion but an approach to its problems.

The Deists appealed to reason, and found its laws supremely manifested in nature. Here was the true and sufficient publication of the truth about God. Here, too, was the perfect manifestation of his law for human life. Matthew Tindal, an able and scholarly fellow of All Souls College, Oxford, wrote one of the most important works inspired by the controversy, proving to his satisfaction that *Christianity [is] as Old as the Creation* (1730). God's work is perfect, and perfectly reveals him. If it needed to be supplemented, it would be imperfect; because it is perfect, nothing can be added to it without casting aspersions on

God's original purpose or on his initial handiwork. Tindal quietly assumed, of course, that, from the first, man was perfectly equipped to grasp this perfect religion. This points to one of the fundamental weaknesses of the Deists. Because they had no sense of history, they oversimplified the problems of human development and the seriousness of the evils which beset it. But it proved to them that no further revelation was necessary, because the initial revelation was perfect. Everyone conceded the reality of natural religion. The crucial question, therefore, was whether natural religion was sufficient. The Deists said Yes; the Christians said No. Revelation, claimed the Deists, was at best superfluous, at worst superstitious. Toland had initiated the controversy in its full-blown form by insisting that there was nothing in Christianity that was mysterious. It contained nothing either above reason or contrary to it. The Christian apologists would concede the second part of this assertion, but not the first. There were many things, they claimed, that we could never know unless God revealed them to us. In the last analysis these truths were perfectly congruous with reason but our limitations might blind us to the fact.

If there is such a thing as revelation, how can we recognize it? The Christians pointed to the 'evidences', as they called them – the unmistakable signs that demonstrate the divine origin of what has been revealed. The Deists, since they increasingly questioned the reality (even the possibility) of revelation, denied the sufficiency of the proofs advanced to support it. These proofs were of two kinds: prophecy and miracles. Did the events contained in the New Testament really fulfil predictions made in the Old Testament? Was the proclamation of the Gospel enforced by miraculous events which proved that it was an authentic disclosure of God's nature and purpose? The Deistic controversy falls into two stages. In the first, the debate concerns nature, reason, and the degree to which Christianity offers anything not already latent in either or both. In the second, the issue at stake was the historical proof of the genuineness of the Christian records.

The Deists raised questions which no one at the time could satisfactorily answer. Since there was no sense of history, no awareness of development, no conception of progressive revelation, the debate resolved itself into futile wrangling. The later Deists felt obliged to prove that the New Testament writers were simpletons or knaves, who were either too naïve to understand the facts, or wrote what they knew was not true. The Christians countered by vindicating the integrity of the evangelists and the reliability of what they wrote. The attacks tended to concentrate on the Resurrection as the crucial instance of the events that never happened, and the replies took the form either of a microscopic investigation of details or of the elaborate legalistic ingenuity of Sherlock's *Trial of the Witnesses of the Resurrection.* Even more distasteful were the aspersions cast on the probity of Biblical heroes (Moses, David, Paul), and scarcely more reassuring was the defence advanced on their behalf. But this was late in the debate, when it was clear that the contestants not merely lacked the means of answering their own problems but had forfeited public interest.

At the height of the controversy, however, there can be no doubt that it attracted considerable attention. It was designed to appeal to the man of average education. The more cultivated Deists wrote in the easy style that coffee house standards prescribed. Their material was often superficial but it was usually readable. This had advantages. Theology could not afford to be abstract; it was compelled to be intelligible. Deism was raising the kind of questions that the common man is likely to ask; the answers therefore had to be addressed to him. Though the Deists were not a large group, and never formed a party in any formal sense, it was clear that they appealed to an extensive reading public. Hence their works elicited a large number of replies. One of Collins' pamphlets inspired thirty-five answers, Tindal's *Christianity as Old as the Creation* at least one hundred and fifty. For a couple of decades (1720–40) the interest in the debate was intense. Then it suddenly waned. Bolingbroke's *Works* (1754–6) attracted little attention and probably deserved no more than they got, but Hume's early philosophical writings, which were of serious and searching importance, were at the outset virtually ignored by the public.

Deism, though worsted in the controversy, really collapsed through its own inherent weakness. Its critical powers far outstripped its constructive capacity. The historical insight of the Deists was limited and their human sympathies were restricted; instead of providing a universal faith, they offered a doctrine which proved to be limited in its scope and temporary in its appeal. In repudiating revelation and exalting the religion of nature, they believed that they were stripping away unintelligible irrelevances, but they ended by making religion itself seem commonplace and poor. They regarded the world as a mechanism devised by God and operated by him; they were betrayed into a false optimism and could offer no explanation of the evils and disasters of life. Because the laws of nature are clear and unalterable, they assumed that man's moral inferences, drawn from nature, must be correspondingly simple and permanent. The greatest weakness of Deism was the easy terms on which it offered religious faith and the complacency which it encouraged in its devotees. Nor had it any answer to the obvious difficulty inherent in the position; if all men can so easily see religious truths without the aid of revelation, why have they so conspicuously failed to do so? The fault, replied the Deists, lies with priestcraft. But this was too simple to be true, and few were convinced.

The opponents of Deism showed themselves superior in most of the arts of controversy. Their scholarship was wider and their logic sounder. But the battle was not really won by the contestants who joined in the confused *mêlée* of debate. Long before the controversy died of inanition, it was clear that there could be no solution to the questions which the age had learned to ask, so long as both sides adhered to the assumptions which limited their outlook. The real answer to Deism came from three men who were able to break out of the restricted orbit in which eighteenth-century rationalism moved, and who therefore set the essential issues in a new light. Law (*The Case of Reason*, 1731), Berkeley (*Alciphron*, 1732), and Butler (*The Analogy of Religion*, 1736) showed that the problems could be solved only through a new understanding of reason and its role.

William Law was a fellow of Emmanuel College, Cambridge, who had relinquished his career because he would not take the oaths to George I. As a non-juror he stood apart from the course of church life, but he had recently shown, in his *Treatise on Christian Perfection* (1726) and in his yet more celebrated *Serious Call to a Devout and Holy Life* (1728), that he possessed unusual gifts as a writer of practical devotional works. He was drawn into the main stream of contemporary controversy by Tindal's *Christianity as Old as the Creation*. Tindal assumed that reason provides the only test of truth, but he did not define reason. Christianity is a republication of the original religion of nature – but what *is* nature? Law pounced on the ambiguities latent in Tindal's use of these key words, and pressed his attack with skill and vigour. As his argument unfolds, his work grows in coherence and power; it has an almost organic unity. But the fascination of the book is not confined to his controversial skill; behind the contest of words and ideas is a contrast of personalities. Law was a believer who felt deeply the majesty of God and the mystery of life. Tindal was a scholar whose understanding of religion was abstract and academic. Law naturally seized on the shallowness of Tindal's view of God. Tindal, he claimed, had really reduced God to the measure of human capacity. The arrogance of presuming to fathom God's nature, of venturing to determine what it is fitting for God to do! With remorseless ingenuity, Law exposed the preposterous absurdity of Tindal's assumption that God must behave according to the strictest canons of human reason. But he pressed the attack too cogently. He depreciated reason to the point where he had little left wherewith to commend the faith to his contemporaries. Admittedly he restored prophecy and miracle to their rightful place, but he did so in a way very different from that which satisfied his pedestrian colleagues. His need of these arguments, no less than his method of handling them, was distinctive. He wrote from a vantage point of insight and experience which few of his contemporaries shared, and when, in succeeding years, he moved farther and farther toward avowed mysticism, an age enamoured of reason felt entitled to ignore him.

George Berkeley believed that he had found an argument which provided a devastating criticism of Deism, but it was originally devised as a fundamental philosophical system, not as a contribution to controversy. Berkeley was one of the most attractive figures, as he was certainly one of the most skilful stylists, of the eighteenth century. As a relatively young man at Trinity College, Dublin (where he was successively scholar, fellow, and tutor), he thought out his basic interpretation of mind and reality. But his interests were not confined to speculation. He was a missionary enthusiast, determined to establish a college in Bermuda, and a churchman who secured high promotion in Ireland. Berkeley was persuaded that his interpretation of the universe was beautifully simple and lucid. Non-experts have usually found it both puzzling and paradoxical, and men of common sense (like Samuel Johnson) have been apt to dismiss it as sheer nonsense. Berkeley's importance consists in this, that he shows us the world from a new point of view. Ideas are the things that really exist, and they are all that we can really know. Material things exist only in so far as they are perceived; in other words, their existence is passive and dependent. Active, independent existence can be attributed only to minds. Spirits, finite minds, and the infinite mind are the only realities for whose existence we have any evidence. It is God, as perfect intelligence, who is responsible for the existence of the ideas which are not the products of our own minds. The order of the existence of ideas is determined by the divine agency, and this is what is meant by the laws of nature.

This elusive doctrine might seem to have little immediate connexion with the issues which the Deists debated. To

Berkeley the relation was as important as it was obvious. He was shocked by what seemed to him the irreligious rationalism of the Deists. To get rid of the tyranny of brute matter was to remove the foundation on which all superficial rationalism rests. The usual arguments for God's existence seemed to Berkeley to be little better than atheism. In *Alciphron*, therefore, he combats one by one the various types of infidelity prevalent at the time, always from the point of view of his spiritual interpretation of reality. He was not primarily concerned to expound the content of revelation, but he emphatically believed that Christian beliefs promote the true welfare of man and are even necessary to the full exercise of his rational faculties.

Bishop Butler's monumental work, *The Analogy of Religion, Natural and Revealed, to the Constitution and Course of Nature*, was the most formidable and the most decisive work that the Deistic controversy called forth. On essential matters it virtually ended the debate; skirmishing continued for some years, but it was clear that the fundamental issues had been settled. Butler seldom mentioned his opponents by name; he was contending with basic ideas, not with their representatives. His work, therefore, was delivered from the circumscribing effect of being tied to the arguments of individuals. But for all its air of Olympian detachment, Butler never lost sight of the Deists. Each of their arguments had been thoroughly considered and carefully assigned its proper weight. He never tried to score a point by evading a difficulty, never claimed for his own views a greater cogency than he felt they carried. It is this judicious quality which gives to his reasoning its air of completeness and finality. Equally notable is the atmosphere of modesty which pervades the work. The Deists, with confident optimism, assumed that they knew all about God's wisdom and purpose, because they read it all quite simply in the pattern of nature. Butler saw, with disconcerting clarity, the perplexities and the irrationalities of life. He looked about him with a sombre melancholy which pierced the façade of the easy confidence which was everywhere prevalent. He took for granted what his opponents were willing to concede. He did not prove the existence of God; the Deists also built their case on the assumption that he exists. Reason, too, must be accepted: it is our natural light, the only faculty by which we can judge of things. But it provides no complete system of knowledge, and in matters of fact warrants only probable conclusions. In ordinary life, probability is the only guide we have. With devastating effect he undermined the presuppositions of the Deists. They had assumed that the religion of nature affords us knowledge which is clear and free from all ambiguity; since we are given such satisfying results in this area, can we not safely ignore the uncertain probabilities which is all that revealed religion offers? Butler ruthlessly demolished the premise of this specious argument. Nature is not a realm in which light and reason are supreme. It is filled with dark areas and regions of unexplained mystery, obscurity and perplexity meet us at every turn. If we encounter such problems in nature, need we be surprised if we meet analogous difficulties in religion? Have we any right to expect the one sphere to yield results wholly different in kind from the best that we can obtain from the other? Butler took a further step. The facts of nature, though failing to provide a basis for assured certainty, form a distinct ground for inferring the probable truth of revealed religion. We know the ordinary course of nature because it is disclosed to us by experience, and find it pervaded by ambiguity and uncertainty; if the precepts of religion are marked by analogous obscurity and difficulty, then it is reasonable to assume that the one kind of knowledge is as dependable as the other. Butler reasoned from what is known of nature to the probable truth of what is contained in religion. This is the analogy which he stressed. The balance of probability, he felt, is in favour of the scheme of religion; this probability is a natural conclusion drawn from an inspection of nature.

Butler has not proved the truth of religion, nor has he shown that God rules the world in perfect wisdom and justice. That was not his purpose. He did not intend to provide a philosophy of religion, he wished to meet certain objections brought against Christianity. But there is no mistaking the line which his interests prompted him to follow. Having shown that probability is the basis on which we normally act, he pointed out that religion is not a theory, but a matter of practice, and we are obliged to follow what seems the right course of action, even though we lack perfect certainty. Butler was one of the great moral teachers of the age. In *The Analogy* his argument in favour of immortality presupposes the significance, here and hereafter, of our conduct. Human nature is so constituted that it finds meaning only in acknowledging an end or purpose. That purpose cannot be achieved through following selfish impulse (as Hobbes had claimed). Man's nature is adapted to virtue. Shaftesbury had taught this; he had made benevolence the true mark of man's life, and had found in 'moral sense' the origin of man's ability to choose right and wrong. Butler developed Shaftesbury's system, and showed that 'conscience' (as he preferred to call it) by its nature claims to rule man's life. Conscience can rightfully claim the ultimate authority. 'To preside and govern, from the very economy and constitution of man, belongs to it.'

The eighteenth century began its course with a confident assurance that reason can resolve all mysteries into simple logic and can dispel the last shadows of darkness and superstition. Persistent criticism had revealed the superficiality of this assumed confidence in light and logic. The great figures of the eighteenth century broke with the Augustan faith in reason and its powers. Law, Berkeley, and Butler represent important stages in that repudiation. John Wesley and the Evangelicals were another stage. And the most drastic philosophical statement of the insufficiency of rationalism came from David Hume.

Hume was the greatest of British philosophers. A consummate master of English prose, he demolished the cherished certainties of his age with an elegant simplicity. The system which Locke fashioned and Berkeley modified reaches its conclusion in Hume. The logical result of his analysis leads not to the reconstruction of thought but to the sceptical

disintegration of knowledge. He demolished all the traditional certainties: God and the soul, nature and matter,
causation and miracles. This did not mean that discussion
of these subjects ceased or that reasonable belief came
abruptly to an end. It meant that a new beginning had to
be made. Locke had been the high-priest of confident
rationalism; Hume showed that his philosophy, when pressed
to its logical conclusions, led nowhere. So a fresh start was
necessary, and in Kant it achieved very notable results,
but belief in the sufficiency of reason was shattered. The
effect of Hume's speculations, though not immediate, was
ultimately profound. His earliest and perhaps his greatest
work (*A Treatise of Human Nature*) 'fell dead-born from the
press' (as he described its fate), and the implications of his
thought were not recognized at once. He himself admitted
that as soon as he left his study he found it difficult to believe
in his own theories. And he was a consistent sceptic, in that
he refused to be dogmatic about his own scepticism.
Gradually, however, his influence made itself felt, and certain of his works which deal specifically with religious subjects aroused considerable interest. His famous essay 'Of
Miracles' (developing the contrast between 'laws of nature'
and violations of those laws) was not wholly consistent with
his own fundamental position, but attracted a good deal of
attention. In the *Natural History of Religion*, he suggested that
the process which results in religious belief is very different
from the theoretical arguments which support it. The
Dialogues Concerning Natural Religion (published posthu-
mously) subject the traditional arguments for religious belief
to searching analysis. The literary form of the work makes it
difficult to be certain of Hume's own position, but the
general trend of the discussion implies the acceptance of
purpose in the universe and points to a vague form of
theism. Theologically Hume's importance lies less in what
he himself taught than in what he henceforth made it impossible for others to say. He destroyed the basis for the
glib rationalism of the early part of the century. The
complacent assurance that man's mind can dissipate all

mysteries and resolve all difficulties could not survive the astringent effect of Hume's cool and searching analysis. Rationalism had attacked superstition, only to be attacked in turn by scepticism.

The second half of the century saw a pronounced decline in the vigour and distinction of English religious thought. There are few important movements and few great names. While the evangelical revival was resuscitating English religious life, no comparable impetus was given to theology. There was, it is true, an attempt to free theology from what was considered the dead hand of the past. A group of liberals believed that the Church of England was badly in need of thorough reform, that its credal statements required revision, that its worship had fallen out of touch with modern thought, that its administrative machinery was so cumbersome and inefficient that it imperilled effective functioning. The immediate point of attack was the question of subscription – the form of undertaking imposed on ordinands and incumbents. The most explicit statement of the aims of these liberals appeared in Archdeacon Blackburne's *The Confessional* (1766); and their one concerted political move was the presentation of the 'Feathers Tavern' Petition in 1771. This was a plea addressed to parliament to allow the clergy to interpret the Bible in the light of reason and conscience instead of being bound by creeds and formulas. The request was rejected, and the strongest speech against the petition was made by Edmund Burke.

This flurry on the surface of religious life is important chiefly because it reflects a tendency at work throughout the century. Latitudinarianism had veered toward various forms of unitarian belief (Arian or Socinian). There was a good deal of unsettlement within the Church of England; outside it, particularly among the Presbyterians, there was a steady drift toward unitarian views. Change, claimed the liberals, was the only answer to this prevailing unrest, and a considerable body of opinion supported them. There was a general desire for greater freedom and flexibility. Many people felt that the church was rigid in its thinking, antiquated in its laws, and intolerant in its attitude to other Christians. The intelligent layman, it was claimed, could be held only by a faith which he understood and respected. But reform was difficult to achieve. Repeated attempts to secure the repeal of the Test and Corporation Acts (felt by the dissenters to be serious grievances) failed – again through the influence of Burke – and the involvement of the established church in politics blocked the removal even of abuses which no friend of the church could defend.

One of the foremost spokesmen of the liberal school was Richard Watson. He had had a distinguished but unusual career at Cambridge. Though no chemist he was appointed professor of chemistry, and mastered enough of the subject to teach it. In due course, he was appointed professor of divinity (though no theologian), and the excessively narrow bounds within which he proposed to restrict the subject illustrates one of the weaknesses of the liberal school. 'I reduced the study of divinity into as narrow a compass as I could, for I determined to study nothing but my Bible, being much unconcerned about the opinions of councils, fathers, churches, bishops, and other men, as little inspired as myself.' When Gibbon published his *Decline and Fall* and so seriously agitated the ecclesiastical dovecots, Watson undertook to refute him, and felt that a month during the long vacation was quite sufficient for the task. He was active in that borderland where university and national politics overlap, and was promoted to the see of Llandaff; but because he continued to champion reform after his political allies had fallen, he forfeited all prospects of further advancement. In all he did there was a curious combination of right ends and wrong means, of real insight and great obtuseness.

Of similar outlook but of much greater consequence was William Paley. Like Watson he was a Cambridge man; if his lectures had the same lucid qualities as his books, he must have been an excellent teacher. In no sense was he an original thinker, but he had unrivalled gifts for marshalling his material. What he says is often derived from other people: his moral and political philosophy from the utilitarians, his reply to Hume from Douglas, his natural theology from Ray and Derham. But he developed his arguments with great skill and expounded them with unequalled clarity. As the eighteenth century drew to a close, Paley accurately reflected its spirit, and epitomized its strength and its weakness: its lucidity, its vigorous intelligence, its robust common sense (trembling on the brink of pedestrianism), its limited outlook, and its obtuseness to mystery and wonder. For his own age he provided a powerful defence against the corrosive influence of Hume, Gibbon, and Tom Paine, and it is a tribute to his skill as an expositor that in the University of Cambridge his *Evidences of Christianity* was a prescribed textbook for the Previous Examination ('Little-go') until 1919.

It was among the nonconformists that the cult of liberty, both in theology and in politics, found fullest scope. In their case, rationalism often passed over into unitarianism. Their more advanced representatives followed Bentham and the utilitarians in ethics, Adam Smith in economics, David Hartley in psychology, and Charles James Fox (for lack of a more radical leader) in politics. Changes in thought came easily in chapels which were loosely organized and where the demand for greater freedom was an honoured tradition. The dissenting academies encouraged new studies and were the forcing ground of new developments in many fields. The outstanding nonconformists of the late eighteenth century were Richard Price and Joseph Priestley. From a pious dissenting home, Priestley passed to one of the academies, then to a congregation, and back to an academy as a teacher, all the while seeking enlarged scope for his insatiable intellectual curiosity. His knowledge was encyclopedic. He wrote on history, politics, economics, philosophy, and theology, and was one of the most distinguished experimental scientists of the day. In his view of man, he was a materialist and did not believe in the soul; he was a necessitarian and did not believe in man's freedom of will; he was a Christian who denied most of the traditional Christian doctrines, and who insisted that he was merely freeing the faith from the accretions of superstition. With irrepressible optimism he believed that man was moving towards a progressively better and fuller life. The shackles of ignorance, bondage, and poverty were being broken. 'Error and superstition', he exclaimed with delight, 'are falling everywhere abroad.' Such a man was naturally a reformer; he would improve people in spite of themselves, making the poor provident, the rich generous the powerful enlightened and progressive. The poor disliked him, the rich and the powerful distrusted him. His radicalism seemed dangerous, and when the French Revolution aroused tempers, the Birmingham mob burned down his house. It is impossible to read his writings before that date without marvelling at his humane spirit, his unruffled confidence, his buoyant conviction that a millennial age was dawning. Coleridge once equated Socinianism with moonlight. The simile suggests clear cold light, but it is hardly applicable to Priestley. His confidence is reminiscent of a warm, bright morning in spring; but when he wrote the dark clouds were already massing on the horizon, and his idyllic dream was shattered by the storm.

The pleas for reform were drowned by the revolutionary din let loose by the great upheaval in France. By the end of the eighteenth century, a reaction had already set in against all the things with which the age is normally associated. Reason was becoming discredited. Clarity, lucidity, balance, equipoise were not virtues that commended themselves to the dawning romantic period. The chief representative of this reaction is Edmund Burke. Historic continuity, organic growth in church and state became so important that the demands for reform were stifled. The foundation of Burke's doctrine is a deep religious reverence. Man's life is undergirded by divine providence; the ways of wisdom are slowly and painfully fashioned in history, and a nation can safely go forward only if it follows the path along which it has hitherto been led. Violent change is therefore evil; anything that weakens the church weakens the element in human society which enshrines the values of the past and consecrates the corporate life in the present. Burke, who had been a reformer in his youth, believed that he was merely attacking revolutionary excesses, but he lent the authority of worthy theories to the fears which dreaded any change, and the eighteenth century ended in a spirit of panic, which, in every sphere, postponed the changes that the new day required.

12

Christianity in the New World

By the middle of the seventeenth century the English colonies on the eastern coast of North America had surmounted the initial problems of settlement, and stood on the eve of a period of expansion. In the oldest colony, Virginia, the Anglicans formed the strongest element, Roman Catholics had settled in Maryland, in New England the Puritans were established and had embarked upon their 'holy experiment', a wide variety of national and religious strains had appeared in the Middle Atlantic region. By 1646, eighteen languages could be heard along the banks of the Hudson River alone, and most of the churches which flourished in Western Europe had been transplanted to American soil.

The vigour and dynamic of English colonizing enterprise showed itself conspicuously in New England. In the minds of many people the beginnings of the American nation are inseparably associated with the Pilgrim Fathers and with the Puritans of Massachusetts Bay. Though similar in aim and purpose, these two groups were different in origin and character. The settlers at Plymouth were separatists who came to the new world after a period of voluntary exile in Holland. The Puritans were reformers, anxious to purify the polity and worship of the Church of England, but with no intention of cutting themselves adrift from it. To them it was still their 'dear mother', and they were 'members of the same body'. In the new world they hoped to erect a church free from the corruptions which in their eyes disfigured the parent body. Yet in practice the two groups were much alike. For both, the bond of social and religious unity was a covenant into which men entered and which bound them together both in church and state. Their religious beliefs determined the character of the society they created.

In practice, each congregation was largely independent and self-sufficient. It was strongly democratic in character; all who professed their faith, accepted the covenant, and joined the church, were entitled to share fully in its life and direction. They elected the officers to whom the well-being of the congregation was entrusted, and debated and decided all matters of policy and government. They cherished the ideal of a godly community and a purified church. The avowed purpose of many of the colonists was to worship God according to his Word. Beyond question there were other objectives. Everyone hoped that economic progress would be compatible with religious reform, but such aims were secondary. There was always the danger, of course, that the intended order might be reversed. Some settlers were greatly concerned with material gain and little interested in godly worship, and they could not be entirely excluded. There was no need, however, to encourage them. Consequently the right to direct colonial affairs was restricted to members of the church. The government was in their hands. Those who were enrolled as members of the congregation were the freemen of the community; they, and they alone, possessed full voting rights. The nature of the 'holy experiment' was determined by the purpose of the colonists. In Holy Scripture God had provided a pattern for man's life in church and state alike. He desired a people pledged to the true worship of his name and to faithful obedience to his revealed purposes. And how could this be achieved? The Puritans were ready with their answer: it could be achieved only through the rule of the saints. Consequently in all the New England settlements the congregation formed the nucleus of the community, and civil power was restricted to its members.

The identification of community and congregation resulted in a distinctive pattern of relations between church and state. The magistrates were the 'nursing fathers' of the churches. They arbitrated disputes between congregations, ruled on the fitness of ministers and determined the location of the congregations where they would serve, supervised the behaviour of the citizens, and enforced the moral law. The ministers, also, had obligations as well as privileges. They guided the magistrates by advice drawn from God's Word, and applied to daily life the insights supplied by Holy Scripture. Ministers and magistrates were thus related to each other by complementary responsibilities; both were answerable to the members of the church, and all together were committed to the ideal that God's will should prevail in the affairs of the community no less than in the lives of its citizens.

On this basis the 'holy experiment' had been launched, but already it had been challenged at a number of points. In a theocratic society the magistrates inevitably had powers of coercion and control, which extended to questions of belief and practice. Roger Williams disputed the right of the state to interfere with matters in which a man must obey his conscience alone. It was proper to observe the Sabbath, but it was not the place of the magistrates to compel a man to do so. Nor should they impose religious oaths merely to confirm their own authority. Roger Williams stood for the freedom of the individual conscience and for the separation of the responsibilities of church and state. His founding of the colony of Rhode Island assured a haven for those who shared his convictions, and guaranteed the continuity and the ultimate triumph of his views. But meanwhile his protest represented the first break in the Puritan experiment.

A settlement dedicated to reform could scarcely expect docile citizens. At all events difficulties multiplied. An able and vocal woman named Anne Hutchison struck at the foundation of the community by attacking the theology of the ministers. As a criterion of truth she exalted the Holy Spirit, which enlightens men either through the Scriptures or beyond them. But the colony was committed to the belief that the truth was revealed in the Bible, and that the ministers, duly called and constituted, were its official exponents. Mistress Hutchison's attitude promised unregulated confusion. She was banished and fled to Rhode Island. The Baptists, too, were restive under the magistrates' control. The Quakers proved even more turbulent. In spite of fierce persecution they persisted in bearing their witness where it was not wanted. Some of the colonists, in search of greater freedom and of better land, left Massachusetts and settled in the lower Connecticut valley.

The challenge from dissident zealots was serious, but a far more dangerous threat was posed by the lax and laodicean elements in society. The holy experiment identified the community and the congregation, restricted political power to those who stood within the covenant. But a new generation was arising which was indifferent to the aims of the founding fathers. The numbers presenting themselves for church membership dwindled alarmingly. Those who should have accepted political responsibility were not doing so because they failed to qualify. They had not professed their faith or owned the covenant. The solution adopted was to recognize the 'halfway covenant'. Those who had been baptized were in a sense members of the church. They could not receive the sacrament of the Lord's Supper, nor share in the shaping of religious policy, but they nevertheless belonged in part – enough to enable them to exercise their citizenship. Such a compromise was fatal to the ideals of the Puritan colonies. The 'holy experiment' had virtually collapsed.

In other respects the New Englanders had already achieved notable success. The Puritans believed in an educated ministry; to provide it, they founded a college – now Harvard University, and one of the great intellectual centres of the world. An educated ministry presupposed an educated people: how could people read the Bible if they could not read at all? To meet this need, the New Englanders established an excellent system of grammar schools. Nor did they wholly neglect the duty of preaching the Gospel to the Indians. Here the obstacles admittedly were great – nomadic life posed many problems; friction between the new and the old inhabitants of the land was endemic and periodically erupted in violence; then enthusiasm for missionary work noticeably cooled. Nevertheless a serious beginning had been made. Roger Williams had shown that sympathy could accomplish much in gaining the trust and confidence of the

Indians. John Eliot, perhaps the greatest of the early missionaries, published the New Testament in their tongue, and gathered among them a covenanted church.

The second half of the seventeenth century was a period of steady growth. The population of the southern colonies was increasing, and in most of them Anglicanism became the official religion. The work of the church was beset with problems. Since the nearest bishop was on the other side of the Atlantic, ordinations were difficult and confirmations impossible. The local vestries seized a disproportionate amount of power, and often became self-perpetuating religious oligarchies. Parishes were large and priests were few. In an attempt to cope with the problems of oversight and discipline, the Bishop of London appointed commissaries – clergymen who were authorized to perform certain episcopal functions – and Thomas Bray (in Maryland) and James Blair (in Virginia) did their utmost to keep the clergy loyal to their ministerial duties. Individuals could do much; organizations could do more, and the founding of the Society for the Propagation of Christian Knowledge (1698) and the Society for the Propagation of the Gospel (1701) opened up new opportunities for effective service. Missionaries were recruited, sent out, and maintained. Even in the Puritan stronghold of New England they founded new Anglican churches.

In the Middle Atlantic colonies interesting developments took place. The Quakers had made their presence felt in unwelcome fashion in New England and in New York, and after George Fox's visit to America in 1672 they began to claim new fields. Their great opportunity came when William Penn founded Pennsylvania in 1681. Penn's plans were bold and imaginative. He renounced the use of coercion, and granted the free exercise of their religion to all who might seek a home in his colony. Those who were persecuted elsewhere were promised a haven in Pennsylvania, and immigrants in large numbers responded to his invitation. Lutherans, Mennonites, and members of the Reformed Church came from Germany, Baptists, Quakers, Anglicans from

England, and Presbyterians of Scottish extraction from
Ulster. In due course many of these groups established
vigorous churches. The Presbyterians steadily grew in
strength, and early in the eighteenth century they began to
build up their conciliar system in the new world. Lutheran
and Reformed communities also multiplied, though their
effective organization was delayed till later in the new century. The polyglot nature of the population proved fatal to
some of Penn's cherished designs. His imaginative treatment
of the Indians did not set a permanent pattern for relations
between the races. His repudiation of force was subsequently
disallowed. But by extending equal rights to people of all
faiths Penn had set a notable example. No group could
claim official status; none could therefore apply coercive
measures, and the American pattern of wide diversity within
a framework of full toleration began to appear. In Rhode
Island, the same policy was pursued. Roger Williams
violently disagreed with the Quakers, but never disputed
their right to sanctuary in his colony.

The steady process of consolidation continued without
serious interruption during the closing years of the seventeenth century and the opening years of the eighteenth. A
wide range of national strains had brought with them a
great variety of religious affiliations. All of them, it seemed,
might expect to maintain in the new world the patterns with
which they had been familiar in the old. A new and powerful influence, however, made itself felt. Revivalism, which
was to affect American religious life so profoundly, appeared
in the early part of the eighteenth century. Initially the
Great Awakening was not a concerted movement. Jonathan
Edwards' preaching at Northampton, Mass., deeply stirred
the whole community. A German called Freylinghausen
was achieving remarkable results in New Jersey; so was
Gilbert Tennent in Pennsylvania. These various strains
were drawn together by George Whitefield, the friend and
associate of John Wesley. Whitefield was a preacher of consummate power; wherever he went he convicted men of sin
and claimed them for a new life. Though an Anglican, he

cooperated readily with all groups; as a visitor from abroad, he was equally at home in all the colonies. By his successive visits he knit into a unified movement, transcending colonial frontiers and denominational barriers, the previously scattered manifestations of reawakened zeal.

The Great Awakening brought to the churches an immense accession of vitality. Many of the churches recorded a phenomenal growth. The Presbyterians and Baptists expanded rapidly. The Methodists, a group new to the country, were launched on the tide of a great enthusiasm, and began the outreach which was to make them one of the largest churches in America. The Lutherans, under Mühlenberg, consolidated their forces, and prepared to move forward. The Reformed Churches, both Dutch and German, had been languishing in apathy; the Awakening galvanized them into life and probably saved them from extinction. In all directions the churches reached out toward those who were outside their orbit, challenging the uncommitted, giving impetus to Indian missions. David Brainerd, though he died on the threshold of his life's work as a missionary, caught the imagination of his contemporaries, and made them aware of a duty which they were neglecting. Though the Great Awakening encouraged the preaching of uneducated men and often appealed to the emotions rather than to the reason, it coincided with a notable expansion of educational enthusiasm. Colleges multiplied in number. The effect of the Awakening can also be detected in the growing opposition to slavery. John Woolman, a Quaker, belonged to a group less affected than most by the revivals, but his witness against slavery certainly found a readier response in an atmosphere profoundly modified by the Awakening.

These results were beneficial; certain others were not. Controversy broke out on every side. The Presbyterians were split between those who favoured revivals and those who did not. The Baptists also were deeply divided. Some of the enthusiasts fell into grotesque excesses and aroused the contempt of those committed to more restrained methods.

A new kind of leadership began to emerge; new groups were formed and rapidly expanded. American religious life was changing its complexion, and was subtly altering its emphasis. The early leaders of the Awakening had stood in a strong theological tradition. Whitefield, though not a profound thinker, was a convinced Calvinist. So was Jonathan Edwards, one of the penetrating and original minds of his age. These men were in no danger of ignoring God's sovereignty or of minimizing his redemptive activity. But their successors were preoccupied with the human response to the divine initiative. As a consequence an exaggerated importance was attached to emotional reactions. Conversion was described in terms of how a man felt, the new life was defined in terms of how he acted. This was more than an emphasis on the moral consequences of obedience to God; it was a preoccupation with man, and it became absorbed in what he did and in the degree to which he promoted righteousness. In a curious way man's activity was obscuring the cardinal fact of God's rule. And in the process a valuable element in the American religious tradition was weakened. The Puritans had stressed the church's responsibility for the whole of life; they believed that every aspect of the community was subject to divine judgement and should be brought into subjection to God's will. Revivalism minimized the role of the church and ignored the religious significance of man's corporate life. Preoccupation with the inner experience of each soul deflected attention from the political, economic, and intellectual implications of the Gospel.

The first part of the eighteenth century was dominated by the Great Awakening, the second part by the War of Independence. The interval between these notable events was a period of turmoil and struggle. The French and Indian Wars brought disaster to the exposed communities on the frontiers, and caused much anxious searching of hearts throughout the colonies. Religious leaders re-examined the basis of their corporate life: how did they differ from the papists and wherein was their liberty better than submission to absolute power? Meanwhile many of the pulpits encouraged the mood of independence which was spreading throughout the colonies, and fostered the growing consciousness of the precious boon of freedom. When the French Wars were over, and the vexatious problem of paying the bills arose, the preachers fanned the popular indignation which greeted any invasion of colonial rights. Many other causes – commercial and political – contributed to the final explosion. The influence of the churches cannot be overlooked; for years they had been fostering an attitude which came to full and free expression during the revolutionary period.

Most of the churches enthusiastically supported the colonial cause. With few exceptions the leaders of the Congregationalists, the Presbyterians, and the Baptists were ardent champions of the revolution. The Quakers, because of their witness against violence, tried to stand aloof, and in the event suffered at the hands of both sides. The Anglicans, especially in New England, were staunchly loyalist, and consequently were seriously discredited in popular esteem. The Methodists, too, lost ground because the populace identified them with John Wesley's opposition to the American cause.

The new nation numbered approximately three million souls. To serve the religious needs of this population there were more than 3,100 congregations; of these, the Congregationalists claimed the largest number, with the Presbyterians and Baptists next in order. It was apparent that the churches shared in the upsurge of vitality with which the former colonies hailed their independence. As the states developed a federal organization, so each of the denominations began to create for itself a national structure and to unify its corporate life. The churches also began to face the problems inherent in their new situation, and of these few were more vitally important than the relation of church and state. Some of the colonies had had an established form of religion – Congregationalism in New England, Anglicanism in the south. In the middle colonies experience had proved that where many churches divide among themselves the loyalties of the people, none among them can claim a favoured status. This was a lesson fraught with important consequences; it affected the practice of toleration and the achievement of complete religious equality. In the years following the revolution, establishment became a controversial issue in Virginia. The Great Awakening had immensely increased the strength of the Baptists and the Presbyterians, and they vigorously attacked the favoured position which the Anglican Church enjoyed. The deism prevalent in certain circles augmented the tide of criticism. Men like Jefferson, while advocating a mild form of belief, objected to the enjoyment of a preferred position by any single body. As a result of mounting agitation, Virginia passed in 1785 a law which placed all churches on an equal footing. A little latter, when the United States of America came into being, the constitution forbade the imposition of religious tests, and provided that nationally no religious body could claim favoured treatment. This did not immediately end existing arrangements nor create a uniform pattern in all the states. In New England the belief persisted that religion was so important a part of life that the state should maintain the church both by legal safeguards and by financial aid, and for half a century longer Congregationalism enjoyed its established status. But the characteristic American pattern had been created: all religions were equally free, none was specially favoured, and all had to claim from their own members the means for their support.

As the eighteenth century drew to a close, the American churches were confronted with a fluid situation in which new problems faced them on every hand. Deism had been introduced from Europe, and made rapid strides. It appealed strongly to the sophisticated easterners, and found favour even on the western frontier. Just as the problem of the frontier increasingly dominated American life, the needs of the west claimed the attention of all the churches. The Congregationalists and Presbyterians combined to provide a trained ministry for the new areas, but the task was far beyond their resources. The Baptists with their lay preachers and the Methodists with their circuit riders were notably successful in following the settlers and in ministering to them.

As the century ended, the country was swept by a great new wave of revivalist enthusiasm. In the east, in more sober guise, it met the challenge of deism and unitarianism and vigorously reaffirmed the doctrines of evangelical Christianity. On the frontier it assumed a more highly-charged emotional form. It met the needs of men and women living in remote, difficult, and often lonely places. The 'camp meeting' assembled them in great companies in which religion gained intense personal significance within a social setting. It gave colour as well as dignity to lives that often were conspicuously lacking in both. Revivalism set its mark indelibly on American church life. It explains the intensely emotional quality which has persisted in certain strains of American Christianity; it is responsible for the slightly defiant repudiation of the intellectual elements in the faith. Undoubtedly it met the basic needs of the frontiersman; the stark simplicity with which it set forth sin and salvation as alternatives demanding an immediate choice were close to his experience and within his grasp. But its excitements lent themselves to serious corruption, and often raised a barrier beyond which it was not easy for the convert to pass. The profounder regions of Christian experience remained outside the grasp of the revivalist. The crudity and violence of frontier life naturally resulted in a strong emphasis on the moral transformation which faith effects. But morality was conceived wholly in personal terms. Its wider implications were ignored, and its attack was often limited to the more obvious evils – drinking, swearing, gambling.

As the period ends we are faced with a vigorous manifestation of a particular type of Christian zeal. It satisfied the immediate demands of a new country and a new day, but it did not coalesce with the older and more substantial traditions which had been the creative forces in an earlier age. It lacked theological depth, but like the society which it served it was possessed of abundant vitality, and had as little doubt of its power to claim America for Christ as of its duty to do so.

French Catholicism, like English Protestantism, came to the new world in the early part of the seventeenth century. Quebec was founded in 1608. Seven years later a band of six Recollects arrived; another ten years intervened before the beginning of the Jesuit mission in Canada. Life was difficult, and the colonies maintained a precarious foothold on the edge of the inhospitable wilderness. The tiny communities of Quebec, Three Rivers, and Montreal struggled to survive. Beyond, in the vast forest regions, the Jesuits had embarked on their heroic mission to the Indians. Among the Iroquois they made little progress. Experience soon taught them that it was virtually impossible to achieve permanent results among nomadic tribesmen, and it became their policy to encourage settled ways of life. At Sillery, outside Quebec, they established a model village, and achieved a modest success. It was among the Hurons – the most peaceful and settled of the tribes – that the Jesuits met with their most encouraging response. It was here, too, when the Iroquois exterminated the Hurons, that the Jesuits wrote one of the brightest pages of their martyrology. In the reports which they sent home – the *Relations* – the Jesuits provided a vivid and detailed account of their work among the Indians. Its inherent interest, together with the heroism which marked some of its episodes, has often obscured the relatively modest scale of this enterprise.

Those responsible for French policy in the new world were eager to see an autonomous Canadian church develop. Progress, however, was slow; to the problems inseparable from a frontier community were added jurisdictional disputes. What was the effective source of ecclesiastical authority? The clergy were not agreed, and only when Mgr Laval was appointed as vicar apostolic in 1658 could any measure of unity be expected. Laval was a man of earnest and upright character, disinterested, zealous, hard-working, and unsparing of himself. He was not conspicuously gifted with psychological insight; he distinguished with difficulty between essentials and incidentals, and he often asserted with little tact the minor rights of his position. It was a tiny church which he had come to govern. The clergy numbered about twenty-five, there were fewer than a dozen churches, institutions were few and struggling. But as the colony developed, the church also grew, and in 1674 Quebec was raised to the dignity of a bishopric. Laval tried to make his seminary a centre of corporate life for his clergy, but his paternalism was at variance with the natural forces which dictated the character of Canadian life. The country clergy were cut off from effective contact with the bishop, and the independence characteristic of the people became equally the mark of their priests.

From its earliest days, the French Canadian church began to develop a distinctive quality. It was unaffected by the controversies which raged in metropolitan France, there was no echo of the debates about Gallicanism and Jansenism. As time passed, there was no disposition to flirt with Voltairean heresies. There was some tension with the civil authorities, and a good deal of inter-clerical rivalry. The French Canadian Catholic was marked by deep faith, pure morals, little interest in speculation, and little taste for learning. A puritanical austerity prevailed; the threat of Hell powerfully reinforced moral standards. The clergy were the natural leaders of the community, the *presbytère* the centre of community life. The priest was in touch with all the affairs of his people, gave them counsel, arbitrated in their disputes, and acted as their legal adviser.

When New France fell to the British, the Canadian church was suddenly thrown upon its own resources. For a short time the future seemed precarious. Would the new rulers try to impose a new faith? Could the anomaly be accepted of a Roman hierarchy in a land governed by English law? The growing unrest in the American colonies compelled a modification of policy, and the British withdrew any decisions which presupposed an assimilation of the French Catholics to English Protestantism. The Quebec Act of 1774 guaranteed the free exercise of the Roman Catholic religion; it replaced the oath of supremacy with a simple oath of loyalty, and allowed those who took it to hold public office. The French Canadians remained loyal throughout the Revolutionary War; they might not love their new masters, but they had no intention of changing them for New England Yankees. It was clear, therefore, that they would be permitted to develop their life along lines already established. Freedom of worship had been conceded; so had episcopal administration. The holding of property remained a problem. A great deal of church property belonged to orders in France, but the law declared that only British subjects could be property holders. The orders, therefore, made over their lands and buildings to their Canadian representatives, and a strong tie with the outside world was severed. The training of the clergy presented a greater difficulty. The British refused permission to recruit in France, and forbade the Jesuits and the Recollects to remain in the colony. The population was growing and, thrown wholly on its own resources, the church was ill prepared to solve the problem. Some help came at the time of the French Revolution: the British allowed into Canada *émigré* priests who provided welcome relief.

The readjustments which the conquest of Canada demanded were of a kind to strengthen the position of the church. The general ruin, as well as the social and administrative changes caused by defeat, deprived the colony of its former leaders. The members of the old seigneurial class had lost their wealth, their favoured position, and their authority in the direction of economic and political activity. The clergy were the natural – indeed, the only – leaders who could consolidate the social as well as the religious life of the country. The position they had already won as leaders of the community assumed an added significance. They were the only surviving group able to maintain French-Canadian unity, and this largely explains the solidity and permanence of Roman Catholicism in Quebec. Protestants had gained a foothold in Nova Scotia before France lost its Canadian possessions; after the conquest, they appeared in Montreal

and Quebec and increasingly gained control of the economic as well as the political life of the country. After the
American War, the Loyalists came in large numbers, and
Canadian Protestantism began to claim the vigorous role it
has played ever since in the expanding life of Canada. But
the French-Canadian population remain unaffected and unchanged. Its leaders saw that their unity would depend on
their retaining their French language, their distinctive culture, and their Catholic faith. The interpenetration of these
three has been the mark of the French Canadian to this day,
and is responsible for many of the pronounced features of the
national life of Canada.

*

Canada was not the only scene of French missionary labours,
and it was certainly not the only stronghold of Catholicism
in the new world. Louisiana began as a French colony, and
though its life was precarious the church established itself
firmly at the mouth of the Mississippi. During the seventeenth and eighteenth centuries the West Indies seemed to
be far more desirable colonies than the mainland of America, but religious activities in the islands produced consistently
disappointing results. The islands were involved in the
intermittent struggle which the European nations waged for
their possession. There was endemic warfare between settlers
and natives. Most damaging of all were the internecine feuds
between the various Catholic orders – the Dominicans
against the Capuchins, the Jesuits against the Recollects, the
regulars against the seculars. This in turn was related to the
diminution of missionary zeal within the French church.

*

The Iberian nations claimed South America as their exclusive preserve. The Catholic Church extended from Tierra
del Fuego in the extreme south across the whole continent,
through Central America and into California; but though it
was impressive in appearance, its roots in the lives of the
people were shallow and precarious. In Brazil the church was

Portuguese in origin and character; elsewhere it was Spanish. By the middle of the seventeenth century it had behind it one hundred and fifty years of experience in the new world. The stage of rapid growth was over, and throughout our period the aim was to conserve rather than to expand. The Latin American church had developed a twofold aspect. Its diocesan system covered the continent. The hierarchical organization was complete, and closely followed Spanish patterns. There were far fewer bishops than at home, the dioceses were sometimes immense, and there was a dearth of clergy instead of a superfluity. The same style of architecture prevailed, and the churches aimed – though without success – at a similar standard of magnificence. In short, they were Spanish churches, and primarily served the Spanish population. Within the parishes the priests tried, with little effect, to penetrate the religious indifference of the natives, and outside the larger towns the incomplete character of Catholic evangelism was painfully apparent. Enormous areas were virtually untouched, and the forward thrust of the Spanish mission had largely ceased.

This does not mean that missionary work had been abandoned. Vast districts were designated as missionary territories and were consigned to the great orders, particularly to the Franciscans and the Jesuits. One of the features of the Latin American church was the vigour and effectiveness of the Jesuit order. It was largely responsible for education, and the training of the lower clergy was almost entirely in its hands. Its internal discipline was strict, and its members were in great demand as directors of conscience. Its highly original contribution to missionary endeavour was the organization of the 'reductions' in Paraguay. These were self-contained communities in the interior of the country, some two score in number, and they enjoyed their greatest prosperity between the years 1650 and 1720. Each village was built round a square, the homes and gardens of the Indians on three sides, the church, school, infirmary, and shops on the fourth. The originality of the enterprise lay not in this serviceable groundplan, but in the relations of the

Indians to the Spanish crown and in the meticulous elaboration of the theocratic paternalism under which they lived. The 'reductions' were created in areas previously unclaimed; because the Indians voluntarily submitted to Spanish rule, they were treated as 'immediate subjects' of the king. Consequently the Jesuits were able to develop entirely self-sufficient communities, from which all intruders were excluded. Within this little world every detail of daily life was minutely regulated. In each 'reduction' there were normally two priests, and every aspect of the community's life was under their control.

The Jesuits' experiment had its critics and its foes. In the early days the 'reductions' were exposed to direct attack from neighbouring districts controlled by the men of São Paulo. Later it proved increasingly impossible to keep these closed communities uncontaminated by the outer world. They could not be indefinitely insulated against contact with the Spanish empire. Even the Indians who marketed surplus produce were often seduced by the attractions of the larger towns. The very success of the Jesuits raised enemies against them. In Europe the attack on their missionary methods was a part of the mounting criticism of their order. Their work was seriously disrupted by a border dispute between Portugal and Spain, and finally, in 1767, the dissolution of the order in all Spanish lands spelled disaster to their Paraguayan experiment.

*

In the Far East, the expansion of Christianity steadily and progressively lost momentum. The period of ardent Catholic outreach – of the initial zeal of the Counter-Reformation, of the marvellous work of St Francis Xavier and his companions – was over; the forward surge of Protestant missions was still to come. In many places the ground once gained by the Jesuits was lost. Almost everywhere progress was hindered by the bitter rivalries of the various Catholic orders. Indeed, with melancholy reiteration these internal feuds intrude on the story of missionary effort in the seventeenth and eighteenth centuries, and one of them – the 'affair of the rites' – re-echoed throughout Europe for many a year.

The Jesuits had made encouraging progress in China. They had won the confidence of the emperor. By their proficiency in science and astronomy they gained the respect of the cultivated classes. They were convinced that Christianity could win the intelligentsia and could readily be incorporated within the framework of Chinese life. Admittedly this would involve a certain amount of accommodation. There was the question of language: could Christianity appropriate existing Chinese terms and 'baptize' them for its own use? More controversial was the problem of customs. The Jesuits were prepared to recognize Confucius as a great ethical teacher, and they claimed that certain rites associated with the Chinese way of life – such as the reverence paid to ancestors – were social rather than religious in character, and were free of anti-Christian implications. They might safely be practised; they could even be incorporated into a Chinese Christian system. Minor adjustments seemed a small price to pay for the glittering prospect of converting the Chinese empire.

Other missionaries saw the matter in a different light. The Dominicans and the priests of the Foreign Mission condemned what they considered a dangerous compromise with paganism. They may have been prompted by jealousy of Jesuit success – as Jesuit supporters were quick to suggest – but at all events they appealed to Rome. The question of the 'rites' was hotly debated not only in the Vatican but in most of the great schools of Catholic Europe. The Sorbonne was drawn into the debate, and conflicting opinions were tossed to and fro. In a series of decisions, Rome clearly ruled against the Jesuit practice. The transmission of the verdict was difficult and slow, its enforcement proved disastrous. The emperor, enraged at what he regarded as an insult to Chinese customs, revoked all concessions and brought Christian missionary work virtually to a halt. The Jesuits, pointing to what they had originally gained and to the prospects that had now been forfeited, felt that their position had been vindicated by events. Their critics claimed that the Jesuits had always beguiled themselves with false hopes; the Chinese had never really intended to embrace the faith, and honest failure was preferable to specious self-deception.

13

The Church in France,
1715–89

WHEN the long reign of Louis XIV ended, his heir was still only a child. Important changes were obviously imminent, and the dying king had foreseen that all his policies – in church no less than in state – might be reversed. He intrigued to prevent it; he failed to do so. During the minority of the new king, power rested in the hands of the regent, and in outlook and aim Orléans was typical of the new day. He boasted of his emancipation from conventional 'prejudices' (moral as well as theological) and was eager to break with accepted traditions. He questioned the doctrines of the church and neglected its practices. His character made him the natural leader of all who had opposed the absolutism of Louis XIV or who had been restive under the austere regime inspired and sustained by Mme de Maintenon.

At the outset the Regency was liberal in spirit, and in one respect at least it was revolutionary in method: it attempted to replace absolute government with committee rule on an extensive scale. Administration was committed to six (later seven) councils, and the one responsible for church affairs was entrusted to Cardinal de Noailles, Archbishop of Paris and the leader of the party opposed to the ultramontane policies of the Jesuits. The experiment was a failure; absolutism had not developed the leaders that a freer system presupposed. In church affairs the regent soon discovered that it was easier to encourage dissidents than it was to control them. The Jansenists had been rigorously repressed during the closing months of Louis XIV's reign; on his death their feud with the Jesuits promptly revived. This, in turn involved a recrudescence of Gallicanism, and both issues were related to the constitutional question of the rights and powers of the *parlements*. Within a few months, therefore, the controversies had appeared which were to distract the religious life of France throughout most of the century.

The ecclesiastical council promptly demonstrated its ineffectiveness. It tried to settle the Jansenist controversy and failed. The dispute about the Bull *Unigenitus* flared up at once, and the struggle once more divided Frenchmen into warring factions. The regent was puzzled and annoyed; he detested noisy enthusiasts, and had little sympathy with the passions aroused. Nor did he grasp the alignment of forces. Voltaire remarked that on one side were most of the bishops, the Jesuits and the Capuchins; on the other, a handful of bishops and all the rest of France. In an attempt to control the situation, Orléans turned to leaders of ultramontane sympathies; the brief experiment in religious and constitutional liberalism was abandoned, and the regency became as absolute and arbitrary as the rule of Louis XIV.

In the troubled and fluid situation which prevailed, two churchmen successively came to power and controlled the affairs of France throughout the remainder of the first half of the eighteenth century. Dubois owed his rise to his unquestioned political ability. He was an astute manipulator of men, a master of expedients and compromises. He was fashionably immoral at a time when moral standards had collapsed; though a bad priest, he was archbishop of the richest see in France, and a cardinal of the Roman church. Saint-Simon, the most graphic diarist of the age, detested him, and effectually blackened his good name. 'All the vices,' he said, 'perfidy, avarice, debauchery, ambition, flattery, fought within him for mastery.' As absolutism reasserted itself, Ultramontanism gained ground, and Dubois threw his weight on the prevailing side.

Fleury, who also received a cardinal's hat, was a better man and a more successful minister. Brought from a remote southern see to act as tutor to Louis XV, he remained, long after the regent's death, to direct the affairs of France. He saw that the country needed peace; to achieve it abroad and to safeguard it at home were the consistent aims of his policy.

He faced formidable obstacles. The church was apprehensive about its special privileges; he gained its support by confirming the tax exemptions which reformers had challenged. He was determined to suppress the semi-religious controversies which had been fomenting bitterness in French life. Of these the most persistent was the Jansenist struggle, and his most pertinacious opponents were the leaders of the Parlement of Paris.

Jansenism had ceased to be primarily a religious heresy and had become a temper of mind. It resented Roman interference and was eager to frustrate its influence in French affairs. It had coalesced with Gallicanism (which had suffered a similar transformation), and the combination provided an excellent shield for the political ambitions of men who were engaged in a struggle for power. The controversy about the Bull *Unigenitus* persisted. The churchmen who protested against its application were gradually suppressed, and in 1730 it was declared to be part and parcel of the law of France. The result was a bitter struggle with the judges, which dragged on through most of the century, and in which the points at issue were far more constitutional than religious. But before considering the role played by the Parlement of Paris, it is necessary to observe the deterioration of Jansenism as a religious force. Persecution often breeds hysteria in its victims, and the Jansenists had been persecuted for many years. Early in the eighteenth century it became apparent that the more extreme members of the party had succumbed to extravagant tendencies. They spoke with tongues. They claimed the power to perform miracles. They lived in a world lit by flashes of apocalyptic prophecy. An earnest young Jansenist had been buried in the cemetery of Saint-Médard, and Parisians were amazed to learn that his grave had become the scene of miraculous cures. In 1732 the government intervened and closed the cemetery, and the wits of the capital coined the famous epigram:

> De par le roi, défense à Dieu
> De faire miracle en ce lieu.

But enthusiasm could not be suppressed by royal edict, and it next erupted in the strange phenomenon of the Convulsionaries. By frightful self-tortures, these extremists worked themselves into a state of frenzy, then prophesied and performed miracles. The reputable Jansenists repudiated them, the police severely repressed them, but forty years later Diderot still found it necessary and useful to ridicule and attack them. In its more legitimate forms Jansenism lingered on in certain convents and in country parsonages, and during the revolutionary period it proved, in the person of the Abbé Grégoire, that it was far from dead.

In the middle years of the century, religious affairs became entangled in an intricate struggle in which the court and the Parlement were the chief protagonists, while Jansenism, Gallicanism, and Jesuitism were complicating factors. One of the crucial problems of the age was how to achieve a due balance of power between the various authorities – political, judicial, ecclesiastical – to which men owed allegiance. The absolutism of the crown threatened to engulf all others, and the defenders of traditional privileges became alarmed. The States-General[1] had not been convoked since 1614, and the Parlement of Paris attempted to step into the breach. It aspired to play a political role, and it hoped to achieve its ends by transforming its right of remonstrance into an effective control of the royal power. The disputes about Jansenism furnished it with invaluable pretexts for protest and intervention. A majority of its members were Jansenist in sympathy and Gallican in attitude. Gallicanism, like Jansenism, had been modified in important ways. It varied with the existing relations of king

1. The States-General was a representative body, similar in origin to the English Parliament and at one time parallel to it in character and function. The *parlement*, on the other hand, was a permanent court of justice, having supreme authority in the cases brought before it. Originally there was only one *parlement* (that of Paris), but the exigencies of the administration of justice led to the creation of a certain number of provincial *parlements*. In addition to their legal functions, the *parlements* also had political rights; they claimed a share in shaping the higher policy of the realm, and regarded themselves as the guardians of its fundamental laws.

and pope, and in particular it was affected by the claim of the Parlement (a body of lay legalists) to control the relations of the national clergy with the see of Rome. The Parlement had established the position that no decisions of the pope could be published in France without royal approval, and it insisted that such approval must be registered by the Parlement itself. In the eighteenth century it declared itself competent to deal with such purely spiritual matters as the conditions under which the sacrament could be administered or withheld. Ecclesiastical Gallicanism thus became inextricably intertwined with political Gallicanism. It was a feature of the eighteenth century that it steadily secularized movements which had originally been inspired by genuinely religious motives.

In the struggle for effective power, the court thus faced the Parlement of Paris. The one side found allies in the Jesuit order; the other appealed to the Jansenist and Gallican sympathies which were prevalent in many sections of the community. But the pattern was not quite as simple as this. Louis XV lacked the resolution to deal decisively with this or any other problem. If he exiled the Parlement, he soon repented and allowed it to return to Paris. His vacillation robbed his actions of any effect they might have achieved. His attitude was always modified by the opinions of those in his immediate circle, particularly by the last person with whom he had been talking. Mme de Pompadour, the royal mistress, was at first bitterly critical of the Jesuits and was strongly opposed to their policies. But even she altered her views, accepted a member of the order as her confessor, and sought to influence the king in their favour.

Advantage had apparently inclined decisively to the side of the Jesuits. In steady succession they had won a series of victories. When Voltaire sought admission to the French Academy, he found it expedient to solicit their support, and the letter he wrote in vindication of the Order is one of the strangest documents of an age not excessively sensitive about literary integrity. At length the Jesuits felt secure enough to strike a decisive blow against their opponents. They obtained

a ruling that no one might administer supreme unction to a
person who had not confessed to a priest who accepted
Unigenitus. There were many parishes in Paris which were
strongly – almost solidly – Jansenist, and death-beds became
the scene of many an unseemly wrangle. The Parlement
reacted vehemently, and prohibited the application of the
rule. In the capital, excitement rose to a pitch of fierce intensity. Popular feeling supported the Parlement, and in an
effort to calm the clamour, the king prohibited all discussion
of *Unigenitus*. The ban was ineffective. The king was per-
plexed, and wavered from side to side. He banished the
members of the Parlement; the result was a perceptible
increase in the unpopularity of the clergy. 'The ministers of
religion', wrote d'Argenson, 'can scarcely show themselves in
the street without a hue and cry after them; and all this arises
from the Bull *Unigenitus* and the disgrace of the Parlement.'

The Jesuits, however, were convinced that persistence
could still ensure victory. They persuaded the king to send
the Parlement to a remoter place of exile, and to institute a
'Royal Chamber' to replace the Parlement and to perform
its functions. They intensified their campaign to deprive all
who rejected *Unigenitus* of the solace of the sacraments. Feeling was so deeply stirred that shrewd observers believed the
country was hovering on the brink of a social and religious
revolution. The imminent clash was averted; Louis XV lost
his nerve, dissolved the 'Royal Chamber', and recalled the
Parlement. It returned in no mood for compromise. It
promptly prohibited any minister of the church, no matter
what his rank, from according to *Unigenitus* the authority of
a rule of faith. For the moment this seemed to destroy the
importance of this controversial document, but it remained
an object of ceaseless debate, and when the humiliations of
the Seven Years' War overtook France, Louis XV ordered
that the Bull be accepted as part of the church's law. Popular exasperation erupted once more. There was an attempt
on Louis' life, variously attributed to the Jesuits and the
Jansenists. A new ban prohibited attacks on religious policy,
but momentary firmness again gave way to vacillation.

Finally, in 1757, it was decreed that no one should publicly mention *Unigenitus*.

For the better part of half a century this celebrated Bull had kept French public life in a continual uproar. It had become a pretext for contention, a rallying point for ardent loyalties and bitter antipathies. It was identified with Jesuit ambitions, and antipathy to the order had been steadily mounting. Their ascendancy in the principal Catholic courts of Europe aroused fierce antagonism, and their constant interference in politics had intensified the opposition to them. The mid eighteenth century saw the tide of resentment rising in one country after another. The story of the overthrow of the order belongs to another chapter (Chapter 14). It may be noted in passing that in France the occasion of its downfall was a lawsuit about commercial losses; but the way had been prepared by incessant struggles with the Jansenist party and with the Parlement of Paris, while the mounting influence of the new philosophy was increasingly thrown into the balance against it. Of these deeper tensions the struggle about *Unigenitus* was merely the surface manifestation.

*

Throughout the eighteenth century the French church was involved in the political and constitutional struggles of the period: its privileges were too extensive and its influence too pervasive for it to remain untouched. The controversies of the age challenged its faith and modified its thought. But the importance of the church in the history of the period lies elsewhere. In its structure and in the character of its life it epitomized many of the features of the age of absolutism; to a greater extent than any of the other churches, it was immediately challenged and ultimately modified by the revolutionary forces which inaugurated a new age.

In the Roman Catholic world the French church occupied position of unquestioned pre-eminence. Numbers alone provide no guarantee of strength, but in this respect it easily outdistanced any of the other churches of western Europe.

Its tradition of intellectual vigour and spiritual vitality gave it a place of unique distinction. It is true that the eighteenth century did not advance, or even maintain, the standards of the recent past, but the French church could tacitly claim an eminence which others were ill qualified to contest. To its prominence in French life, the great number of churches and convents bore silent but ubiquitous testimony. It claimed the service of perhaps 130,000 persons, and for their support it could rely on vast possessions steadily accumulated during many generations. Nor was great wealth its only privilege. Many church dignities carried with them their appropriate feudal counterpart: bishops were often temporal lords, and religious and secular powers were intimately intertwined. In addition the church claimed certain specific privileges. It was conceded the place of highest precedence, and constituted the first estate of the realm. To conduct public worship was its exclusive right. In 1685 the revocation of the Edict of Nantes had deprived the Protestants of the concessions they had once enjoyed; throughout the eighteenth century semi-tolerance alternated with unpredictable spasms of repression, but there was never any doubt that Roman Catholicism was the official and favoured faith of France. In certain areas the Catholic church also enjoyed the privilege of exclusive jurisdiction. Most prominent, and to many people most vexatious, of all its privileges was its exemption from taxation.

The responsibilities of the church were as extensive as its privileges. Its influence was all-inclusive; it touched life at every point. All acts of civil status – births, deaths, and marriages – were under its control. Its right to shape the public conscience and to mould public opinion was unchallenged; royal ministers, even when openly Deist in outlook, regarded the clergy as the normal medium for commending to the people the policy of the government. The church administered all forms of charitable assistance. It operated all hospitals, infirmaries, and alms-houses. It had virtually complete control of education. But it failed to perform these duties with an efficiency sufficient to preserve i∕

from severe criticism. Public aid was well-intentioned but haphazard and ill organized. The presuppositions of its educational programme were openly challenged and the scale was condemned as grossly insufficient. And certainly when the Revolution subjected every aspect of French life to searching scrutiny, it revealed the fact that the great majority of the people were illiterate. Here, it was felt, was clear evidence of the deficiencies of the teaching which the church had provided.

Its critics insisted that the church performed these duties badly in spite of the fact that it possessed ample resources to perform them well. Beyond question the church was rich. Much of the land of France was in its hands. In some of the poorer southern districts its holdings amounted to no more than 4 per cent, but in northern dioceses the figure rose sharply to 30 per cent in Picardy and to over 60 per cent in the Cambrésis. It is difficult to determine the exact income of the church, since contemporary statistics often concealed rather than revealed its true extent. Some modern authorities place it at 60 million livres; others estimate it at nearly three times that amount. It was not the extent of this wealth which constituted the grievance, but the immunities which accompanied it. As the financial position of the kingdom deteriorated, the church's refusal to accept its due share of the national burden became increasingly intolerable. It is true that it made voluntary grants to the royal treasury, but these were never commensurate either with its own vast wealth or with the country's desperate plight. The church occupied a highly favoured position, and resolutely refused to make concessions. On the eve of the Revolution, when the situation was manifestly dangerous, Cardinal Loménie de Brienne, then the first minister, suggested to his fellow-churchmen a sum which he regarded as their rightful contribution to a crying need; in response they offered a quarter of what he asked. This determination to retain privileges which could be justified only by services which the church did not adequately perform, aggravated the hostility with which it was regarded in many quarters.

The church's attitude on such matters can be understood only in the light of its character and constitution. Power rested in the hands of the higher clergy, and many of the bishops no longer conformed to any pattern that the ideals of the Christian community could sanction. Generalization, of course, is as dangerous as it is easy. It is unjust to bring an indictment against a whole class, since there are always exceptions to every rule. There were bishops who conscientiously administered their sees and faithfully shepherded their flocks, and some of them led lives of apostolic simplicity and sincerity. But these men usually held the poorer and remoter sees. Certainly they were not the ones who attracted public attention and who determined the character of the church under the *ancien régime*.

The more favoured bishops were usually non-resident. Many of them visited their sees as seldom as possible; some of them never appeared among their people at all. A cynic remarked that it was boredom which drove them to the capital. Certainly the richer bishops could hardly expect to spend their immense incomes except at court. If they had been willing to curtail the extravagance of their expenditures the church might have discharged more adequately the tasks which it was condemned for neglecting, but such a change would have presupposed a revolution in outlook. Many of the greater prelates enjoyed incomes of 100,000 *livres* or more; the highly favoured ones received twice or even four times that amount. These figures mean little except by comparison with other clerical stipends. A bishop resident in a distant diocese might receive 7,000 *livres*, while 300 *livres* was the statutory minimum for a priest. The wealthier bishops, with princely incomes, lived like worldly princes. They accepted without demur the standards of the court of which they aspired to form a part. They acquiesced in the current adulation of absolutism, and were seemingly content to see the church in servitude to the world. They conformed to the frivolity which ruled in society, and to support the standard of living which they considered appropriate they were constrained to be greedy as well as secular.

These were the men who were chiefly responsible for bringing discredit upon their order. Their attitude could never have gained currency had it not been for a serious change in the character of the episcopacy. In the days of Bossuet and Fénelon scholarly eminence and distinction in the pulpit had still been accounted the appropriate attributes of a bishop. The decline in preaching power had been pronounced, and this had coincided with an increasing tendency to restrict the episcopacy to the nobility. On the eve of the Revolution, out of 130 bishops only one was a commoner. A see, in fact, had become the recognized way of providing for the younger sons of the aristocracy or for those among them (like Talleyrand) who were precluded by deformity from making their way in more desirable careers. It inevitably followed that the church, as represented by the higher clergy, steadily lost contact with the common people.

By no means all the worldly bishops lived frivolous and useless lives. Some posed as statesmen, and a contemporary divided the bishops into two classes – those who 'administered the sacraments' and those who 'administered provinces'. Talleyrand declared that 'the French clergy consisted of men of whom some were genuinely pious, others were distinguished as administrators, and others again were merely worldly, and, like the Archbishop of Narbonne, delighted to put off the attributes of their office and live as great nobles'. But the Archbishop of Narbonne was a notable administrator, indefatigable in encouraging trade, improving agriculture, draining swamps, buildings roads, and digging canals. This same archbishop was typical, too, of those who prided themselves on their enlightened views and posed as *philosophes*. The Cardinal Archbishop of Strasbourg, Rohan, was similarly emancipated in outlook. 'A mere priest', said Chamfort, 'must believe a little, or he will be considered a hypocrite, but he must not be too sincere in his beliefs or people will call him intolerant. A vicar-general may permit himself a smile when religion is attacked, a bishop may laugh, and a cardinal may give his cordial assent.' Such a comment contains a large element of exaggeration but also more than a grain of truth. The spirit of the age inevitably infected men who entered the church from motives which were seldom primarily religious. Cardinal Loménie de Brienne accepted the current philosophy in order to win the applause of its chief exponents. When the archbishopric of Paris was sought on his behalf, Louis XVI demurred: 'No,' he said, 'the Archbishop of Paris must at least believe in God.' When faith was apathetic and a sense of religious vocation was weak, it was natural that some men should devote themselves to a life of ambition and intrigue. The inducements were great, because the prizes were glittering. Some sought, and won, high position in the state. Others sought less creditable triumphs. Loménie de Brienne and Talleyrand are good examples of the former class, Cardinal Rohan of the latter. Rohan, indeed, was the central figure in the notorious episode of the 'diamond necklace' – a scandal which rocked society because it was taken to imply that a prince of the church would contemplate seducing the Queen of France.

It must be emphasized that the evils from which the church suffered sprang from the intimate association of the higher clergy with the classes among which indifference and apathy had made the most rapid strides. The infection of contemporary standards insensibly pervaded the church. Even the exemplary bishops, who did their duty and were devoted to the public good, often appeared self-conscious about their position and slightly apologetic regarding their faith.

The monastic orders occupied an intermediate position between the higher clergy and the parish priests. Their standing in the community had been gradually declining. A host of titular *abbés*, who drew their incomes from monastic houses but who avoided participation in monastic life, flocked to the capital and were content with a life of worldliness. Among the monks themselves morale was low. They were conscious of the mounting criticism directed against their way of life. To the *philosophes*, they epitomized the superstitions bequeathed by a benighted past, and such attacks shook the confidence of those who had no clear vocation for the monastic life. In 1765 twenty-eight of the most learned monks of Saint-Germain-des-Prés asked to be relieved of their habit, which (they said) degraded them. In the monasteries internal discipline was often lax, and abuses had multiplied. In extreme cases, conventual standards had been virtually abandoned; the canonical hours were not observed, visitors entered at pleasure, and the monks went abroad at will to mingle with the world. We read of mixed parties in the monasteries, of banquets and masked balls. Numbers declined. Year by year, fewer novices sought admission. The average population of the monasteries had fallen to seven or eight. Famous abbeys, once flourishing centres of the monastic life, could muster a mere handful of monks: six at Longport, five at Mont-Saint-Michel, four at Igny, three at Juvigny. Valcroissant's sole occupant was a farmer. Some houses and some orders were less affected than others, but the prior of Saint-Pierre at Chartres spoke for many beside himself when he confessed that 'we are but the shadow of our former selves'. The monasteries, however, were not left to dwindle away without interference from the outer world. A commission was established under Loménie de Brienne, and it applied drastic measures. On the grounds that reform was necessary it closed nearly 500 deserted houses. It dissolved orders which it regarded as redundant, raised the age at which men might take monastic vows, and facilitated the return to secular life of monks who had lost their sense of vocation. Such a programme failed to restore discipline; it merely accentuated the desire of the indifferent for a wider degree of latitude. The women's convents were relatively immune to the influences of the age, but in general the picture was depressing.

The cleavage between the higher and the lower clergy was deep and for the most part impassable. In origin, in outlook, and in way of life they were poles apart. The abuses of the bishops bore with oppressive weight on their less fortunate brethren. It was little consolation that in popular esteem the village priest had been sentimentalized into a model of humble devotion and virtuous poverty. Beyond question many priests were bitterly poor. Late in the century the government finally took steps to compel the church to pay its country clergy a living wage; in this the initiative came wholly from lay sources, and the ecclesiastical authorities showed little enthusiasm for reform. The priests sprang from the people and remained in intimate touch with them. As the century progressed and their alienation from the higher clergy became more complete, there appeared among them a democratic – almost a revolutionary – temper. It was fortified by a growing tendency to appeal to the equality which was regarded as the distinguishing mark of the primitive church. The impact of this democratic sentiment was far from negligible; the numbers of the lower clergy, the justice of their claims, their devotion to the faith, and their pastoral zeal, all lent weight to their protests against prevalent abuses. Yet they achieved no immediate reforms. The position of the lower clergy remained unchanged: they had no share in the government of the church and no voice in its affairs. In effect they were merely subjects of the higher clergy, and were treated by their superiors with a pride which sometimes bordered on contempt. But their protests were important for the future, and bore fruit in the revolutionary movement. A distinguished French historian, P. Sagnac, claims that the antagonisms within the church had intensified to the point where they virtually constituted a state of civil war. An offensive of the lower clergy was in preparation against their detested leaders. The bishops silenced their critics by means of *lettres de cachet*, but this was neither a permanent nor an effective answer to genuine grievances.

A church thus divided was in no position to withstand the attacks to which it was increasingly exposed. The certainty of its faith and the quality of its spiritual life had been corroded by the secular temper of the times. Socially, administratively, and financially, it stood in urgent need of reform, but there was neither the will nor the power to effect from within changes which the times demanded. The

church had given hostages to its opponents, and had delivered itself into their hands. The cleavage among its
clergy prevented it from facing its critics with a united
front. This gave the *philosophes* their opportunity, and they
seized it. The tactical advantage which they thus acquired
was heightened by the prevalent hatred of the Jesuits. The
leaders of the new thought were not the only people who detested the disciples of Loyola; the other religious orders, the
secular clergy, the legal profession, and the *bourgeoisie* were
united in their antipathy to the Jesuits – yet the Jesuits were
the most aggressive arm of the church. One thing is clear:
the influence of the clergy was waning. Interest in theology
declined even among those committed to its study. Science
and humane learning claimed more attention, dogmatics
and biblical scholarship received less. The clergy remained
a source of enlightenment and of good taste; Voltaire, for
all his bitter hatred of the church, was willing to concede as
much. But their doctrines were attacked by the *philosophes*
and their privileges by the economists, and in the eighteenth
century most intelligent men regarded themselves as belong-
ing either to the one category or to the other. In meeting
this challenge the clergy showed themselves diffident and
inept, and all too often they abandoned the field to their
foes. Within their ranks the churchmen no longer numbered
controversialists comparable with those who had flourished
in the seventeenth century, and only ability can reply effectively to ability. The church did not lack men of intelligence,
but they declined to exercise their gifts in theological debate.
Moreover, the pervasive influence of freemasonry met certain needs for the satisfaction of which men had formerly
turned to the church, and perhaps weakened the hold of
Catholicism on some men's minds.

It is an error to assume that on the eve of the Revolution
France was a country from which the influence of the church
had been largely eradicated. The religious life maintained
itself in vigour. Criticism was not always hostile even though
it was increasingly vocal. But the deficiencies of the church
and its failure to discharge the obligations it had accepted

came more and more under unsparing attack. The growing exasperation of the middle classes found its pretext and its justification in the defects of antiquated institutions. The inarticulate frustrations of the peasants were attributed to the burden of superannuated privileges. The new ideas which the literature of the day diffused throughout society intensified the restlessness which permeated the nation. Ambitious commoners demanded a wider freedom and claimed a fuller participation in the life of France. The clergy were not prepared to guide these aspirations, were too deeply committed to the old régime. But they were unable to resist them. Because some of the higher clergy had posed as the spokesmen of a new day, they had disqualified themselves as champions of the privileges to which the church had clung so tenaciously and for so long. Neither were they willing to identify themselves with the lower clergy in their clamour for reform. As the nation moved toward the revolutionary crisis, the church was paralysed between the claims of the past and the demands of the future. In the early days of the Revolution, the leaders of the clergy showed that they were not unwilling to face the needs of a new age, but the day of moderate counsels was brief. The leaders of the revolutionary movement soon discovered that they had behind them a redoubtable and unpredictable force – the aroused and undisciplined passions of the hitherto submerged sections of the nation. Moderate reform was swept away by the excesses of the Terror, and the church which survived was chastened by adversity, inured to poverty, and purified by suffering.

14

Church and State in the Age of the Enlightened Despots

THE eighteenth century was the age of the enlightened despots. The relations between church and state assumed a characteristic form, and in the areas affected the history of the church becomes largely a record of its response to the new views of kingly responsibility.

The papal territories, cutting across central Italy in a broad band, occupied a unique position in the European political system. Here was a state which was a church, a church which was a state. Its ruler had temporal as well as spiritual relations with other sovereigns, and this determined the kind of pressure to which he was often subjected. Before considering the prevailing pattern of relations between church and state, we must examine this exception to the rule.

Many contemporaries were bitterly critical of the papal states: no area, they said, was so backward, so benighted, so priest-ridden, or so completely a prey to superstition. Weakness and stagnation were balanced with a nicety unparalleled outside the Ottoman domains. In part this was merely the accepted mythology of a self-consciously enlightened age; like all exaggerations, it contained an element of truth. The ruler of the papal states was usually old, and was normally surrounded by rapacious relatives. Papal procedures were dilatory, complicated by personal rivalries, and frustrated by competing interests. The principal administrators were clerics, better versed in canon law than in economic theory. Because there was no consistent policy at the top and little imaginative direction at any level, trade languished and poverty increased. But there was another side to the picture.

It was unfair to insinuate that corruption had undermined what torpor had not already destroyed. The papal court had a reputation for unhurried competence. Society was not sunk in unrelieved apathy, nor had intellectual interests perished.

No one was tempted to minimize the difficulties of the papal states. By the end of the seventeenth century the excesses of favouritism and nepotism had been curbed; the evil could not be entirely eradicated, but never again would the patrimony of Peter be so openly a prey to papal relatives. Throughout the eighteenth century the papacy was involved in a dull and discouraging struggle with the other side of the problem, the heritage of debt bequeathed by the past. The prevailing financial chaos was reduced to some degree of order, but administrative reforms consistently lagged behind fiscal needs. The papacy was constantly driven to expedients which proved as pernicious in effect as they appeared to be inescapable in character. When the French Revolution finally destroyed the eighteenth-century world, the papacy was tottering on the verge of bankruptcy.

The eighteenth-century popes were worthy and respectable men, but they lacked the capacity to check the decadence which had overtaken the church. With the exception of Benedict XIV (1740–58), few of them were men of intellectual distinction. It was about Clement XI that Victor Amadeus of Savoy made his celebrated comment ('He would always have been esteemed worthy of the papacy if he had never obtained it'), but it could have been applied just as appropriately to most of the other popes of the period. What these men lacked was zeal. They exerted little moral force, and the scope of their influence was relatively small.

Benedict XIV exemplified the strength and the weakness of the eighteenth-century papacy. He combined unquestioned ability with conspicuous charm. He was affable and witty, easy of approach and with a gift for friendship. He recognized the need of a sound economic policy and did his best to enforce it, but his primary interests lay in literature and the arts. He was a brilliant conversationalist and wrote in a polished style. He preserved the artistic treasures of Rome, inaugurated the catalogue of the Vatican manuscripts, encouraged education and research. He closely approximated to the eighteenth-century ideal of an enlightened ruler; it is not surprising that Hume and Montesquieu, Voltaire and Frederick the Great sang his praises. But Benedict himself was quite aware of his impotence in certain spheres. He could not arrest the processes of disintegration, nor stem the tide of change. He knew that the authority of the church was weak; a conciliatory attitude toward secular rulers might gain concessions which Rome was in no position to demand. 'I prefer to let the thunders of the Vatican rest,' he said; 'Christ would not call down fire from Heaven. . . . Let us take care not to mistake passion for zeal, for this mistake has caused the greatest evils to religion.'

The pope was more often regarded as a petty Italian prince than as a spiritual leader with world-wide responsibilities. This was a weakness, but it had certain compensations. Because Italy was not a political entity, the pope's position as the ruler of a minor principality saved him from obvious dependence upon any of the major powers. To that extent his temporal sovereignty still guaranteed an international independence. This independence was often more apparent than real. There had been a steady decline in the authority of the papacy. Its claims, if they were to be effective, presupposed a deferential response which the Middle Ages had been prepared to give, which had been declining since 1300, and which at last the eighteenth century was content publicly to withhold. Papal authority, indeed, was too vaguely defined to impose effective demands on men's loyalties. Most Catholics were prepared to concede to the pope a primacy of honour, but many of them believed that in matters of faith the ultimate authority lay with a General Council. Only Italian theologians were ultramontane in outlook. In France it was still argued that the pope, by himself, could err in questions of faith and morals. When even bishops adopted a distinctly independent attitude in religious matters, it is scarcely surprising that Catholic princes disregarded the political pretensions of the church. The pope had little or no control over the rulers who theoretically recognized his authority. Often they simply ignored him, and certainly they did not intend to let him interfere in their affairs – even in their ecclesiastical affairs. The dignity of the Roman Church was compromised – indeed almost wholly destroyed – by the attacks of Roman Catholic rulers. The Bourbon powers – France, Spain, Parma, Naples – showed a fixed disposition to override the temporal interests of the papacy. At international gatherings, the pope was refused a voice. His representative was excluded from the negotiations at Utrecht. Sicily's fate was settled without the slightest reference to Rome's traditional claims to suzerainty. When Clement XII asserted similar rights over Naples, his claims were simply swept aside. From 1648 onward, every readjustment of European boundaries was effected without reference to the wishes of the pope. Sometimes he was quietly ignored, sometimes he was brusquely rebuffed. Not for two centuries had the political prestige of the papacy sunk so low. As a power in European politics it had been almost entirely effaced. The overthrow of the Jesuit Order – the papal militia ever since the Counter-Reformation – illustrates the aggressive confidence of the Catholic princes and the relative impotence of Rome.

The magnitude of the Jesuits' contribution to the Catholic cause was beyond dispute. They had turned back the tide of the Reformation; in country after country they had regained the rulers (and consequently the people) to the obedience of Rome. Their devotion, discipline, and intrepidity were beyond praise. Their schools and colleges had gained them an unchallenged educational prestige. They had shown extraordinary skill in winning the confidence of the great, were the confessors of kings, and the chosen counsellors of the noble and the rich. All this power and influence they placed unreservedly at the disposal of the Curia; surely the obvious responsibility of the pope was to protect such effective and obedient servants. But the Jesuits had overplayed their hand. They had been addicted to intrigue, and men had begun to suspect their motives. Their moral teaching had exposed them to damaging attack. They had shown an appetite for power, and had been phenomenally successful in satisfying it. Those who are strong and wealthy are likely to have foes; the Jesuits had created them in such prodigal fashion that the Society was beginning to prove a liability to the papacy rather than an asset.

Diffused hostility became dangerous because of the conjunction of several powerful influences. Eighteenth-century rulers were intent on extending their own authority; they resented any attempt to consolidate the authority of the pope. The philosophers, who created the prevailing climate of opinion, were the sworn enemies of the Jesuits. In France, Jansenists and *parlementaires* were awaiting an opportunity of settling old scores. In most Catholic countries, power was in the hands of men who had little sympathy with papal aims. It was in Portugal that the initial blow was struck. Pombal, who virtually ruled the country, accused the Jesuits of usurping royal prerogatives in the colonies, and an attempt to assassinate the king gave him a chance to take decisive action. The evidence of Jesuit participation in the plot was flimsy, but it was the more readily accepted because Jesuit moral doctrine seemed to condone regicide. At all events, in 1759 the Society was driven from the country. In certain French circles, the ejection of the Jesuits from Portugal was hailed with delight. The pretext for launching a similar attack arose because of the financial embarrassments of a Jesuit father named LaValette, who had become deeply entangled in commercial ventures in Martinique, and was ruined by the hazards of war with Great Britain. His creditors insisted that the Society as a whole was responsible for debts contracted by its members. The Jesuits refused to pay; the case came to trial, and the verdict was given against them. This inspired a demand that the Jesuit statutes should be investigated. It was discovered that legally the Society was present in France on sufferance only. Proceedings against the Jesuits multiplied in number and in scope. The moral and political teachings of the Society were condemned. Their

schools were closed, their property confiscated, their foundations dissolved, and in 1764, under the pressure of a public
opinion inflamed by the philosophers, Louis XV issued an
edict which decreed that the Society should no longer exist
in France. After Portugal and France came the turn of
Spain. The Jesuits had reputedly been engaged in intricate
intrigues, and Charles III, though a devout monarch, distrusted them. When an outbreak of violence occurred in
Madrid, a secret inquiry into its origin laid the blame upon
the Jesuits. Aranda, the chief minister, persuaded the king
that the Society was disloyal to Spain and had been plotting
against his life. In great secrecy the expulsion of the Jesuits
was planned; in 1767, with dramatic suddenness and with
complete success, the Society was suppressed, and all its
establishments, both in Spain and in its colonies, were
abruptly closed.

The overthrow of the Jesuits had apparently been
achieved; only inveterate malice could wish to crown the
humiliation of the proud Society with complete extinction.
But the Catholic princes were not content. The Bourbon
powers were determined that the pope should dissolve the
Society. They had a common policy and a common plan.
Their diplomatic representatives at Rome applied unceas-
ing pressure to the pope. When Clement XIII died, they
used every artifice to ensure the election of a successor predisposed to yield to their demands. With some skill Clement
XIV (1769–74) manoeuvred to gain time. He hesitated,
proposed alternatives, made timely but limited concessions,
and discussed ways of satisfying the Bourbon kings. His
Fabian tactics merely postponed the day of reckoning. The
ambassadors of the Catholic powers prodded the pope incessantly and in the sharpest terms. They talked of severing
diplomatic relations; when he continued to procrastinate,
they threatened to invade the papal states. A decision could
not be indefinitely evaded, and by the Brief *Dominus ac
Redemptor* (1773) Clement XIV dissolved the Society of Jesus.

In ultramontane circles the decision was greeted with dismay. The interests of the Jesuits were so closely allied with

those of the Curia that the overthrow of the Society seemed the most shattering blow that papal prestige had suffered since the Reformation. Yet even in Catholic countries there were many who received the news with satisfaction. Certainly the temper of the absolute rulers was not mollified by the pope's compliance with their demands. They regarded this success as a foretaste of further triumphs. During the next few years extensive changes took place. Sometimes they were made with the pope's reluctant consent; often they took place in spite of his strenuous opposition. As the period ends, we see Pius VI struggling to check the ravages of reforming movements such as Josephism. To understand these developments, it is necessary to consider in greater detail the way in which political trends affected the church.

Enlightened despotism was a characteristically eighteenth-century form of absolute government. Many of the controls to which kingly power had been subject had ceased to function. In most continental countries representative assemblies were moribund or in abeyance. Legal and theoretical checks had changed in character and had often lost their force. Kingly rule now appealed to different kinds of sanction. There was little disposition to rely on the divine justification of autocratic power; the theories which had supported the court absolutism of Louis XIV of France seemed as obsolete as those on which the confessional absolutism of Philip II of Spain had relied. The Lutheran conception of rule by divine right, which had played so important a part in German political theory, made no appeal whatever to Frederick the Great. In his eyes monarchy was justified by its effectiveness as an instrument of government. He saw himself as the first servant of the state; if he faithfully discharged his duties, he could safely ignore religious sanctions. Frederick was more cynical as well as more candid than his colleagues, but all eighteenth-century rulers tended to appeal to motives far more secular than those which had served a previous age. Theory, of course, was not wholly despised. The rationalist philosophers were ready to devise political doctrines which would justify the rule of their patrons.

Often the trend of their thought seemed to presuppose an extension of popular rights, but their speculations were disciplined by reference to hard facts. In some utopian future, things might be different; then the wisdom and maturity of the people might warrant their claiming a share in government, but until that happy day power should remain wholly in the hands of the prince. He would be guided, no doubt, by the intellectual leaders of the nation; the philosopher-king would provide the surest and shortest road to social happiness. Power should be exercised by those most likely to accept the most enlightened advice. 'The greatest happiness of a nation', wrote d'Alembert, 'is to have those who govern it be in accord with those who instruct it.' Holbach was the chief architect of this theory, Voltaire its most influential exponent. Some of the enlightened despots paid lip-service to theories of human rights and popular government, but usually the world of stubborn facts intervened between fine talk and concrete achievement. The cynical realism of Frederick the Great despised any concessions to democratic sentimentalism. He harboured few illusions about human nature. If he conferred any benefits upon his people – liberty of conscience or the advantages of education – these were gifts prompted by his own generosity, they were not concessions to any theory of human rights.

Though enlightened despotism might appeal to theory, its application was governed by practical considerations. An enlightened ruler had to balance reforming zeal against the resistance of social groups on whose support he still relied. The privileged orders – the feudal aristocracy and the higher clergy – were the chief obstacles in the way of change. Any attempt to create an efficient system of centralized government was certain to run foul of the traditions and the autonomous rights of the nobility and the church. In spite of its wealth and its apparent strength, the church proved particularly vulnerable to attack, and in one country after another was the primary target of reforming zeal. Few rulers could resist the temptation to deflect church revenues to purposes which seemed more in keeping with the spirit of the age, and they justified such seizures by stressing the inability of the older guardians of social well-being to cope with the problems which a new day was creating. Poverty was widespread, and the remedial charity which the church dispensed was no longer adequate to meet the need. In the great kingdoms of central and eastern Europe, capitalistic agriculture had disrupted the old patterns of peasant life. An enlightened and absolute ruler might be able to solve the difficulty; the privileged orders manifestly could not

The enlightened despots tended to curtail the power of the church and to circumscribe its influence. The pattern varied from state to state; in all alike the wealth of the church was diminished or expropriated and the activities of the clergy restricted. Religion virtually ceased to be a factor in international affairs. When England and Prussia concluded the Convention of Westminster (1756), French and Austrian observers feared that a new day of confessional alliances, and consequently of religious wars, was dawning. But to Frederick the Great such concepts were wholly obsolete. No one, not even women, he assured d'Argenson, would now grow fanatical about Luther or Calvin. Frederick might wish to expropriate ecclesiastical states or secularize the lands of prince-bishops, but this was a matter of power politics, not of religious expansion. For such purposes he relied upon his military strength, and ignored religious loyalties. Parallel with this decay of ecclesiastical influence was a corresponding corruption of political morality. Frederick William of Prussia ('the Great Elector') pursued a policy in which selfishness and bad faith were combined in nicely balanced proportions. He proved himself 'a political egotist so penetrating, adroit, and callous' that he amply compensated for his other defects. If a devout Calvinist could act in this spirit, it is scarcely surprising that Frederick the Great demonstrated the limits to which an opportunist devoid of scruple was prepared to go. In the partition of Poland we can see the extremes to which this cynical disregard of right and obligation could be carried. At the time, that piece of calculated brigandage aroused relatively little protest, so quiescent had the conscience of Europe become! By anticipation and on a limited scale, the eighteenth century forecast the fate which would overtake a community of sovereign states which devoted scientific ingenuity to the cultivation of military power, without learning to submit to any law higher than selfish expediency.

Certain characteristics were common to all the enlightened despotisms, but each of the continental countries had its own particular pattern of development. By the middle of the century, Frederick the Great had achieved a preeminent position, and his brilliance as a military leader had fixed the eyes of Europe on his kingdom. Prussia appeared to be the supreme example of the benefits of absolute rule. But appearances were deceptive. Frederick had indeed brought the civil service to a high degree of efficiency and had organized the life of the country in a way congenial to a military martinet. Though he was anxious to improve the peasants' lot, he could not translate his theories into facts. His reign resulted in an actual increase in serfdom. His rule rested on assumptions which were already obsolete long before the advent of the French Revolution. It is true that by illiberal means he achieved certain liberal ends. He abolished torture; he promoted education; in the fields of politics and economics he applied the principles of the Enlightenment. He had no sympathy with Christianity and little patience with its devotees. He regarded the service of the state as an adequate substitute for Christian faith and life. He advocated toleration on the ground that all religious beliefs were equally absurd. As an enlightened sceptic he believed that he could release the humanist values latent in eighteenth-century philosophy. He failed to do so: though emancipated, he was fundamentally illiberal in outlook, and merely consolidated a social structure that needed to be radically reformed.

Inevitably the lesser German states were drawn into the orbit either of Prussia or of Austria. Among these minor principalities a wide diversity prevailed. Some, like Brunswick and Saxe-Weimar, were models of enlightened progress; others were not. In the ecclesiastical electorates traditional patterns of life and thought had been less openly challenged than elsewhere, but even here a new spirit was stirring. The question of the nature of the church and the source of authority within it had been seriously raised. In 1763 von Hontheim, a high ecclesiastical official of the elector of Trier, published (under the pseudonym Febronius) a book called *Concerning the Condition of the Church and the Legitimate Power of the Pope*. The pope, he insisted, is not infallible. So far from being exalted above the whole church, he is subordinate to it, and an appeal from his decisions can always be carried to a General Council. In every country the authority of the church should be exercised by national or provincial synods of bishops. Such a doctrine presupposed a decentralized church and accorded to the pope merely a primacy among his fellow bishops. Febronianism gratified the growing sense of national independence which was stirring in many countries, and seemed in accord with the spirit of the age. In Catholic circles it won considerable support. The 'Articles of Coblenz', signed by the three Rhineland electors, protested against the arrogance of Rome and the extortions of the papal chancery. When, in 1786, a much more representative gathering ratified the 'Points of Ems', it was really reaffirming the position which the leaders of Catholicism in western Germany had already adopted.

Austria, though increasingly challenged by Prussia, was still regarded as the leading power in the Germanic world. In Vienna, no less than in Berlin, the principles of the Enlightenment were gaining ground. Joseph II, the most ardent of the enlightened despots, was neither a cynic nor an unbeliever. His reforming zeal had a distinctly religious quality; he might sometimes seem to be an insubordinate son of the church, but he insisted that he was (and intended to remain) a sincere believer. Frederick, with his flair for caustic comment, called him 'my brother the sacristan'. Even during the lifetime of his mother, Maria Theresa, there had been premonitions of change. No one doubted the piety of the empress (that 'apostolic hag', in Frederick's expressive phrase). She banned the teaching of English in her universities 'because of the dangerous character of this language in respect of its corrupting religious and ethical principles'. She abhorred dissent, since she saw in the church the bulwark of her throne, but she conceded that the temporal power of the church might advantageously be checked. Some of her decisions were in the authentic spirit of the Enlightenment. She amended the penal laws and restricted the use of torture. She fostered intellectual life (within discreet bounds) and regarded education as a responsibility which the state could not surrender to the church. She chose as her advisers men of liberal outlook, who in turn trained their successors in the school of enlightened reform.

Joseph II promoted with zest the changes which his mother conceded with reluctance. For fifteen years before her death, the empress had accepted her son as co-ruler, and tensions had been severe. He wished to remodel education along lines more drastically secular than she was willing to accept. 'The state', he said, 'is no cloister, and we have, in good truth, no monks for our neighbours.' When Maria Theresa's ambiguous policy towards the Bohemian peasantry caused an uprising, Joseph intervened. He was shocked at her sporadic attempts to suppress dissent. Persecution was foolish and wasteful: enforce it, and 'many bodies will be sacrificed which we need and might have used'. But he did not appeal merely to such utilitarian arguments. Coercion of men's consciences was human arrogance flouting the patience of God; it was humbler and more appropriate, he assured his mother, to recognize the limitations which God has placed on the authority of rulers, and leave the Holy Ghost to change the hearts of men. 'Such, as your Majesty is well aware, is my creed: and the strength of my convictions will hold me to it as long as I live.'

During the decade from 1780 to 1790, Joseph was free to develop the implications of this creed. Austrian Enlightenment now passed into its militant phase. The emperor was determined to press to their logical conclusion the reforming movements which the spirit of the eighteenth century had inspired and which he had already inaugurated. Reason was to govern affairs, and the power of the state was to act as the servant of reason. The state therefore would be the agent of reform, and its effects would be felt in every department of the nation's life. He proposed to fashion a form of absolute government in which uniform rules and practices would be founded on the principles of reason, unaffected by traditions derived from faith or history. In Joseph, the influences at work in the Catholic world to limit the power of the papacy and to restore the church to its 'primitive constitution' amalgamated with the ideals of the Enlightenment. His programme was inspired by motives appropriate to a national ruler, an orthodox economist, and a self-conscious rationalist in the later years of the eighteenth century. His enthusiasm and his zeal were beyond praise. His efforts were doomed to failure because of the defects of his good qualities. A doctrinaire inflexibility, an injudicious haste, a self-confident pride, an administrative ineptitude, a tendency to be beguiled by theories, a naïve belief that his subordinates were as disinterested as himself – in combination these proved fatal to his schemes of comprehensive reform.

The emperor's programme touched almost every area of life. He had long been aware of the problems of the peasantry; greater freedom, a juster system of land tenure, a fairer share of the burden of taxation were his answers. The legal and administrative systems of the empire were reformed. He introduced a programme of compulsory education organized on a secular basis, and Austria achieved the highest rate of school attendance in Europe. In reforming the universities he magnified the role of practical subjects (science, medicine, law) at the expense of speculative subjects like philosophy and theology. He abolished the censorship; superstition, instead of sheltering behind ancient immunities, should be exposed to criticism. 'I have weakened deep-rooted traditions', he wrote, 'by the introduction of enlightened principles.' He advocated nothing less than a fundamental re-alignment of human relations, and his programme reflected the invincible optimism which marked eighteenth-century thought in its most confident mood.

Such a programme created consternation in Austrian religious circles. All types of faith opposed his scheme of secular education. At certain points the emperor's plans directly affected the rights and privileges of the Catholic Church. The Catholic clergy had already been forbidden to correspond directly with Rome, and papal Bulls could be promulgated within the empire only with the ruler's consent. Such measures, though they seemed alarming enough to some, had scarcely prepared the public for the Patent of Toleration of 1781. The edict recognized the dominant position of the Catholic Church, and reserved to it the sole privilege of conducting public worship, but it granted dissenters the right of worshipping in private. The Lutherans, the Calvinists, and the Greek Orthodox were permitted to build churches – so long as they avoided such distinguishing marks as steeples. For the first time, those who did not conform to the official faith could claim the rights of citizenship. They were allowed to practise law or medicine, they might engage in trade and become members of corporate bodies, they could proceed to academic degrees, and by special dispensation they might be admitted to public office. It is true that these new privileges were beset with limitations. The edict offered little to the Jews, and nothing to the Unitarians and the Deists. The Patent was a dramatic reversal of traditional Hapsburg policies. It was conceived in a generous spirit and represented an important step toward a more liberal attitude. Dissent could no longer be treated as a breach of the law.

The papal authorities watched these developments with dismay, and in 1782 Pius VI took the unprecedented step of travelling to Vienna in order to bring the emperor to a better mind. The journey was not a success. The pope was received by the emperor with formal courtesy, by the chancellor Kaunitz with bare civility, and by the populace with enthusiastic devotion. But the Patent of Toleration was neither revised nor revoked, and the reforming zeal of the emperor was not even temporarily restrained. Indeed, it was apparent that it would touch the privileges of the church at many additional points. The emperor claimed the right to cancel certain papal Bulls; on occasion he exercised it. He required bishops to take the oath of allegiance to him. He undertook to reorganize episcopal sees. If the income of a bishop seemed to him excessive, he reduced it. He prohibited pluralism. He reorganized parishes. He studied with care the means of securing an adequately educated clergy. The diocesan seminaries seemed unsatisfactory, so he suppressed them. A proper training, he believed, should include secular branches of knowledge as well as theology and canon law. A revised curriculum could most effectively be taught at a few well-organized institutions; therefore he founded five general seminaries. These, he was convinced, would provide young priests with a sound and comprehensive education, solid in content, liberal in outlook, compatible with the latest advances in science, and in touch with the best learning of the age.

These seminaries were subject to the authority of the state; the training of the priesthood had thus been transferred from episcopal to civil control. Joseph, indeed, had been steadily transforming the church into a department of state, and the results of the change became increasingly apparent. The emperor disliked the international character of the great religious orders; he decreed that within his domains their members should no longer be subject to foreign generals. He was dissatisfied with the condition of the monasteries: for men to devote themselves wholly to contemplation violated the principles of rational economics. As a disciple of the physiocrats, he objected to waste of any kind, and it was obviously wasteful if men did not work. So he drastically reduced the number of convents. Out of a total of 2,163 monastic houses, over 700 were suppressed. The number of monks fell from 65,000 to 27,000. Only orders devoted to practical duties, such as teaching or the

care of the sick, were permitted to survive. Joseph's zeal was
not content to interfere in major affairs alone; he could not
rest so long as the smallest details were unreformed. He
believed that simplicity had been the mark of primitive
worship; the extravagance of baroque display was oppressive to him. So he interfered with the pattern of church
services. He objected to 'superstitious practices' like pil-
grimages and the observance of saints' days. Nothing was
too trivial to arrest his attention, no area so remote as to
escape his concern.

Such an all-embracing, omnicompetent paternalism was
certain to create resentment. In Hungary disaffection flared
up in troubles which persisted for five years. In the Austrian
Netherlands, the smouldering anger caused by Joseph's well-
intentioned but ill-advised religious reforms broke out in
revolt when civil changes touched the structure of secular
life. Inescapable signs already pointed to Joseph's failure to
persuade his subjects to support his programme. Such evidence rapidly multiplied, and when the emperor died in
1790, it was obvious that the schemes he had so ardently
promoted would promptly collapse. Many of his reforms
were wholly ephemeral; and yet even the tide of conservative
reaction could not entirely efface the work of the reformer
whose good will had so consistently outstripped his good
sense.

Emperor Leopold, who succeeded his brother on the
Hapsburg throne, had already had a notable career as the
enlightened reformer of the grand duchy of Tuscany. He
shared Joseph's enthusiasm for the new philosophy and was
equally convinced of the need for thorough-going reform.
He, too, was fond of order, efficiency, economy, symmetry,
and was passionately interested in the smallest details of his
schemes. Few could deny that his grand duchy was ripe
for reform. The cultural pre-eminence of Florence had been
destroyed by obscurantism. The Inquisition ruled unchallenged, and its activities were supplemented by the
minute surveillance of conduct and morals which the friars
maintained. In few countries had freedom been so largely

suppressed; nowhere was a reforming ruler so certain to clash with the overweening power of the reactionary elements in the church.

Leopold was determined to place the relations of church and state on a new footing. Like Joseph, he believed that the temporal ruler had the right as well as the duty to direct and supervise the work of the church. But his aims extended far beyond a redefinition of the respective functions of the civil and ecclesiastical powers. The church itself needed reform; only when purged and purified could it raise the people from their spiritual torpor. Leopold's programme was both courageous and comprehensive. He deprived the Inquisition of the right to regulate literature; in response to its angry protests, he suppressed it altogether, and allowed its revival only in the limited form in which Venice tolerated its presence. He taxed clerical incomes. He restricted the transmission of funds to Rome. He modified the powers of church courts: their jurisdiction was restricted to spiritual matters, the right to impose temporal penalties was withdrawn, the nuncio's court was abolished, and appeals to Rome were forbidden. At various other points the direct influence of the Curia was reduced: its use of patronage was strictly controlled, and its power of interference in the affairs of the religious orders was restricted. Some restraint was imposed on the activities of begging friars. Hospitals were transferred from religious to lay control. The problems of the secular clergy received careful attention. Patronage was reformed, clerical non-residence was attacked, the low level of many stipends was raised, the standards of clerical education were improved. Nowhere was the need of reform so clamant as in the monastic houses. Their number was excessive, and the condition of some was an open scandal. Upon charges of immorality, doubtless justified, and without consulting Rome, Leopold suppressed the Tuscan convents of nuns under the control of the Dominicans.

Leopold regarded his ecclesiastical reforms as the crown of his entire programme. They were far from popular. The pamphlets in which he commended his schemes did not touch the populace which had long been subject to the friars in their most obscurantist mood. His chief adviser was Bishop Scipione Ricci of Pistoia and Prato, and together they tried to enlist the support of the clergy by reviving the synodal system of church government. A synod held at Pistoia in 1786 indicated that a more general participation in church government appealed to the parish priests, and the resolutions adopted by the gathering were strongly liberal in tone. In the following year, when Leopold convoked a general assembly of the Tuscan bishops, he met stubborn opposition. Clearly he was attempting to achieve too much too quickly, and the leaders of the church were determined to resist further change. The fruits of Leopold's efforts bore no adequate relation to the disinterested zeal which inspired them. He showed considerable understanding of the problems of his age and some grasp of the ways in which they might be solved. He pursued his mission with self-denial as well as industry. In a small and unified kingdom, the ideals of enlightened despotism confronted the fruits of lethargy and superstition in their worst forms. The results of their encounter were inconclusive. When Leopold left Florence for Vienna, a reaction, partly clerical, partly popular, was already threatening his schemes. Before long the tides of Revolution swept them away.

In Russia, Peter the Great had spread a thin veneer of civilization over an absolute but semi-barbaric state. When Catherine the Great appeared as a champion of the Enlightenment, one kind of despotism challenged another, and the contrast fascinated her contemporaries. In her youth she had studied the works of the French philosophers, who confirmed her instinctive conviction that the secret of rational government lay in the principles of enlightened absolutism. She was heart and soul a child of the new age, but her ardour never blinded her to realities. She was as devoid of moral scruple as of mystical insight. In fashioning her policies she relied entirely upon a clear, rationalistic intelligence. The country obviously needed reform. Bad government, reinforced by an administration of justice as unpredictable as it was cruel, had caused widespread disaffection. The misery of the peasants was darkened by hatred bred of religious persecution. Catherine believed that she had an unparalleled opportunity of securing for her people the blessings which would accrue from the liberal doctrines of French philosophy. A clear legal code was a paramount necessity, and her first, perhaps her most striking, contribution to progress would be a revision of the laws. Her *Instruction*, issued to the commission entrusted with the task, became a classic of the Enlightenment. It was infused with a benign optimism which delighted in the prospect of indefinite human advance. It spoke in eloquent terms of the law of nature and of the responsibilities of enlightened rulers. But this glowing programme was quite irrelevant to the Russian situation; it did not touch its problems, and was useless as a guide to codifying Russian laws. This soon became apparent, and Catherine realistically accepted the fact. Though she delighted to talk in exalted terms of progress, she did not let her own enthusiasms deceive her.

In dealing with the church, Catherine pushed forward the policy which her deposed husband, Peter III, had initiated. Church lands were secularized, and as a result two million serfs passed under state control. She established a commission to administer the sequestrated lands; some of the income was designated for ecclesiastical purposes, but much of it was deflected to schools, hospitals, and asylums. The church, more clearly than ever, was subjected to secular control. The clergy had little chance of exerting an independent influence in social and political life. They might resent their subordinate position, might even try to foment disaffection, but they were inescapably sinking to the status of salaried servants of the state. Nor did a church policy dictated by reasons of state benefit the serfs who had become the government's responsibility. This was one of the gravest problems facing the nation. Catherine was adept at appealing to the ideals of the Enlightenment; like Frederick the Great, she failed to apply these high-sounding principles to the steady amelioration of her people's lot.

The northern countries bordering on the kingdoms of the enlightened despots felt the impact of the new ideas. Poland, in endemic political turmoil, had found in mounting intolerance a certain compensation for its increasing weakness. The history of the country during the years before the first partition reads like a sustained invitation to disaster. The Roman Catholic majority unquestionably treated the Lutheran and Orthodox minorities with a severity out of keeping with the ideals of the Enlightenment. The enlightened rulers to the east and to the west of Poland found in such intolerance an added pretext for intervention. At all events, liberty of conscience came to Poland as compulsion from without, and for a few years the country reluctantly became one of the most tolerant nations in the world. But a rising tide of patriotic resistance was the chief result, and the interplay of renewed intolerance at home and increased intervention from abroad contributed to the final downfall of the kingdom.

Denmark experienced a variety of forms of government, all of which affected religious life. In 1660, a weak monarchy, supported by the Lutheran Church and by the burghers of Copenhagen, acquired absolute power, and steadily tightened its grip on every aspect of the nation's life, including the work and worship of the church. In the early eighteenth century, the pattern of royal paternalism was dictated by the ideals of Pietism. The most trivial details, such as the appointment of organists in provincial churches, received the king's attention. Sabbath restrictions were stringent and minute. Christian VI believed that a reformation guided by the king and enforced by the state church would guarantee a sound national life. An austere sobriety would be achieved through uncompromising regulation. It was this system – shaken indeed by the collapse of royal morality during two successive reigns – which was briefly but dramatically challenged by Strauensee. This brilliant adventurer, the son of a pastor, began his career as a doctor, but his hold over King Christian VII and Queen Caroline soon gave him powers rarely enjoyed by any minister. Though not himself a despot, his programme was certainly inspired by the ideals of the Enlightenment. He aimed to give Denmark a benevolent autocracy which would break the power of tradition and eradicate the evils of privilege. Anything which interfered with the application of his emancipated principles was swept away. The fashionable philosophy of the age must be given the freest scope. Many customs, sanctioned by the church and dear to the people, were abolished. A spate of new laws revolutionized Danish life. Every citizen was to be guaranteed the freedom to live whatever life seemed best to him. For Strauensee himself liberty was apparently synonymous with the abrogation of all moral restraints. His cosmopolitan humanitarianism left most Danes untouched: the combination of doctrinaire abstractions and ill-digested laws merely convinced them that he was an enemy of faith and morals. After a meteoric career of less than two years, he was deposed and executed. Under the younger Bernsdorff, Denmark experienced government which was enlightened but moderate, which paid little heed to the shibboleths of the day but which solved the problem which baffled most of the enlightened despots – the position of the peasants.

Sweden, in 1772, provided Gustavus III with as fair an opportunity as a reformer could desire. Persistent misrule had brought the country to the brink of disaster. By a *coup d'état* the king gained effective power, and embarked upon a programme which conformed with the best traditions of enlightened despotism. Torture was abolished, restrictions on religious liberty were lifted, freedom of the press was introduced. The Lutheran Church forfeited its exclusive position, but gained compensating advantages. It had suffered from fiscal and judicial abuses. Its charitable funds had been misappropriated. Scores of parsonages had fallen into ruin. Episcopal visitation had been neglected. In effecting his reforms, Gustavus III relied chiefly on two churchmen whose political gifts he discovered and on whose aid he increasingly relied: Bishop Olaf Wallquist and Carl Gustaf Nordin.

In both Spain and Portugal the new despotism stirred the somewhat stagnant pools of national life. The tensions which it caused were primarily concerned with the relations of church and state, not with the clash of competing ideas. The new philosophy made little impression and left the church virtually untouched. There was no such crisis of thought and conscience as France experienced. The crucial problem concerned the extent to which the church's influence could be allowed to affect affairs of state. This perennial issue had widened till it challenged all ancient restraints upon the initiative of the civil power.

Spain was the most fervently Catholic country in Europe. Statistics alone indicate as much. There were 160 sees and at least 400,000 clergy. These figures are far larger than the comparable ones for France, though Spain had a smaller population and less wealth. In a real sense the church was the centre of the people's life. Monks and friars formed an unusually high proportion of the clergy. Ardent faith was a distinguishing mark of the Spanish church; so, unfortunately, was superstition, and the religious orders tended to inflame the one and confirm the other. The Inquisition had long restricted any free activity of the spirit, and it did its utmost to isolate Spain from the contagion of foreign thought. The need to preserve absolute orthodoxy had become an obsession. The higher clergy were less aristocratic and less worldly than their counterparts in France; they were also less interested in art, in learning, or in any kind of intellectual pursuits. The village priests were often as poor as the peasants whom they served, and their outlook was equally marked by ignorance and fanaticism. They did their best to make religion vital to the people, but often what they offered was tinctured with primitive and even brutal superstition.

Such a church was likely to resist change of any kind. In Charles III it faced a ruler who had little doctrinaire enthusiasm for new ideas. He was not interested in current philosophical trends, though some of his advisers were. To his contemporaries he seemed to be two men in one. Sincerely religious in outlook, he dedicated his domains to the Immaculate Conception of the Virgin, and lived the simple, frugal life appropriate to a member of the Franciscan Third Order. But his personal devotion did not modify his undeviating pursuit of policies likely to strengthen the Crown. Before coming to the Spanish throne he had served a long apprenticeship as ruler of the Kingdom of the Two Sicilies. He had shown that he could respect the church's dogmas while he resisted its claims. As King of Spain he relied on a succession of able administrators whose views were well in advance of his own, but with whom he could work for certain clearly defined objectives. Floridablanca was a diplomat, an economist, a disciple of the French philosophers. So was Aranda, the enemy of the Jesuits. Campomanes was a classical scholar, a jurist, a historian, and an economist, as well as an eager reformer and a skilled administrator. In Jovellanos, the same aptitudes and outlook were combined with a deep interest in education and a firm belief that here the state must retain the initiative. These men were the champions of the Enlightenment in Spain. They believed that royal absolutism offered the only pathway to reform, and they entirely agreed with Charles's aims.

As he increased the power of the crown, the king depressed the position of the church. He claimed the right to nominate to ecclesiastical positions. He admitted papal Bulls only if they had first been submitted to him for approval. He limited contacts with Rome, curtailed papal interference in his domains, and never missed a chance to restrict the privileges of the clergy. Welfare services, so long the preserve of the church, were opened to lay participation. Charles even restrained the Inquisition, and reduced its dreaded power to a shadow of its former self. All the while he increased his revenues at the expense of the church. Charles was not a man of great intellectual capacity, but his persistence in pursuing a limited range of objectives made him one of the chief rulers of the age and one of the ablest of the kings of Spain.

In Portugal, too, the tension between church and state resulted from a sustained attempt to strengthen the position of the crown. The central figure, however, was not the king, but his chief minister. Pombal was one of the ablest statesmen of the age. Professor Gershoy has called him 'the most spectacular and dynamic ruler of the eighteenth century', which is high praise if we consider those who compete for the designation. Ignorance and superstition were so prevalent in Portugal that Pombal regarded the monarchy as the only possible instrument of reform. He knew that the crown would have to be strengthened, and he realized that most of his schemes, whether in commerce, finance, or education, would bring him into conflict with the church. His bitterest foes were the Jesuits and the aristocracy, with which the Jesuits were closely allied. These two, he believed, were the twin sources of Portugal's weakness and the cause of its degradation to the status of a fourth-rate, priest-ridden power. The Jesuits were powerful and rich, and hitherto had largely directed state policy both at home and abroad. Pombal struck at them without fear and without mercy. More than any single man, he was responsible for the overthrow of the Society of Jesus. Henceforth he was free to pursue his reforming programme. He had already curbed the power of the Inquisition. He so drastically curtailed the influence of the papacy that throughout the second half of the eighteenth century the Portuguese church was virtually cut off from Rome.

Absolutism intent upon reform was thus a characteristic feature of eighteenth-century life. A common intellectual atmosphere diffused certain basic convictions. It was customary to pay lip-service to freedom of thought, but the exercise of that freedom was severely restricted. 'Newspapers must not be worried if they are to be interesting,' remarked Frederick the Great, but censorship was relaxed only on non-political subjects. 'Pray do not tell me about your Berlin liberty of thought and writing,' said Lessing; 'it merely consists in the liberty of circulating as many witticisms as you like against religion.' Any kind of foreign influence over the church was discouraged. In Catholic countries, ties with the Vatican were reduced to a minimum, and there was some disposition to favour national churches which would largely be independent of Rome. Governments freely intervened in church affairs. They reorganized monasteries, suppressed orders, reformed ecclesiastical procedures, and expropriated church funds. These changes were initiated from above. They were not prompted by popular demand nor did they correspond to any articulate desire within the churches. They were inspired by 'the spirit of the age', yet this spirit was dominant chiefly within the restricted circles responsive to prevailing cultural forces. Hence the surprisingly evanescent character of enlightened depotism itself. The French Revolution swept away the old régime and many of its rulers. It discredited the aims and the methods that had served the eighteenth century. As the tides of violence receded, the extent of the conservative revulsion became apparent; the ruling classes sought reassurance in forms of absolute government which made no concessions, in theory or in practice, to the ideals of reform, and it was assumed that the church would be at hand to sanctify reaction.

15

The High Noon of Rationalism, and Beyond

THE eighteenth century was self-consciously an enlightened and emancipated age. Throughout much of its course, it was not a period remarkable for creative thought. Its debt to the seventeenth century was immense; it drew upon medieval sources to a far greater extent than it realized. The ingredients of eighteenth-century thought were borrowed from others, the pattern which they assumed was original and new. The Age of Reason was remarkable less for the doctrines which it propounded than for the manner of thought which it encouraged. It was secular in spirit and destructive in effect. It diffused a scepticism which gradually dissolved the intellectual and religious patterns which had governed European thought since St Augustine. It proclaimed the autonomy of man's mind and his infinite capacity for progress and perfectibility. In the principle of causality it believed that it had found the key which would open all the secrets of knowledge and lay bare the essential nature both of the universe and of man.

The thought of the period was largely English in origin but predominantly French in character. Its basic concepts had been fashioned by Locke and Newton; they were publicized by Bayle and Montesquieu, Voltaire and Diderot. A cosmopolitan culture had evolved; its capital was Paris and its mother tongue was French. Ideas circulated freely; a universal language gave them the widest possible currency, and their French endorsement lent them added weight. From France came the social institution which aided the wide diffusion of new ideas. The *salons* were centres of literary and social life, often ruled and directed by some woman of culture, and dedicated to the free discussion of current thought. To a degree unparalleled before or since, the social and intellectual leaders of Europe were united in a community of thought and interest.

In addition to diffusing thought, the *salons* determined its character. The *philosophes* of the age were not formal philosophers devoted to a particular academic discipline. They were men of letters who were also men of the world. They moved easily in society, received its homage and set its tone. In their sight it was more important to be intelligible than to be profound. Ideas would command attention if they were clear and interesting. Some of the *philosophes* were scientists, some were historians, economists, psychologists, while some were merely able publicists. Among them were men of great talent, a few were men of genius. For these men philosophy was not one branch of knowledge among many, but the spirit which animated every branch. Their aim was the diffusion of knowledge and the creation of an emancipated spirit. 'It gives me pleasure to note', wrote Grimm, one of the foremost interpreters of the movement, 'that an immense republic of cultivated spirits is being formed in Europe; enlightenment is spreading on all sides.' The Age of Reason was dominated by a few cardinal ideas which were arranged with strict precision and whose implications were developed with logical consistency. The thought of the *philosophes* was always clear; it was often abstract as well. Grimm recognized the danger, and realized that it was a weakness. 'All our knowledge', he said, 'consists in generalizing our ideas, in imagining relations which exist only in our head, which, while they honour our imagination or our wisdom, are none the less chimerical; in formulating, in a word, on the basis of a few particular facts, inductions from which we establish so-called eternal and invariable laws that nature has never known.'

The zest which marked eighteenth-century thought was due to its confidence, and this confidence was inspired by the belief that man's mind had discovered a new and marvellous instrument. This much-prized tool was reason – not man's mind as such, but the way in which his rational faculties

could be used to achieve certain specific ends. Descartes
had relied on deduction; Newton had used inductive analysis in penetrating to the great secret of nature's marvellous
laws, and the spirit and method of Newtonian physics ruled
the eighteenth century. Nature was invested with unparalleled authority, and it was assumed that natural law
ruled every area into which the mind of man could penetrate. Nature was the test of truth. Man's ideas and his
institutions were judged by their conformity with those laws
which, said Voltaire, 'nature reveals at all times, to all men'.
The principles which Newton had found in the physical
universe could surely be applied in every field of inquiry.
The age was enchanted with the orderly and rational structure of nature; by an easy transition it was assumed that the
reasonable and the natural must be synonymous. Nature was
everywhere supreme, and virtue, truth, and reason were her
'adorable daughters'. The effect of this approach was apparent in every sphere. In France history, politics, and
economics became a kind of 'social physics'. The new outlook can be seen in Montesquieu's *The Spirit of the Laws*;
thenceforth the study of man's institutions became a pro-
longation of natural science. The emphasis fell increasingly
on the practical consequences of knowledge: man is endowed
with reason, said Voltaire, 'not that he may penetrate the
divine essence but that he may live well in this world'. Even
in ethics, natural law reigned supreme; morality was a
science which substituted independence and autonomy for
submission to the divine will. The natural and the reasonable
became the secular as well. The Age of Reason was chiefly
interested in the elaboration, elucidation, and exposition of
this analytical procedure derived from Newtonian physics.
Its most brilliant achievement was the *Encyclopedia* (1750–
1770). Diderot, the directing genius of the enterprise, explained its purpose. He and his colleagues were not primarily
interested in communicating a specific body of knowledge;
rather, they aimed at effecting a fundamental revolution in
the prevailing pattern of thought.

This was a deliberate challenge to accepted beliefs. The

theology and ethics of the churches were subjected to a criticism more merciless than any which they had hitherto faced. The appeal to reason and to natural law was closely related to the desire for freedom from traditional patterns of authority. The old forms of feudal power were disintegrating; the old forms of belief which had provided their sanction were discredited. The new age refused to follow the old guides. What men wanted, however, was a change, not a revolution. For all its destructive appearance, the thought of the Enlightenment was curiously conservative. The *philosophes* were members of the middle class, believing in order and security, and wanting a stable society. The idea of a disordered universe was abhorrent to them. Hence, for convenience sake, they retained the kind of God that Deism in its later phases could countenance. He was scaled down and domesticated; his majesty was no longer disconcerting, and he was useful as a guarantor of order. He was abstract and remote; he was no longer inconvenient because he no longer encountered man with an exacting personal demand. 'I believe in God,' said Voltaire, 'not the God of the mystics and the theologians, but the God of nature, the great geometrician, the architect of the universe, the prime mover, unalterable, transcendental, everlasting.' Such a God stood entirely outside the drama of human history; he could not be connected with anything that happens on this insignificant planet. He built the machine, and set it in motion, but the machine now runs its predetermined course in complete independence of its maker. The *philosophes* therefore denied the fact of revelation. They dispensed with the Holy Scriptures and the holy church. The God they retained inevitably faded into the abstraction of a first cause. This was the natural consequence of their glorification of the Newtonian revolution; having 'deified nature', they 'denatured God'.

The critical scrutiny of authority developed in four distinguishable stages. The first phase in the attack on traditional beliefs is represented by Pierre Bayle (see p. 49). No matter what the subject, he tabulated the reasons against belief in exhaustive detail. He claimed that he was just as meticulous in enumerating the grounds for faith, but his protestations did not convince his contemporaries. Certainly his works provided an almost inexhaustible reservoir from which lesser critics could freely draw. The second stage of the attack is represented by the *Encyclopedia*. This great enterprise, the rallying point of the *philosophes*, both exemplified their methods and diffused their point of view. Diderot's article on Christianity professed the profoundest regard for the transcendent religion of Jesus, but its effect (and probably its aim) was to excite in the reader an equally profound contempt for its social morality. But the aridities of pure reason were provoking a reaction, and Jean-Jacques Rousseau was the prophet of the new approach. Logic alone could not satisfy the heart of man, and emotion claimed its rightful place. In the name of sensibility, Rousseau advocated a simple religion of reverence for God and love for mankind. Feeling was more important than thought. Nature was fundamentally good; man had been corrupted by the evils of society, but an easy solution lay to hand: he need only recognize and return to the *Social Contract* on which our life is rightly founded. Rousseau, it might appear, was far more sympathetic to Christianity than the rationalists against whose teachings he reacted so vehemently. In his 'Creed of a Savoyard Vicar', he set forth a view of religion which is simply Deism permeated with emotional enthusiasm. Though he doubted the value of revelation and questioned the adequacy of the proofs advanced in its support, in the Gospels and their teachings he found a beauty and a holiness in striking contrast with the arrogance of the rationalists. Yet Rousseau was at best a dangerous ally for Christianity. His religion of feeling stripped away all the distinguishing marks of the historic faith, and encouraged a diffused form of theism. The fourth stage of the attack on religion reflects the confusion which had overtaken thought by the reign of Louis XVI. The influence of Voltaire encouraged a complete denial of God; the disciples of Rousseau propounded a vague worship of nature and of the Supreme Being who stands behind it. 'Illuminism' (a movement which combined theosophical and mystical elements and relied heavily on allegorical methods of interpretation) is characteristic of the strange cults which were arising. Even quacks, like that colourful knave Cagliostro, who toured Europe dispensing his elixir of youth, reflected the restless hunger of the times. The ridicule of the *philosophes* had shaken confidence in the ancient forms of faith, and the aspirations of man's soul were seeking satisfaction in strange and unexpected ways.

The influence of Voltaire cannot be restricted to any one of these stages of the attack on traditional beliefs. For the better part of half a century he was the most powerful influence in European thought. He was a superb critic but a mediocre philosopher. In his earliest phase, he drew heavily (and not always exactly) on the English Deists, and gave their views the widest possible circulation. Long after they had been virtually forgotten at home, they were affecting the intellectual climate of the continent. From the Deists, Voltaire drew the arguments with which he attacked miracles, prophecy, and the authority of Scripture. He popularized the views of Locke and Newton. Here, too, he was profoundly influential in determining the pattern of eighteenth-century thought. He emphasized the simplicity and sublimity of Newton's laws – and gave a superficial and inaccurate account of them. The inferences which he drew from them were important: man's mind, he claimed, has now been emancipated from authority, from innate ideas, and from revelation. Into the place thus left vacant, reason stepped, and brought with it a method which used a few simple principles to account for everything that could be explained. As concerning other things – the inscrutable regions of mystery or paradox – Voltaire airily dismissed them as of no account. In the early stages of his long career he accepted the abstracted kind of deity in whom Deists could plausibly believe. 'I am not an atheist,' he said, 'nor a superstitious person; I stand for common sense and the golden mean.' But as time progressed, Voltaire's golden mean was increasingly obscured by violent antipathies. The idea of Providence – of God's watchful care of individual lives – he dismissed as absurd. His attacks on the organized church grew more and more vitriolic. Instead of relying on his usual weapons of supercilious ridicule and urbane sarcasm, he resorted to angry denunciation.

In this respect, Voltaire did not stand alone. All the *philosophes* participated in this bitter vendetta against established religious authority. The contrast with English thought is conspicuous. In England the Deists had been met with a willingness to discuss their case, even a readiness to compromise at certain points. In France they were opposed by an unbending orthodoxy which held in reserve the ancient weapons of imprisonment and persecution, and which was ready enough to use them. The church expected the secular authorities to apply a repressive policy; its attitude inevitably provoked resistance to a religious system in which intolerance played so large a part. This lurking threat of persecution explains a certain oblique disingenuousness in Voltaire, a readiness to hide behind the authority of others and to imply that he accepted more than he really did. He was sometimes abusive, sometimes cringing. He used abuse when he felt brave; he resorted to lies when he felt timid. But it also accounts for the violence, even the extravagance, into which the champions of reason and common sense allowed themselves to fall. When it was safe to do so, they attacked the strongholds of superstition with volcanic energy. Nothing was so sacred as to escape their ribald criticism, nothing so mysterious as to defy their confident analysis. The beliefs, the prescriptive rights, the ancient prerogatives of the church were incessantly attacked. The failings of the priesthood were magnified into a deliberate conspiracy against reason and the elementary rights of man. '*Écrasez l'infâme*' was Voltaire's battle cry; he repeated it with the monotony of an unvarying refrain. '*L'infâme*' was not God, nor Christ, nor Christianity, nor even Catholicism. Probably what Voltaire meant by it was privileged and persecuting orthodoxy. In this particular respect, that attack of the *philosophes* was almost wholly destructive in purpose; they did not worry about the casualties they inflicted on what they called the empire of superstition.

Their consuming desire was to free the élite from the bondage of authority. But this deliverance would extend to the enlightened alone. Voltaire wasted no sympathy on democratic aspirations, and both his hatred of Christianity and the deliberate class-consciousness of the Age of Reason are admirably conveyed by his words to Frederick the Great: 'Your majesty will do the human race an eternal service in extirpating this infamous superstition [Christianity], I do not say among the rabble, who are not worthy of being enlightened and who are apt for every yoke; I say among the well-bred, among those who wish to think.' In certain areas this violence was beneficial. The *philosophes* attacked theology because they wished to establish the freedom of scientific inquiry. They sought a science which would be free from theological preconceptions. Voltaire attacked the physics of the Bible in a way that betrayed bad taste, but his purpose was clear enough. There was no appreciation of the fact that theological and empirical methods might be different, yet valid in their distinct areas. Only gradually was the distinction recognized between different disciplines, and meanwhile Voltaire and his friends were intent on establishing the fact that there were certain areas in which ecclesiastical authority was irrelevant and where coercion could not legitimately be applied.

In his pleas for toleration, Voltaire's more generous instincts coalesced with his hatred of traditional authority. The whole bent of his mind made him an enemy of coercion, and a particularly flagrant case of religious persecution aroused him to launch his notable attack on intolerance. Though the French Huguenots had few legal rights, they were not consistently repressed. Their freedom was limited and precarious; at any moment unpredictable circumstances might precipitate a fresh outburst of persecution, and the fate of Jean Calas was an extreme example of what could happen. In 1761, Calas' son committed suicide. The father was a respected member of the community; the young man had been suffering from melancholia and was known to be of unstable mind. But the Catholics claimed that Calas had hanged his son in order to forestall his conversion to Romanism. Popular feeling was fanned to a fierce intensity and the case came to trial in an atmosphere charged with emotion. The Toulouse Parlement found the family guilty, and with a refinement of cruelty out of keeping with the spirit of the age, sentenced the father to be broken on the wheel. Voltaire's interest was aroused. He examined the evidence and satisfied himself that a flagrant miscarriage of justice had taken place. This was a case which gave full scope to his superb gifts as a publicist. Its tragic circumstances lifted him above the faults of violence and ribaldry into which religious controversy usually betrayed him. With passionate but disciplined intensity and with a clarity which never left the essential issues in doubt, he brought the matter to the bar of public opinion. The reaction which followed was too powerful to be ignored. The verdict was reviewed by the king and council and was reversed. Belated justice was done to Calas' memory and to the members of his family, but of greater importance was the effect upon the European mind. Intolerance suffered a mortal blow, and it was fondly assumed that the judicial punishment of religious beliefs had been discredited for ever.

The *philosophes* were anti-Christian but not necessarily irreligious. They attacked the church with every weapon at their disposal, and fashioned the kind of anti-clericalism which has had such a vogue in certain European countries. Clearly in attacking God they were attacking the pretensions of priestcraft; it is equally obvious that in their own way they cherished beliefs and aspirations which can only be described as religious. They detested dogma but hankered after an awareness of God which would be as all-embracing as the universe itself. In the very process of seeking to define these non-Christian truths, the Age of Reason laid bare the insufficiency of reason. The problem of evil in a world apparently so good could neither be evaded nor resolved. They repudiated the explanations advanced by the theologians, but had nothing to substitute for them. Hume had shown that the resources of reason are restricted; to certain questions the human mind, if left to its own resources, can find no answers. Before the eighteenth century had half run its course the arrogant confidence in man's unaided reason had been chastened. To this was due the enthusiasm with which men turned to more practical matters. The reforming spirit of the *philosophes* increasingly sought satisfaction in ethics rather than in metaphysics. Diderot's concern with morality was not exceptional; most of his associates also wished to be considered 'men of virtue'. Their opponents represented them as enemies of virtue. What more effective answer could they offer than the assurance that they were replacing an outworn morality with a new and effective one? 'It is not enough', said Diderot, 'to know more than [the theologians] do; it is necessary to show them that we are better, and that philosophy makes more and better men than sufficient or efficacious grace.' Moreover, useful studies would in all likelihood prove much more rewarding than abstract speculation. Hume turned from metaphysics to history and economics, and thus established a pattern which many others followed. This was more than a shift in interest. Here, too, we can detect the desire to change and improve the world. History was regarded as philosophy teaching by example. The didactic motive was strong, and behind it lay the conviction that society was in need of regeneration. One of the marks of the age was its desire to set things right and it was increasingly clear that reason alone could not effect the needed change. An increasing emphasis was therefore placed on practical measures to improve the world. The Abbé Saint-Pierre is remembered because of his ambitious plan to establish universal peace, but he was fertile in schemes of all kinds, and in his zeal he was conspicuous but not exceptional.

The religious concern of the *philosophes* carried them beyond an emphasis on ethics and an interest in practical studies. They rejected traditional doctrines but did not necessarily repudiate religion itself. Holbach might parade his atheism but he spoke for a relatively limited coterie. The chief ingredients in the outlook which the *philosophes* encouraged are clearly religious in implication, however far removed they may be from Christian belief. To begin with, they taught that by nature man is good, not bad. There is no native bias which predisposes him to evil; he is not born with a propensity to sin. The right comes as naturally to him as the wrong; encourage him with a favourable environment, and his propensity to good will assert itself. It will then be seen that he is easily enlightened, susceptible to reason's guidance, and disposed to be generous and humane. We have already noted that this basic tenet made it difficult for the *philosophes* to deal realistically with the problem of evil. Frederick the Great, with his cynical assessment of 'this damned human race', could pierce at a single glance through the naïve benevolence of this enlightened estimate of man, but few who shared his general outlook could bring themselves to accept the hard realism of his view of human life. In the second place the *philosophes* insisted that our primary concern is with the life we now live, not with some hypothetical existence hereafter. They were contemptuous of preoccupation with heaven, though many of them retained a belief in the immortality of the soul. They wanted to alter the centre of interest; instead of regarding this life as a mere probation for another, men should strive to achieve the good life here and now. And this good life is within our reach; with the light of reason and the guidance of experience to show us the way, we can reasonably expect to achieve perfection. The necessary steps to this goal are few and simple: we must break the tyranny of ignorance and superstition, and overthrow the oppression of feudal authorities.

In their attack upon Christianity, the *philosophes* appealed both to the past and to the future. They wrote history in order to point a moral: the Dark Ages coincided with the period of Christian ascendancy. Their facts were often subordinate to their theories. When Raynal wrote his immensely popular *Philosophical and Political History of the Indies*, he gave a facile summary of all the virtues of other civilizations, and proved that contact with Christian intruders had invariably destroyed them. If the *philosophes* regarded the Christian past with aversion, they looked to the philosophic future with confidence. Man's true fulfilment lay neither behind him (in the golden age of antiquity) nor ahead (in the Christian expectation of paradise). It would be achieved when men substituted true values for false ones – self-fulfilment for vicarious atonement and the love of humanity for the love of God. By the latter part of the eighteenth century, the smiling confidence of its earlier years had been displaced by a restlessness which looked beyond the imperfections of the present to a future in which all wrongs would be righted – by man. God had been dethroned as judge, and posterity was exalted in his stead. It would be more than a time of fulfilment; it would provide the true vindication of the aspirations and endeavours of all enlightened men. 'Posterity', wrote Diderot, 'is for the philosopher what the other world is for the religious man,' and he could invoke its blessings in the spirit of ardent worship: 'O Posterity, holy and sacred! Support of the oppressed and unhappy, thou who art just, thou who art incorruptible, thou who wilt revenge the good man and unmask the hypocrite, consoling and certain idea, do not abandon me!' The circle of the devout might be small, but the effects of this faith were significant. This belief in an enlightened and liberated humanity strongly possessed the early leaders of the French Revolution – a political upheaval 'which functioned in the manner and took on in some sense the aspect of a religious revolution'.

This movement of thought, directed against traditional Christianity but inspired by religious motives of its own, had other important results. It challenged the principle of supernatural authority. It denied divine revelation, scoffed at miracles, and assaulted the chief dogmas of the faith. It profoundly affected the way in which religious authority was conceived and broke the coercive spirit in which theological systems had been enforced. Intolerance was discredited: the individual could no longer be compelled to submit to prevailing ecclesiastical systems. The churches forfeited their controlling influence in the intellectual life of Europe, and science was free to pursue its autonomous course. It encouraged far greater freedom in the pursuit of truth. It gave a new dignity to individual insight, even to intellectual heresy. It did so at the cost of aggravating the confusion in religious values which has been so conspicuous a feature of modern life. And it profoundly modified the standards and methods of all the churches.

So serious a threat to Christian convictions demanded a corresponding effort on the part of Christian apologists. The challenge was not entirely ignored, but in Catholic countries it bore no adequate relation to the danger. No one arose who could rebuke unbelief with the authority of Berkeley or Butler. Religion had lost its sense of immediacy, and in France there was no counterpart to Wesley. Church leaders were not indifferent to the rising tide of infidelity, but they tried to check it with methods which were harmful and ineffective. They appealed to the secular authorities. They invoked the regulations against those who wrote and distributed 'dangerous' works. This was merely an irritant; censorship was out of keeping with the spirit of the age, and even so massive a work as the *Encyclopedia* circulated in spite of everything that could be done to check it. Attempts were made to encourage the production of books which would answer the attacks on Christianity, but they achieved a limited success. In France there was an effort to answer ridicule in kind, but ridicule is not the best instrument of Christian apologetic, and against an adversary like Voltaire it proved to be a dangerous weapon. Serious works suffered from even more serious defects. The authors were too often unaware of what had been happening in the scientific fields to which their opponents appealed with special confidence. The *philosophes* had chosen the ground for the encounter. They also dictated the weapons that would be used, and the Christian apologists were usually unfamiliar with the chief issues involved. Their confusion was aggravated by the tendency of the critics to widen the debate to include legal, political, and economic issues. The apologists fell into errors of tactics, and forgot that successes at minor points did not constitute a major victory. Their weaknesses could often be attributed to faulty training. The long primacy of the Jesuit colleges had taught the clergy to rely unduly on authority alone, and it had also confused the distinction between words and things. They appealed to arguments either which carried little conviction, or which no one was disposed to dispute. Late in the century we find them implying that the truth of Christianity was less important than its usefulness, and that its high morality made it unnecessary to stress its theological claims. The enemies of the faith were scoffing at the absurdity of Christianity; its champions were busily defending secondary positions. This was a grave blunder in strategy. 'We cannot deny', wrote Benedict XIV, 'that today there are people who are notable for capacity and learning but they waste too much of their time in irrelevant matters or in unpardonable disputes among themselves, when it should be their sole aim to resist and destroy atheism and materialism.'

French culture was cosmopolitan in character, and the French language had become the language of cultivated Europe. Because French thought had so wide a vogue it is a temptation to assume that other continental countries merely aped the fashion which prevailed in Paris. But this would be an oversimplification. Germany, in particular, developed its own form of rationalism, and in due course produced much the most authoritative answer to the limited outlook of eighteenth-century thought. Here, as in France, English influence was very strong. Newton and Locke were supplemented by the Deists; when the latter had ceased to carry any weight at home, they still powerfully affected continental thought. Leibniz, however, was the chief source of the new outlook. He had been a kind of German counterpart to Newton, with a comparable authority in his own country, and his philosophy thoroughly permeated German thought. Unlike France, Germany had experienced a movement which revitalized religious life, Pietism. Many of the early exponents of rationalism had been reared in the traditions of Pietism and some were in conscious revolt against them. Tendencies which were strong elsewhere began to appear in Germany. Religion, it was claimed, could profitably be simplified; its traditional doctrines merely obscured the few essential truths which it proclaimed, and were the products of priestly fraud. God is pure reason; our reason, reflecting his, is a sufficient guide to all the problems of thought and conduct. The most influential of the early rationalists was Christian Wolff, who established the new views at Halle, the centre and citadel of Pietism. The claims of Christianity, he taught, had been advanced in an extreme form; there are many types of religion, and much can be said for most of them. If you doubt it, study the wisdom of Confucius: it vindicates the claims of human reason, and proves the sufficiency of moral principle. Among the middle classes such views found a ready welcome. Scepticism became fashionable and disbelief was rife.

In spite of this tendency the Enlightenment in Germany was, to a far greater extent than in France, a movement of reform within the churches rather than an attack on them from outside. For this reason, German rationalism did not merely attack the Scriptures; it studied them in a new spirit. A remarkable group of scholars pointed out the differences between the Old and New Testaments, and between the different parts of each Testament. They raised questions of authorship, examined the accuracy of disputed texts, and detected various strata in what had hitherto been accepted as flat and undifferentiated uniformity. They subjected prophecy and miracle to rigorous examination. Some of this was necessary pioneering work; much of it was vitiated by the limitations of the age. In defending the use of reason in biblical studies, the critics gave the impression that nothing else was needed. In dealing with revelation and with the miraculous or the supernatural, they applied canons of judgement which condemned their findings to superficiality. They lacked historical perspective and were devoid of any sense of wonder. Some of them were men of extreme, even of unbalanced, mind. Of one of them (K. F. Bahrdt) it has been said that he possessed great learning, but had neither sense, nor tact, nor humility, nor morals. But Semler, who was one of the most influential scholars of the later eighteenth century, did not outgrow his Christian faith, while Ernesti, Michaelis, and Eichhorn showed that it was not necessary to be a sceptic in order to be an able biblical scholar. Some of this criticism seemed extreme and even dangerous, but much of it came from within the Christian community. Its great service was to awaken a critical interest in Christian origins and in the figure of the founder of the faith. Both in spirit and in intention it was very different from the attacks launched by the French *philosophes*.

The most representative and perhaps the most widely influential figure in the development of the German Enlightenment was Gotthold Ephraim Lessing. His literary gifts were very great; he was the chief inspiration of the remarkable galaxy of poets and philosophers who for a few years gained for Germany an unchallenged pre-eminence in the intellectual world. Moreover, he profoundly affected German theology, and through it much of the thought of modern Protestantism. He turned to religious controversy when he was a man of established reputation, and his views were reinforced by the great authority of his name. In the years 1774–8 he published, under the title of the *Wolfenbüttel Fragments* (he was then librarian of the Duke of Brunswick's library at Wolfenbüttel) extracts from the works of Reimarus, a rationalist critic of the Bible of somewhat radical tendency. During the controversy which ensued, Lessing did not defend Reimarus's views. His primary object was to uphold the right of free discussion even of the most sacred subjects. Christianity should not be equated with the Bible; long before it had a written literature, the faith had shown itself a triumphant and transforming power. Christianity is thus greater than its documents. The convincing evidence of the truth of Christianity is the way it meets the needs of human nature, and as a result the religious spirit can regard without dismay the findings even of the most radical critics. Lessing's views did not carry conviction save in a rather limited circle, but their effect was seen in the much greater latitude thenceforth permitted theological writers. Lessing had also suggested new and important fields of investigation. The early history of the church, the formation of the New Testament canon, and the essential nature of the faith would all have to be re-examined. Lessing obtained even wider circulation for his characteristic views through his famous play, *Nathan the Wise* (1779). True religion, he implied, consists of love to God and man, and the true seeker can find God equally through any of the great faiths. Christianity, Judaism, and Mohammedanism are all avenues which lead to the truth. The distinctiveness of Christianity and its unique claims vanish; the consequences of such relativism appeared in the attitude of the provost of Berlin Cathedral, who taught that the Jews are really 'true Christians', since they believe in God, in immortality, and in virtue.

Lessing's last and most stimulating work was a little treatise called *The Education of Mankind* (1780). Its basic premiss is that no dogmatic creed can be regarded as final. Those who do not allow for development cannot appreciate the growth of religion. Every historical faith has played its part in developing the spiritual life of mankind. History reveals a definite law of progress. Occasional relapses may occur, but even they have a necessary share in leading the world onward to its ultimate goal. Only gradually could men grasp the fact that conscience is an inner voice, that virtue is its own reward, and that immortality is the necessary counterpart to the infinite value of the human soul. Such views were revolutionary to an age which had known only the rigidity of unyielding orthodoxy and the negative attacks of scepticism. The unhistorical rationalism of the early eighteenth century was discredited, and Lessing opened in all their attractiveness the significance of history and the importance of development. In doing so he gave a new direction to religious philosophy.

Immanuel Kant stands between two ages and in a sense belongs to both. He gathered together the significant strains in eighteenth-century thought and showed how they could be reconciled. He also opened the way for the developments which made the nineteenth century so brilliant a period in the history of philosophy. Kant, who lived an uneventful life as a professor at Königsberg, was a kindly man, convinced that the world can be made a much better place than it actually is. He was a product of the Age of Reason; he used its thought-forms, yet transcended its limitations. He saw the significance of natural law as Newtonian physics had unfolded it. He also appreciated the importance of Rousseau, who had revealed new depths in human nature and had exposed the meaning of man's moral nature. The two seemed poles apart. Yet Kant knew that as a matter of experience they could be held together. In one of his most celebrated sayings he declared that two things excited his awed reverence: the starry heavens above and the moral law within. He undertook to show that these two experiences could be united within a single framework of interpretation. He believed that he could concede the claims of scientific knowledge and yet acknowledge the rights of moral obligation; man could know the nature of a universe governed by natural law and yet experience the freedom of obeying the moral law.

Kant's first step was to define the way in which we know facts. He did not question the reality of scientific knowledge: the authority of Newton was too great to permit of any doubt on that score. Kant admitted the force of Hume's argument that the observation of nature entitles us to believe in probability but not in the uniformity of necessary law. By reason we cannot penetrate to the principles which rule the world. But Kant believed that such principles exist, even though he admitted that reason cannot find them. So he turned the problem around: he argued that instead of reason venturing out into the world to discover the laws which operate there, the facts of experience become knowledge only when they are organized by the principles which the mind itself provides. Whatever material sensation supplies to us must be thought out according to the categories which the mind itself affords. By reversing the way in which the mind is related to things Kant introduced a revolutionary change, and one result of this was to postulate a system of mechanical necessity. Kant, it will be seen, has deliberately limited knowledge in order to make it invulnerable to the kind of attack latent in Hume's thought. Thus there are many things of which, in the strict sense, man can never have exact knowledge. Whatever lies outside the realm of sensible experience, all the categories used by metaphysics and by natural theology, cannot be described as 'regulative'. But in addition to the realm of 'phenomenal' reality, Kant recognized another, that of 'noumenal' existence, and deliberately restricted the scope of the former in order to establish the validity of the latter. Insight is really more important than exact scientific knowledge, and Kant believed that what our moral experience discloses carries us far beyond the truths which phenomena reveal. 'I have therefore found it necessary', he wrote in a famous sentence, 'to deny *knowledge* in order to leave room for *faith*.' Our awareness of inescapable moral constraint is no less definite and much more important than the understanding of the material world as our senses reveal it to us. The moral law is unchanging and duty is an enduring and timeless absolute.

Having established the conditions which determine knowledge, Kant undertook to show how man's sense of obligation operates. Here his contrast between the phenomenal and the noumenal gains added importance. Man's awareness of the demands of duty is possible because he belongs to the noumenal no less than to the phenomenal world. This is what makes freedom possible, and without such freedom obligation would have no meaning. But freedom itself depends on other great realities, especially on the existence of God and the certainty of immortality. Kant has thus distinguished two realms of experience. In the world of phenomena man is subject to the necessities of natural law, but in the noumenal world he is free. The unity of man's life derives from the fact that these two spheres are distinguishable but in practice are related one to another. Moreover, in the final analysis, the realm of nature (governed by necessity) is subordinate to the realm of ends (ruled by purpose). This estimate of the relative significance of these two areas of experience is of primary importance in determining the character of Kant's thought. The wonder inspired by the starry heavens is great, but it is less than the reverence awakened by the moral law, and obedience to duty carries man far more deeply into the appreciation of reality than his grasp of the phenomenal world can possibly do.

We have already noted that Kant epitomized the spirit of the century that was passing and determined the objectives of the period about to begin. He was a child of the Age of Reason; and the theology which he erected on the foundation of moral obligation dealt with God, freedom, and immortality in terms suggested by that age. He differed from his age in asserting that we cannot *know* God or freedom or immortality in the sense in which the eighteenth century was convinced we could; but since they are the condition of our freedom we must always *believe* that they exist. Kant's problem was to re-establish the grounds of certainty, so rudely shaken by Hume's scepticism. He found it ultimately in God, where it can always be found. Because he was so firmly rooted in the eighteenth century, he could not begin with God; the presuppositions of the Age of Reason dictated that revelation must be earned by strenuous mental effort. So Kant started with man, and in human nature he found the way that led to the absolute. But he delivered the whole concept of reason from the narrow limitations which the eighteenth century had imposed upon it. Moreover, by affirming the supremacy of spirit over matter he bequeathed to the nineteenth century the problems with which it would chiefly be concerned.

Kant revitalized eighteenth-century thought from within, and so led to its ultimate transformation. There were other intellectual forces at work which, though not specifically theological in character, affected religious thought because they modified the outlook of the age. The Romantic revival radically altered the concept of 'nature'. Earlier writers had seen it as a sphere subject to the laws of science. By the end of the century it was regarded as the supreme manifestation of 'the sublime and beautiful'. The sense of wonder returned; the awe and majesty of mountain scenery were no longer despised as uncouth or barbarous. Nature even proved to be an incentive to worship, but it was not always the Christian God before whom men bowed in adoration. A vague pantheism became popular. Sentiment was more important than logic. The emotion might be religious in tone (as in some of the lyrics of 'Novalis'), but at best the relations of romanticism with Christianity were nebulous and ill defined. The supreme representative of the late eighteenth century was Goethe. His works clearly reflected many of the tendencies which modified the thought of the period. The amplitude of his mind and the range of his interests made him far more than a leading poet; he was one of the great spokesmen of his time, and he helped to fashion the temper of the new age. His early writings are typical of the *Sturm und Drang* (tempest and turmoil) movement, with its sentimentalism, its emotional confusion, and its defiance of convention. After his visit to Italy, classical and even pagan elements appeared in his thought. But fundamentally his outlook tended toward a Spinozan view of nature as 'the living garment of God', and this combined with a vague faith (derived from Leibniz) in the divine mission of human life. Following the end of the ascendency of rationalism there was unquestionably a revival of religious feeling, but some of it was scarcely Christian at all. The reinterpretation of the faith to an age which was seeking new bearings would be the task of Christian thinkers in the period that was about to begin.

In the closing years of the eighteenth century, the German people were awaiting a prophet who could relate with authority a living message to their sense of need. Frederick Schleiermacher proved to be that prophet. In a unique degree he possessed the gifts necessary for reinterpreting the Christian faith to a generation weary of rationalism and disillusioned by the course which the French Revolution had taken. His theological position was marked by strong emphasis on the subjective element in Christianity. In his *Speeches to the Cultured Despisers of Religion* (1799) he pointed out that the essence of the faith was not dogma but intuition and feeling. To cultivate philosophy and the arts was no substitute for maintaining the life of the soul. Those who prided themselves on their cultured emancipation from religion were as much the slaves of external appearances as the most conventional dogmatist. In his *Monologues* he declared that the free man is uncontrolled by any authority external to his own soul. The inner life should grow and flower with the free spontaneity of a plant, but Schleiermacher was persuaded that this kind of satisfying personal life was possible only in society. This emphasis on the individual and his realization within the community made Schleiermacher's message particularly acceptable to his age. In the renascence of German national life, his powerful preaching was a factor of great significance. To a unique degree, he understood the religious aspirations of the Prussian people, and satisfied them. But his influence was far more lasting than that of any patriot preacher. His *Speeches* rank with Kant's *Critiques* and Goethe's *Wilhelm Meister* as one of the most creative works of the period. His great work on *The Christian Faith* carries us beyond the bounds of our period, and indicates the way in which Schleiermacher not only dominated early-nineteenth-century thought but enriched the theology of Christendom.

16

Christianity and Culture
in the Baroque Age

ARTISTIC taste is proverbially inconstant. In the Victorian age it was fashionable to despise the art of the eighteenth century. Baroque architecture violated all the canons of criticism enunciated by John Ruskin. Rococo represented the final collapse of standards which were already degraded and debased. Eighteenth-century painting was dismissed as elegant but trivial. It was even assumed that eighteenth-century music suffered by comparison with the compositions of the nineteenth-century giants. A strong reaction, gathering momentum since the second decade of this century, has rectified the balance and has resulted in a juster appreciation of eighteenth-century achievements in all these fields. This change has been parallel to the recognition that the church life of that age cannot be ignored simply on the assumption that it was stagnating in torpor and sloth. Since many aspects of eighteenth-century art affected religious life and in turn were modified by it, the relationship between church and culture cannot be ignored. In certain areas the church was still a patron of the arts, and this was particularly true of the three fields in which the Baroque age achieved its greatest triumphs: architecture, sculpture, and music. Moreover, artistic achievements faithfully reflected the prevailing spirit; even where the influence of the church was least pronounced, the culture of the period cannot be neglected in a book like this: it indicates the nature of the world in which the church attempted to maintain its witness and worship.

Baroque architecture developed with a clear consciousness of its artistic aims, and with the assurance that it was supported by a strong tradition. Baroque owed its character to a combination of seemingly incompatible forces. It was the product of an age of contrasts. It developed in a society in which extremes balanced each other in uneasy equipoise. Blatant self-indulgence was matched by the ascetic self-denial of new religious orders. Science was extending its empire; so, apparently, was superstition. Charity flourished side by side with crime. It seemed as though the chief characteristics of civilization were splendour and squalor. Baroque architecture was the result of the interplay of a wide variety of aesthetic, religious, and social influences. It was the favoured style for great churches and for the palaces of princes, was considered appropriate both for monasteries and for courts. The large number of Baroque churches in southern Germany reflects the desire of churchmen to keep pace with secular rulers in appropriating the style which Louis XIV had established as the norm for kings. But Baroque was also the architecture of the Counter-Reformation. It spread across Europe with the Society of Jesus. At first it was cautious and restrained, a style suitable to the outposts of an army intent on reconquering lost ground. The note of assured triumph was present; it needed only the encouragement of success to rise in the high Baroque to a resonant chorus of victory. The style was thus the counterpart in stone and stucco of the Counter-Reformation; it stood for the church militant. It was also a style easily assimilated to the secular spirit.

Rome was the capital of Baroque art. Here it developed its distinctive features. Lavish decoration became the mark of the unfolding style; all details received the same richness of treatment, and could apparently claim the same degree of importance. The churches were embellished with painting on a scale to which there had hitherto been no parallel. The effect thus produced was enhanced by the lavish use of coloured marble. Metal work achieved a new intricacy as well as a new importance. The development of Baroque was the work of many architects and artists, but two of them gained unchallenged pre-eminence: Borromini (d. 1667) and Bernini (d. 1680). Borromini was the more fearless innovator of the two. His influence encouraged Baroque to venture on bold and even reckless departures from the conventions which had governed Renascence architecture. Bernini accepted the traditions which had recently prevailed, and within them created a school marked by dignity rather than by daring. He was unquestionably the commanding exponent of Roman Baroque in its full amplitude, and his influence remained pervasive till the advent of neo-classicism. In his finest creations he attempted to achieve an overwhelming emotional effect through a synthesis of various artistic media. Architecture and sculpture were brought into an intimate interdependence, and though painting had a subordinate role, it was used to heighten the sense of dignity, splendour, and movement. This synthetic approach to art was the most conspicuous characteristic of the Baroque period, and it formed the notable contribution of the Roman school.

The new style spread rapidly to every part of Europe. Italian architects carried it to France, Spain, Austria, Poland, and even to Russia. Wherever it went, it showed conspicuous powers of adaptation. Local schools fashioned variants of the style adapted to their building methods and materials, and to the temperament and tastes of each country. The Spaniards, with characteristic ardour and intensity, developed a type of Baroque which was arresting but extreme. In its capricious waywardness, its intricate elaboration, its reliance on fantastic decoration, it reached a point beyond which further progress was impossible, and the name of its chief exponent (José Churriguera, d. 1725) became a by-word for eccentricity allied with ornate ornamentation. French Baroque rapidly established its independence even of Italian example, and exerted an influence second only to that of the Roman school – if, indeed, it was second to any. When Bernini was invited to France to confer with Louis XIV about the building of the Louvre, his journey was like a royal progress, but the plans which he submitted were rejected. Louis felt that he had architects in Paris who could do just as well, if not better. The vogue of

French Baroque was due to its Gallic regard for the practical necessities of life, and hence to its greater attention to the arrangement and adornment of interiors. It reached its full splendour under Louis XIV. His palace at Versailles was more than the epitome of a particular style; it was the symbol of an entire era. It was lavish and pretentious, slightly false in feeling yet undeniably impressive in effect. That this, in all its pomp and pride, should be the setting for the court of 'the Most Christian King' suggests how thoroughly the secular standards of the age had permeated Christendom. Contemporaries associated French architecture chiefly with palaces and ornamental parks, but French architects designed a number of great churches which have become an important part of the Paris scene; the Invalides, the Val-de-Grâce, and Sainte-Geneviève (now the Panthéon).

In the Spanish Netherlands, Baroque enlisted the services of a great painter in Peter Paul Rubens, whose vast canvases typify many of the qualities which attract or repel the ordinary observer. Here we find the magnificence and movement, the pride and the pomp, the brilliant colouring and the technical versatility after which most Baroque painting aspired. Even the sensuousness of his very fleshly nudes was characteristic. In other fields Flemish art in this period was derivative and not entirely successful. It drew upon Italian, French, Spanish, and German sources, but its syncretism seldom represented a true synthesis.

German Baroque architecture was vigorous and impressive. It was the style favoured by every princeling who wished to see his court embellished in the fashionable manner. It is astonishing to notice how many German towns have a 'Residenz' or a 'Schloss' designed in imitation of Versailles. Often ancient cities acquired a wholly new character. In Dresden a series of brilliantly successful buildings – churches, palaces, public buildings – made the city one of the showplaces of the age. The Zwinger is still one of the most graceful of all attempts to capture in stone the courtly grace which eighteenth-century society accepted as its ideal. Würzburg, Bayreuth, Ansbach all show the way in which the new spirit changed the face of old cities. Not only individual towns, like Karlsruhe and Mannheim, but whole districts acquired a courtly atmosphere.

In Bavaria and Austria, the Catholic South of the Germanic world, Baroque art flourished with a warmth and splendour which has few parallels. It came from Italy and retained the grandiose dignity allied with airy movement characteristic of the finest Roman work. It was distinctively the art of princely circles. The palaces of Vienna – the Belvedere and the Schönbrunn – reflect the era when the Turkish menace had at last been driven far from the city gates. Salzburg was rebuilt as a Baroque town by Archbishop Wolf Dietrich, and in this he acted as a prince rather than as a churchman. And his colleagues, the abbots and bishops of Bavaria and Austria, were prompted by the same spirit. The buildings of ancient monasteries were swept away and replaced by resplendent new ones in the current sumptuous style. At Melk, where Prandtauer rebuilt the abbey, the magnificent marble hall, the sumptuous 'Golden Library', the fantastically colourful church embody the Baroque dream in its richest elaboration. The works of famous architects like Fischer von Erlach, Balthasar Neumann, and Prandtauer are scattered in marvellous profusion over southern Germany and Austria. But masterpieces like Fürstenfeldbruck and Vierzehnheiligen (the pilgrimage church of the 'Fourteen Holy Deliverers') tell only half the story. Almost every Bavarian village has its charming onion-towered church, often enriched with carvings and frescoes of genuine distinction.

Baroque architecture shared with other eighteenth-century media three conspicuous characteristics. In the first place, it stressed technique as an end in itself. With meticulous concern it concentrated on style, and valued ornament for its own sake. Secondly, it had a keen sense of pattern. It confined artistic creation within the bounds of conventional forms, such as the heroic couplet or the fugue. Thirdly, it valued what has been called 'eloquence' – an emphasis on expressiveness rather than on any attempt to stir profound emotions. This accounts for its almost pathological fear of 'enthusiasm'.

In architecture these basic principles explain the way in which space itself was treated. Buildings were part of the setting in which they were placed. The planning of open squares, the perspective given to streets, the use made of colonnades and fountains were regarded as inseparable from an entire conception of the way in which the works of man could be related to their environment. Baroque is also 'the art of the façade'. It had a keen perception of the monumental possibilities inherent in the outward face of a building, but it found in any flat space an opportunity for embellishment and decoration. Its use of clustered ornament and of surfaces broken up to provide sharp contrast meant that strong light was necessary to achieve to the full the architect's desired effect. Within as well as without, Baroque relied upon an abundance of elaborate elements: highly ornamented altars, intricate stucco work, painted ceilings, metal grilles, organ cases. At times they seem to break loose from all the restraints imposed by a sense of reality. At worst they degenerate into a confused orgy of twisting forms and brilliant colours; at best they culminate in a wonderful symphony of light, radiance, and exuberant joy. In such a style pictorial effects naturally predominate. Masses are arranged in a manner that will be deliberately spectacular. Dramatic movement, rather than stability, is the effect after which the architect strives. The whole church becomes a riot of light, colour, and movement, and this culminates in the high altar. Here the straining after the spectacular becomes most pronounced. Above the altar at Weltenburg on the Danube, St George on his charger slays a dragon which writhes in the contortions of death; the gilded figures are silhouetted against a brilliantly lighted background, and the whole is enclosed by dark twisting columns, which are crowned with gilded capitals and enriched with garlands of fruit and flowers. From the shadows the figures of holy men watch with wonder the deliverance which the saint effects.

It is daring in its lavish use of colour, contrast, and move-ment, and brilliant in the effect which it achieves. Unques-tionably it borders on the theatrical, but after its own fashion it is also devout. Man is human and must have his ideals expressed in human form.

As a focal point of attention, the cupola was second in importance only to the altar. It gave to the silhouette of the building the swelling lines beloved of Baroque architects. In the interior it offered unrivalled scope for the play of light and colour. In Salzburg cathedral the nave is kept deliber-ately subdued in order that the flood of light in the dome and the choir may be duly emphasized. At Neresheim, the cupola is so lavishly covered with frescoes that it seems as though the heavens have opened and the celestial hosts are hovering just above the congregation. But this brilliant style, so prodigal in its use of light and colour and movement, raises certain disconcerting doubts. There is no suggestion here that the service of God – and consequently his worship – has any place for austerity or discipline. The pomp and pride of high Baroque are unchastened by any disturbing sense that 'the lust of the flesh and the lust of the eyes and the pride of life' are passing away. The golden saints, the stucco clouds, the marble cherubs belong to no world save this. The angels have a solidity and even a sensuousness which emphatically belie their celestial nature, and the spectator cannot suppress the wish that 'this too, too solid flesh would melt . . .'. It may not be necessary wholly to repudiate the world; it is hardly desirable to come to terms with it with such enthusiasm. Baroque architecture had achieved its most conspicuous triumphs in the palaces of kings. Versailles was its supreme symbol, and in the service of the church it never wholly escaped from the secular spirit which had infected it in the courts of princes. It had begun its course as the architectural counterpart of the Counter-Reformation. By the beginning of the eighteenth century its achievements no longer glorified God; they magnified the kings who ruled by divine right.

Along certain lines Rococo pushed the evolution of

Baroque art to its logical extreme. Individual imagination was freed from all restraints. Absolute freedom became the distinguishing mark of the new phase. Flexibility and movement passed into irregularity of rhythm. The love of broken lines was pushed beyond the point which the monumental qualities of Baroque could sanction. There was a subtle change, as more intimate and elegant forms replaced the pomp and dignity of the older style. Gracefulness and charm became the conspicuous features of architectural detail. A playful waywardness marked the subsidiary arts which played so large a part in eighteenth-century civilization. Rococo was partly a reaction against the dignified pomp of the Baroque age; the grandiose palaces were not comfortable places in which to live, and Rococo aimed at providing a domestic setting where comfort could be combined with elegance and charm. The frivolous and sophisticated spirit reflected in Watteau's paintings and in Louis Quinze furniture affected church architecture as well. An unrestrained gaiety is the distinguishing feature of Rococo decoration in churches no less than in villas. Fantasy bids defiance to rules and symmetry. Carving and ornamentation multiply without restraint, and decorative ingenuity is carried to its furthest limits. In 'Die Wieskirche' ('The Church in the meadow' which Zimmerman built near Oberammergau) and at Zwiefalten, Ottobeuren, and Waldfassen, the style reached its culmination.

A reaction was inevitable. In the final phase of Rococo, much of the playfulness disappears. Balance and calm reappear, without displacing gracefulness and charm. The revived interest in classical art was already chastening the waywardness of fantasy in ornamentation. The reaction gathered momentum; by 1780–90 the severities of the neo-classical movement had replaced the warmth and colour of Baroque and Rococo.

In England, the Restoration opened a period of great architectural distinction. The Fire of London (1666) created such an opportunity as fortune has seldom afforded an architect, and in Sir Christopher Wren England was fortunate enough to have a man capable of turning it to full account. The latter part of the seventeenth century thus saw the establishment of a school of church building faithful to the spirit of the age and admirably adapted to the needs of the Church of England. It is in churches that we can study most fully the growth and development of the English variant of Baroque architecture. This outburst of creative effort does not subside until the middle of the eighteenth century. In it there are two distinguishable phases. For more than a generation Wren dominated the picture. Thereafter, for an equal length of time, a succession of able men carried on the tradition which he had inaugurated. All of them were profoundly influenced by him. In 1708 Wren wrote a famous memorandum on the building of churches. The extent of his authority can be judged by the degree to which his successors were content to be governed by the principles he laid down.

Wren had an opportunity such as comes to few men of artistic genius. Probably no other architect has left such splendid and extensive evidence of his powers. Yet in architecture Wren was an amateur. He had had no such intensive professional training as James Gibbs received in Italy. Wren was a scientist and a mathematician, and had proved his capacity in both fields. When he first began to ponder the problem of repairing the ruinous Old St Paul's, he made a trip to Paris. He met Bernini. He had a chance to study the work of the elder Mansard, who was just completing the Val-de-Grâce. It is important to remember that the great English architects of this period – Wren, Hawksmoor, and Vanbrugh – all looked to France for artistic inspiration. It is even more important to observe the highly individual way in which Wren used the ideas which he borrowed.

Though the Fire gave Wren a magnificent opportunity, it did not assure him free scope. He laid out a composite plan for a new London; for all its far-sighted imagination it foundered on vested interests and the intricacies of land titles. His first and favourite design for St Paul's was rejected. The persistence of the ancient groundplan of the City complicated his task at every point. Narrow streets and congested conditions robbed him of the asset which Baroque architects particularly coveted: the kind of setting which would impart the maximum impressiveness to the buildings which occupied them. Wren's churches had to be designed for a great variety of sites, usually small in size, often irregular in shape, and seldom standing free of other buildings. In one sense this simplified his task. It was not necessary to design churches in which every part would require equal consideration. With unfailing skill Wren fixed upon the elements which deserved attention: the tower, the interior, perhaps a façade. This was a blessing in disguise. The pressure of work would have made it impossible to design in complete detail so many churches.

As soon as the rubble was cleared away, the immediate task was to provide inexpensive 'tabernacles' in which the people could temporarily worship. Four years after the Fire serious rebuilding began. An increased tax on coal provided the necessary funds, and work began with a rush. Wren built fifty-four churches in London. (Thirty-four of them survived till 1940.) The initial pressure can be judged by the sums spent on construction. In the first seventeen years of the rebuilding programme (1670–87), over £264,000 of public funds were required; in the next thirteen years, only £53,000. These figures, of course, tell only half the story, since they do not include the money provided by vestries and by individual parishioners. Private gifts would be forthcoming as business life returned to normal, and they would be inspired by the need for furnishings and decoration. A remarkable feature of the vast enterprise was the skill with which Wren husbanded his financial resources. He never spent money without making sure that its expenditure would contribute in the greatest possible measure to the total effect. His churches represent an ingenious combination of strictly utilitarian building with lavish decoration where it would serve his purposes. Of even greater interest is the way Wren solved in his churches an infinite variety of architectural problems. The irregularity of the sites meant that no basic pattern would serve all his needs. To study the groundplans of his churches is to be astonished at the ingenuity with which he experimented with arrangements of internal space. St Stephen's Walbrook (1672-3) is essentially a small rectangular room; by dexterous handling of various features Wren created the effect of nave, aisles, and crossing, and the use of slender columns to sustain a graceful dome gives an impression of dignity and spaciousness in marked contrast with the apparently meagre opportunity the site afforded.

Wren's resourcefulness is particularly apparent in his towers and spires. Many of them were built later than the churches which they adorn; his mastery of his medium had fully matured, and he was free from the kind of pressure to which he had been subject immediately after the Fire. Some of his towers are perfectly plain; some have parapets enriched with urns or obelisks; some have bell turrets, often ingeniously elaborated, often placed on domes, pyramids, or steps; some are surmounted by spires, often built up step by step, sometimes forming a true spire in stone, sometimes sheathed in lead, sometimes concave in outline, sometimes convex. One tower (St Magnus the Martyr) has lantern, dome, and spire. Yet any attempt at classification falsifies the picture. Each of Wren's towers is different from all the rest. The same can be said of his churches – he never duplicated his designs – and his fertility in conception appears most fully where the scope might seem to be most restricted.

Wren's masterpiece, of course, is St Paul's. For over two hundred and fifty years its great dome, crowned by a stone lantern and golden ball and cross, has dominated the London skyline and has been the symbol of the City's life. The west front consists of a double-storey portico flanked by two lesser towers, beautifully proportioned and skilfully designed to emphasize the rotundity of the dome. The external walls continue the double-storey treatment of the west front, and the transepts have graceful porticos of their own. In the interior, Wren supported his dome on eight magnificent arches, resting on eight massive piers, and forming an octagon at the crossing of the nave and transepts. By creating a great sense of space and height, Wren achieved a notable degree of dignity. The Baroque character of the building appears particularly in the decorative ornamentation, which is both sumptuous and restrained.

Quite apart from his cathedral and his churches, Wren left enough work to justify a distinguished reputation. Greenwich Palace, the new part of Hampton Court Palace, and the library of Trinity College, Cambridge, all illustrate his versatility and his power, but probably his church architecture gives the best indication of the quality of his work and of the greatness of his achievement. We have already noted that Wren was in a sense a self-trained architect. He rapidly gained a complete mastery of his profession, but increasing competence in no way diminished his inventive fertility. His work never became stereotyped. He never became the victim of his own facility. Imaginative freshness was as much the mark of his later and more assured achievements as it was of his earlier and tentative experiments. The forms he used were those which the Renascence had bequeathed to him. The Palladian tradition (domesticated in England by Inigo Jones) appealed forcibly to him, but he used familiar elements in a strikingly resourceful and individual way. Above all, Wren was a structural artist of unrivalled skill, and in addition knew how to endow structure with proportion and style. He had the secret of imparting grace to his buildings. He was helped by the spirit of his age, with its sense of balance; he was fortunate in the materials he used – Portland stone, or warm brick set off by stone trimming. But the true secret of his success was his own consummate sense of proportion. The distinctive quality of his achievement can be appreciated by comparing the English variant of the Baroque style with its continental counterpart. Southern Baroque was ruled by ideals of dramatic movement and of masses arranged in a deliberately spectacular manner; Wren's work is characterized by serenity and a sense of repose.

From the Restoration to the Regency Wren dominated

English architectural standards. His example was largely responsible for the colonial style in the American colonies. He has been called 'the first of the moderns', and Professor Richardson has pointed out that contemporary Swedish architecture follows Wren's principles 'almost to the letter'. For most people his great achievement was to endow the City of London with a magnificent silhouette. This is his fitting monument.

The first half of the eighteenth century saw the tradition of Wren carried forward by a number of able architects. Sir John Vanbrugh, indeed, forms an explosive interlude. Much of his work, with its vigorous movement, its sensational scale, and its sense of drama is closer to continental Baroque architecture than it is to the school of Wren. In Hawksmoor and Gibbs the building of English churches pursued the line of development which Wren had laid down. Nicholas Hawksmoor was an architect of great merit and of strong individuality, but even in his most original churches (such as St George's, Bloomsbury) he follows to the minutest detail the principles laid down in Wren's memorandum on church building. In Hawksmoor English Baroque reached its fullest development. He built in an age which was avid for sermons. Wren's churches, too, were primarily designed to make certain that the congregation would hear the preacher, but Hawksmoor imparted to his churches an added rhetorical quality which accentuated the purpose which they were designed to serve. There is a sombre magniloquence about his churches which contrasts strongly with the serene repose of Wren's best work. It was James Gibbs's good fortune to build some of his finest churches on some of the most conspicuous sites in the world. No visitor to London can miss St Martin-in-the-Fields or St Mary-le-Strand, and few churches have acquired a greater fame. In St Martin's, Gibbs designed a splendid portico and surmounted it with a tower and steeple in which an impression of stability is combined with a great sense of skyward thrust. In Gibbs's work many of the qualities of eighteenth-century architecture appear to their greatest advantage. It is obvious that a distinguished tradition is under firm control; its marks are distinction, serenity, reticence, and admirable finish.

Most of the important church architecture of the period from 1660 to 1750 is to be found in London and its suburbs. Here the need was greatest; reconstruction after the Fire and the growth of the capital made building an urgent need. But after the turn of the century fewer churches were erected in London than might reasonably have been expected, and elsewhere little was done. The old market towns were sufficiently provided with ancient churches, and few recognized the challenge posed by the cities springing up in the midlands and the north. Gibbs built a fine church at Derby. Archer (one of the ablest of the later exponents of the school) built St Philip's, Birmingham (now the cathedral). But for the most part the eighteenth century showed little zeal for building churches. Georgian architecture was mainly domestic: impressive mansions and attractive country houses. Bath is the supreme example of what the eighteenth century could achieve in orderly and elegant town planning. This serene and stately kind of architecture is a reflection of the spirit of the age. It valued dignity, elegance, personal prestige and comfort; it was not interested in church construction.

A distinguishing feature of Baroque religious art – in England as well as on the continent – was the wealth of decoration with which it was enriched. The subsidiary arts of sculpture, wood-carving, joinery, and plaster work achieved a high level of excellence and contributed to the impression of sustained luxuriance created by the churches of the period. Protestantism, of course, imposed a measure of restraint from which Latin craftsmen were free. There was no place for the riot of statuary and painting which marked Catholic churches in southern Europe. In the Church of England, the wood-worker could embellish the pulpit, the lectern, the font cover, usually the organ case, and sometimes the reredos. The plaster-worker had his opportunity in the ceiling. The sculptor executed memorial tablets and tombs. The craftsmen sometimes worked under the immediate supervision of the architect; sometimes they were

allowed considerable independence. The best known practitioner of these lesser arts was Grinling Gibbons, who for half
a century (1670–1722) was the leading wood-worker in
England. He executed the stalls and screens at St Paul's, the
reredos at St James's, Piccadilly, and the decorations in the
libraries of Trinity College, Cambridge, and Queen's College, Oxford. In addition to wood carving, Gibbons worked
both in marble and in bronze, and at the height of his fame
operated what was in effect an extensive business in church
furnishings. This type of craftsmanship was strongly influenced by the schools of Holland and Flanders. In tomb
sculpture, Baroque example was especially apparent. In the
second and third decades of the eighteenth century, a
number of important artists appeared in England. Rys-
brach, Scheemakers, and Roubiliac were highly accomplished sculptors. The first two brought with them the outlook as well as the skills of the great Flemish school; the third
had been trained in France and south Germany, and consequently represented a closer contact with Bernini, who in
all types of sculpture was the most powerful source of
Baroque inspiration. All three men are represented by
tombs in Westminster Abbey. The building is not a suitable
setting for Baroque sculpture, but even those who dislike the
Baroque spirit can appreciate the skill with which a daring
subject is often handled – as in Roubiliac's Nightingale
monument. No one is likely to depreciate the contribution
of this school who knows Roubiliac's marvellous statue of
Sir Isaac Newton in the ante-chapel of Trinity College,
Cambridge.

The musical eminence of this period is unquestioned; it
showed itself only intermittently in the field of church
music. In the Roman Catholic world polyphonic liturgical
music had reached a culminating point in Palestrina (d.
1594). During the seventeenth century, new forms of expression were developed. Opera opened up exciting possibilities.
The spirit of the Counter-Reformation encouraged musicians
to widen their appeal by experimenting with these novel and
arresting forms. Popular taste supported this tendency. In

church the public expected a type of music comparable in richness of texture with what they heard in the opera house. Secular standards and a secular spirit began to invade church music. By its histrionic potentialities, the mass invited dramatic treatment; when composers responded with music conceived in the same spirit as the opera, worshippers tended to become an audience rather than a congregation. Pergolesi (d. 1736) wrote both secular and sacred music, and in his *Stabat Mater* his style differed in no essential respect from that which he used in comic opera. Technical skill was no longer closely related to the meaning of the words. Whether the occasion was frivolous or solemn, the character of the music remained much the same; it had ceased to be a great medium for the expression of religious emotion.

The change which was taking place can best be appreciated if we compare Haydn or Mozart with Palestrina. In the eighteenth century, the musician is far less dependent on the church both for his livelihood and for his medium. Music has achieved a far greater technical range, and is better able to speak wholly for itself. This is apparent in the development of the orchestra and in the works written for it. Even in sacred compositions, such as Haydn's masses, the music stands in its own right and can be enjoyed for its own sake. It may intensify the meaning of the words with which it is allied but this is not always so. Haydn had a genuine, if not particularly profound, religious feeling, and there is no trace of insincerity in what he wrote. But his music is not the inevitable expression of intense emotion, and a work like the *Creation* does not awaken a deep religious response in the listener. Its beauty is above question, but it is not the inevitable expression of genuine faith. Music, written primarily for the joy of making music, remains secular, no matter what its ostensible purpose may be.

Since Mozart was apparently incapable of writing poor music, his compositions for the church contain much highly expert and very beautiful work. They belong to his early period; they were the product of his humiliating service at the court of the Prince-Archbishop of Salzburg. They show a firmer intellectual grasp than Haydn's work in the same field, and they probe religious feeling more profoundly. The fact that Mozart sought lay rather than clerical patronage, and that by preference he found an outlet for his transcendent gifts in instrumental or operatic, not in ecclesiastical, compositions, reflects the new relationship in which music and the church now stood. But in his *Requiem Mass*, his last and one of his greatest works, poignancy of religious feeling reaches an overpowering intensity. Mozart composed it on his death-bed, apparently with the conviction that it was his requiem in more respects than one. The music interprets the words so profoundly that its beauty is always subordinate to its penetrating truth.

In the Protestant world, church music attained during this period a peak of supreme distinction. This was particularly true of Germany, but is partly true in England also. The turmoil of the middle years of the seventeenth century interrupted the smooth development of the English school of music. William Byrd and Orlando Gibbons had been expert in polyphonic composition. Their music had been marked by solemnity and restraint, but to the new generation it seemed deficient in range. Restoration music had far greater powers of expression. It could convey a wider range of ideas and emotions. The new media were not entirely appropriate to church music, nor were they always under firm control. Blow, Wise, and Humphrey wrote fine anthems, but they were lacking in technical resourcefulness, and their inability to sustain and develop the themes which they introduced creates a disjointed effect. Perhaps this resulted from the interruption of the English musical tradition. Even Henry Purcell, the most eminent composer of this period, was not wholly free from this defect. He composed many anthems, often in the prevailing style of short solo verses alternating with choruses, but he could successfully venture on a much grander manner. His *Te Deum and Jubilate in D* (for voices, strings, trumpets, and organ) is an impressive epitome of the notable characteristics of Restoration church music. He achieves a wonderful variety of expression; his music, which is always marked by freshness and vigour, interprets the words with insight as well as fidelity.

Handel, though not an Englishman by birth, was certainly one by adoption. His German musical background had been modified by Italian influences, especially by the prevailing enthusiasm for opera. Its visual and dramatic possibilities strongly attracted him. When circumstances compelled him to turn to oratorio, he did not wholly abandon the operatic style. Opera and oratorio have different aims: instead of directly representing a dramatic incident, an oratorio reflects in the heroic vein on past events. Its appropriate mood is thanksgiving for deliverance or exultation over victory achieved. Most of Handel's oratorios are based on Old Testament incidents, which he used as a pretext for introducing elements which are frankly operatic in character. Probably prevailing fashions rather than personal preferences persuaded Handel to write religious music. He never wholly subdued the theatrical style appropriate to the stage. He most nearly succeeded in the *Messiah*. This was his only oratorio based on a Christian theme; here the inner significance of his subject, rather than its external features, arrested his attention. But the triumphant security which marks his music is usually secular rather than religious in spirit.

The magnificent achievements of German church music are primarily due to Johann Sebastian Bach, but Bach can be understood only as the culmination of a great tradition. The Reformation opened a new line of musical development. Germany was cut off from cultural dependence on Rome, and was untouched by Palestrina's complex and mystical type of church music. The worship of God, said Luther, must be intelligible to the people, and this presupposed a new beginning. The members of the congregation must be able to understand the words and to participate in the music. Hymn-singing was not an innovation, but Luther made it the foundation of a new type of church music. Once established, it proved itself a creative and adaptable tradition. The seventeenth century saw a notable outburst of

vitality in both poetry and music. Johann Heermann (d.
1647) composed the hymn ('O blessed Jesus, how hast thou
offended') which, set to music by Johann Crüger (d. 1662),
was incorporated with such effect in Bach's *St Matthew
Passion*. J. Rist (d. 1667), J. Franck (d. 1677) and, above all,
Paul Gerhardt (d. 1676) greatly enriched German religious
poetry, while Schop, M. Franck, and Crüger provided
music comparable in quality with the words.

Church music was not restricted, of course, to congregational hymns, but few composers escaped the influence of
these chorales. Many had no desire to do so; a few responded
to the ideas coming from Italy. Though the strength of the
Lutheran tradition made it relatively impervious to secular
influences, a number of distinguished composers were ready
to explore the possibilities of the new style. G. P. Telemann,
a contemporary of Bach, was director of the opera house at
Hamburg, and achieved great fame by his operatic compositions. Heinrich Schütz (d. 1672), who had studied in Italy,
believed that the best features of various types of music
could successfully be combined. His limited use of chorales
probably reflects his Italian training, but he was certainly
no slavish imitator of foreign fashions. He had mastered the
new techniques, and his creative capacities taught him to
fashion from them a personal medium of expression. The
impressive feature of his work is the skill with which he
handled it. Even when it apparently offered him least latitude, his music never suggests that his creative fertility has
been cramped. In *The Seven Last Words of Christ*, Schütz
composed a work of solemn beauty and great imaginative
boldness, but when he turned to the Passion story he reverted
to a more archaic manner. Perhaps he detected the threat to
German religious music latent in Italian operatic style.
Within the somewhat straitened limits of the older liturgical Passion narrative, he composed three settings of the
story which for sureness of touch and dramatic power are
worthy forerunners of Bach's great Passions.

The chorales remained the central element in the Lutheran musical tradition and their educational influence was

great. They were well known; even a musical phrase or two could awaken profound emotions. They could consequently be used in a great variety of ways. Association made even very complex polyphonic composition intelligible. A chorale melody might provide the theme for an organ prelude, and thus this abstract type of music would be invested with a wealth of religious meaning. Chorales could be used in cantatas. They could be incorporated in settings of the Passion. The chorale, indeed, had become the most important structural feature of Lutheran church music. Buxtehude was one of the composers who appreciated the immense potentialities latent in this form of music. The great hymn tunes belonged in the churches and would awaken emotions appropriate to worship. The love of the familiar would lead the congregation to appreciate what was new. Buxtehude used the chorale prelude as a means of confirming the religious experience and enlarging the musical knowledge of the people.

Bach was not an innovator. He distrusted the ornate Italian style which had been gaining ground. He was content to rely on traditional German methods, but he used them with a skill and flexibility which were unique, and infused into them a new and vital spirit. In particular he proved that the possibilities of the chorales were almost unlimited. Handel and Telemann were prepared to dispense with them because the new age had no place for their antique dignity. Bach, however, showed that they could be used in an infinite variety of ways, and that they provided an inexhaustible source of religious and musical inspiration.

As cantor of the school and church of St Thomas in Leipzig, Bach was expected to compose cantatas as well as produce them. In this field alone his output was staggering. In his cantatas he often used both the words and tunes of chorales as the basis of his work, but he did not restrict himself to any single pattern or to any one source of inspiration. Sometimes he based his cantatas on the Christian Year, sometimes on a Biblical incident, but his object was always to encourage reflection on the inner meaning of his theme. His melodic inventiveness, his harmonic skill, his ingenuity in weaving together the human voice and its instrumental accompaniment never fail, but the notable feature of his religious music is its combination of thoughtfulness with spiritual integrity. In his organ preludes he also made impressive use of themes from the chorales. Some of these preludes were merely introductions to the hymns when sung by the congregation in church. Others were elaborate movements closely related to what he had already done in his cantatas. Still others were complex compositions in their own right. All illustrate Bach's unrivalled power of exploring the nobility and beauty latent in these great religious themes. In his Passions also Bach showed the sensitivity and skill with which he could introduce chorales into a massive and intricate work. Here they served two important functions. They gave the congregation a part in the performance: a part which ordinary people could understand and in which they would participate. They also promoted reflection; the onward sweep of the tragic events was halted to permit the people to meditate on what they had heard.

Bach composed at least two settings of the Passion story; he may have written others, but if so they have not survived. At this point Bach inherited and developed a musical and liturgical tradition of considerable antiquity. In its oldest forms, the Passion was a dramatic narrative set forth in plainsong, and forming a part of the celebration of the mass during Holy Week. This strain reached its culmination in the great Latin works of Palestrina and Byrd. Allied to it, but presented in the vernacular, were the Motet Passions of the seventeenth century. A new type, the Oratorio Passion, offered greater scope in every respect. Its range was far greater and its dramatic possibilities were immense. It was a form of service which could stand in its own right, independent of other liturgical elements. Its impact on the hearer was powerful and perfectly exemplified one of the points at which Lutheran church music departed from Catholic practice. It did not attempt to shield the worshipper from direct contact with the uncompromising realities of the tragic narrative. Whereas much Roman liturgical music enveloped the central events in a mystical atmosphere, Lutheranism saw in the stark realism of the story an essential ingredient in the believer's education. More and more the Passion had become a distinctively German and Protestant medium. It had also become highly complex. Recitatives based on the Gospel narrative were interrupted by meditative arias, duets, chorales, symphonias. The shouts of the crowds were rendered with dramatic intensity, yet always with profound psychological insight.

The range and power of Bach's Passions defy analysis. But these works were written for performance as an act of worship. When we turn to his *Mass in B Minor* we are probably in another realm. Most of his Latin church music (his Magnificat and his masses) was written for performance as part of Lutheran worship. But the scale of the *Mass in B Minor* transcends the limitations which a church service necessarily imposes. Bach drew upon every resource available to him; with skill and power he exploited every type of composition, and throughout he holds the attention of his hearers by the religious intensity with which every part of the liturgy is felt and interpreted. This is an ideal of musical worship which oversteps all considerations of time and place. It is an act of devotion and praise which Bach, and Bach alone, could have composed.

Bach's greatness is compounded of many elements. He could combine the sacred and the secular without jeopardizing the mystical wonder of the one or the dramatic intensity of the other. He could fuse in one the popular elements supplied by the chorales and the aristocratic elements represented by consummate technical skill. He could carry realism to its utmost limits, yet he never overstepped the bounds of liturgical propriety. He was at once a daring innovator and a 'perfect formalist' – the master of both his subject matter and his form. He showed that Palestrina's beauty (always mystical but often vague) and Handel's vigour (forceful but somewhat material) could be fused in an art which surpassed the farthest reach of either. He accomplished it with an authority which imparted a touch of finality to almost everything he wrote. The firm assurance is more than a product of supreme skill. Bach offers an interpretation of life which transcends the limitations to which the work of lesser men is subject. The central thread which unifies the amazing skill, subtlety, and penetrating insight of his works is the motif of faith. He was fundamentally a religious man. To compose music was an act of faith; to perform it was an act of worship.

Bach was the greatest of church musicians. In a sense he was also the last. As we have seen, the relationship between the church and music was changing. Other patrons competed for the service of the arts; often they offered greater latitude and seemingly more exciting opportunities. Those who now composed religious music regarded it as one interest among many others, and the contagion of the secular spirit increasingly affected what they wrote. In Catholic society the change had taken place even earlier; Palestrina was the last of the great musicians who found their vocation in the service of the church. In Protestant Germany the great Lutheran tradition began to crumble under the eroding effect of new influences. In the latter part of his life Bach relied on methods and appealed to standards which his contemporaries were forsaking for the more elegant music favoured by the Age of Reason. In religious music Bach represents the summit of achievement; after him the descent was rapid.

17

Epilogue

THE age which esteemed reason, order, and stability above
all things ended in one of the most convulsive upheavals of
human history. The French Revolution was not a sudden
revulsion against the aristocratic setting of eighteenth-
century life. It was the product of forces long at work. It
drew its inspiration and its guiding principles from the Age
of Reason. Many of its leaders were animated by the spirit
of Voltaire and Rousseau, and dreamed of a society re-
fashioned according to the pattern which the philosophers
had devised. In trying to rebuild they often destroyed, and
when the cataclysm was over, most of Europe had to recon-
struct the fabric of its life. In the light of what happened,
how are we to assess the consequences of the Age of Reason
for the Christian Church?

In visible status the church had suffered seriously; no
further reverses seemed likely to depress its position. Everywhere its independence had declined. The authority of the
pope had sunk so low that in international affairs he had
ceased to count even as a moral force. He could either be
ignored or harried with high-handed insolence. In dealing
with church affairs the enlightened despots had consulted
their own convenience. They had initiated such reforms as
suited them, and had reduced to a minimum the contacts
of their churches with Rome. In their attacks upon the
Jesuits they had shown with what contempt they were prepared to treat the champions of papal authority. But this
process had not yet reached its nadir. Before Napoleon, no
one had dared to drag the pope at the chariot wheels of
imperial power. Yet the humiliation of Pius VII paved the
way for subsequent developments. Legitimate monarchs,
who had shared a similar fate, looked with a new sympathy
on the legitimate head of the church. The pattern of the new

age would be an alliance between throne and altar: monarchy would uphold the church, and the church would
consecrate lawful authority. The evidence that a new day
had dawned was furnished by the respect with which
Cardinal Consalvi was received at the Congress of Vienna.
In the preceding age, papal representatives had been firmly
excluded from every important international conference.
But appearances can be deceptive. After all, in England the
alliance between church and state had been correspondingly
intimate. Since both had suffered, each had relied on the
other for support. Yet by the eighteenth century it was clear
that the state could act as though the church were its
department of religious and moral affairs. The religious
revival which followed the French Revolution remained in
its official phases a pragmatic programme. Restored rulers
were glad enough 'to wrap the tendrils of tradition about
their shaken thrones', but their attitude to religion itself
was no more sincere and no more enthusiastic than that of
Napoleon. The ancient problem of church and state was not
solved, it merely reappeared in a different guise. It assumed
one form under the enlightened despots, another under the
revolutionary governments and the empire of Napoleon, and
yet another when legitimacy became the watch-word. The
contribution of the Age of Reason persisted. Rationalism
and traditionalism were still at enmity; the city of man
eclipsed the City of God; the authority of reason was
regarded as superior to the authority of revelation. Secular
governments invoked the church insofar as it suited their
needs; they were very cautious about endorsing traditional
doctrines. De Bonald claimed that in civilized society religion established order on a theocratic foundation. Joseph de
Maistre treated papal supremacy as the cardinal doctrine of
the new traditionalism, but such attempts to derive lay and
ecclesiastical authority from a common religious source carried limited conviction. There could be no agreed philosophy of reaction. The ancient problem merely assumed its
modern guise.

The prevailing spirit of the church likewise changed, yet

it still bore the stamp of the eighteenth century. In England the sober virtues of the Hanoverian church were distasteful both to the Evangelicals and to the Tractarians of the next century, yet the Church of England did not quickly escape the influence of Joseph Butler and even of William Paley. The temper and outlook of the Roman Church were similarly modified. The security of the eighteenth century had vanished. The churches that had passed through the fires of adversity were far more alert to the needs of the age, far less content to rely on inherited resources or traditional authority. For the papacy the Age of Reason had been a period of impotence, even of humiliation, but temporal weakness had been compatible with a humane and tolerant outlook. After the great upheaval a new temper prevailed. The spirit of the Curia was reactionary and illiberal. It was preoccupied with authority, with prestige, and with power; and its crowning achievement was the proclamation of the infallibility of the pope.

It is too easily assumed that during the period with which we have been concerned the religious life of Christendom was largely moribund. The facts do not support the assumption. It is true that revivalism and rationalism were in uneasy tension. The authority of reason often encouraged an attitude which was complacent when it was not arrogant, and which despised mystery because it was enamoured of logic. But this is only a part of the story, a part often exaggerated and caricatured. Many of the greatest devotional classics in the English language were written in this period. In hymnody the Age of Reason stands pre-eminent. In comparison with the hymns of Watts and Doddridge, the Wesleys, Cowper and Newton, the praise of the nineteenth century seems lush, sentimental, and introspective. The Methodist movement and the evangelical revival contributed mightily to the awakening of religious vitality. Even the contribution of Bishop Butler, reasonable and slightly sombre though it be, has enriched the spiritual resources of the Anglo-Saxon race. In Germany, we find rationalism and the evangelical spirit in the same uneasy equipoise. Pietism was a form of zeal peculiarly susceptible to distortion; in some quarters it created a disposition to be content with private experience, preoccupied with personal triumphs or failures, and indifferent to the needs of the world. But it never left rationalism an undisputed field, and both these forces powerfully contributed to the modern outlook. In France the confident rationalism of the eighteenth century awakened no adequate reply. Official Christianity seemed nerveless and confused. The champions of orthodoxy were mute. But this is no fair test of what the Roman Church accomplished in replenishing the reservoirs of spiritual life. In the early part of our period, a number of notable religious orders were founded, some of the most distinguished of them in France. In St Alphonsus Liguori the Italian church produced a religious leader whose qualities have endeared him to many of his fellow-believers, and whose order (the Redemptorists) has been active in mission preaching and in works of mercy. These spiritual reserves were to be urgently needed in the days of trouble. Their quality is indicated by the way in which the church came through the fires of adversity: tried, indeed, but refined and purified.

More difficult to assess are the ways in which the churches responded to the intellectual movements of the period. The authority of reason was challenged and its undisputed authority was overthrown. This happened long before the upheaval which ended the age. But reason, though chastened, was still powerful. Even during the Revolution it was assumed that only such beliefs, customs, and institutions as could justify themselves at the bar of reason had a right to exist. The assumptions of eighteenth-century thought have remained as a pervasive influence in each subsequent period, and it is sometimes startling to realize how many of our unexamined presuppositions are a direct bequest from the Age of Reason. In particular, the free spirit in which scientific investigation is pursued and the assumptions which govern much of man's intellectual quest are the direct result of eighteenth-century forces. The atmosphere in which religious thought would henceforth be conducted was profoundly modified.

Nevertheless, an intellectual war of liberation was under way. The naïve and shallow faith in the perfectibility of man, so popular in the eighteenth century, rested on the cult of reason. Rationalism, as popularly understood, affirmed that all reality can be known by the mind. Right reason could reduce society to the harmonious pattern ordained by nature and by nature's God. Once mankind accepted this liberating truth, the golden age would be at hand. This was the theory. After twenty-five years of revolutionary turmoil and warfare, Europe decided that the fruits of this philosophy were discord, violence, and disillusionment. Consequently, a resolute attempt was launched to overthrow the self-evident certitudes which had seemed so deceptively obvious to the Age of Reason. If for no other reason, the philosophy of reason must be wrong because it had lost its moral bearings. Reason could dissolve the basis of religious faith, but it could provide no comparably satisfying sanction for good behaviour. In metaphysics, no less than in ethics, the breakdown of rationalism was apparent. Beginning with Kant, fundamental philosophical and religious problems were re-examined. The nature of the crisis determined the pattern of the answer. Religious issues were discussed in a predominantly philosophical setting.

Others besides philosophers and theologians revolted against the rationalist picture of life. The Romantic movement was the protest of the non-specialist against what the Age of Reason had made of human life. In many fields men protested against the inference that common sense was preferable to emotion or that correct and formal values could compensate for the loss of freshness and joy. Mystery and wonder, beauty and spontaneity asserted their right to a place in any adequate conception of a satisfying life. These have important religious overtones; to reaffirm them is not to recover the Christian faith. Romanticism might be a useful ally; it might equally prove to be a powerful rival.

The Age of Reason had carried men over the threshold of

the modern world. It had shown them the inadequacy of the old conception of man and the universe, and had furnished them with the essentials of a new outlook. It had shown that scholastic orthodoxy, rearranging the pieces of an ancient puzzle, was not a sufficient instrument of thought or life. It had demonstrated the attractiveness and the limitations of reason; it had even revealed the power of the Romantic spirit. It had not actually provided the answer to man's perennial religious problems, though at one stage it was confident that it had. It provided many of the ingredients that would have to be incorporated in a new interpretation of the faith; it suggested the method that might profitably be used; but it bequeathed to the new age the task of restating the ancient faith in terms intelligible to modern man.

BIBLIOGRAPHICAL NOTE

General histories of the period provide valuable background material as well as considerable detail about religious development. *The Cambridge Modern History* (IV, V, VI); *The New Cambridge Modern History* (VII); Methuen's *History of England* (volumes by Trevelyan and Robertson); Methuen's *History of Europe* (volumes by Reddaway); Harper's *The Rise of Modern Europe* (volumes by Nussbaum, Wolf, Roberts, Dorn, Gershoy) are all useful. For some of the European countries little is available in English except general histories.

GENERAL CHURCH HISTORIES

Relatively little is available. J. W. C. Wand, *A History of the Modern Church* (1930) and J. H. Nichols, *A History of Christianity, 1650–1950* (1956) are both helpful. K. S. Latourette, *A History of the Expansion of Christianity*, vol. III (1939) is primarily concerned with missionary development, but its scope is wider than its title might suggest. The volume by Preclin and Jarry in Fliche and Martin, *Histoire de l'église* (t. xix) is concerned exclusively with the Roman Catholic world. F. Nielsen, *The History of the Papacy in the Nineteenth Century*, vol. I (1906) is invaluable for the eighteenth century. In L. von Pastor's *History of the Popes* vols. XXX to XXXVI cover our period. F. Heyer, *The Catholic Church from 1648 to 1870* (English translation, 1969) is a useful survey.

FRANCE

Many of the most useful books are available only in French. G. Goyau, 'Histoire religieuse' in Hanotaux (ed.), *Histoire de la nation française* is valuable. The chief works of the great French writers of the period – Pascal, Descartes, Voltaire, Rousseau, and the various French leaders of European thought – are readily available in English. Part of Fénelon and Bossuet has been translated. On Jansenism, N. Abercrombie, *The Origins of Jansenism* (1936) is critical of the movement. Sainte-Beuve, *Port-Royal* is political rather than religious in emphasis, but remains an important work. R. A. Knox's *Enthusiasm* (1950) is useful on the Quietists and the Jansenists. E. K. Sanders, *Bossuet* (1921); H. F. Stewart, *The Holiness of Pascal* (1915). J. McManners' *French Ecclesiastical Society under the Ancien Régime* (1960) gives a fascinating picture of church life in a provincial city.

ENGLAND

R. S. Bosher, *The Making of the Restoration Settlement* (1951) deals with the early years in great detail. An older book, covering the Stuart period, is Hutton's volume in Stephens and Hunt, *A History of the English Church* (1903). In the same series, the parallel volume for the eighteenth century is by Overton and Relton (1906). Of contemporary works, G. Burnet, *History of My Own Time* is a graphic account by an eye-witness. For the later Puritans, nothing takes the place of such works as Bunyan's *Pilgrim's Progress*, George Fox's *Journal*, or Richard Baxter's *Autobiography* (an abridgement of his *Reliquiae.*) G. F. Nuttall's *Richard Baxter* (1966) is a sympathetic study of an important figure. G. R. Cragg, *Puritanism in the Period of the Great Persecution* (1957) is concerned with the social history of the later Puritans.

For the eighteenth century, the works of Norman Sykes (*Church and State in England in the Eighteenth Century, Edmund Gibson, William Wake,* and *From Sheldon to Secker*) have been primarily responsible for much recent revaluation of the period. Parson Woodforde's Diary is easily available.

The literature on Methodism is immense. There is no substitute for John Wesley's *Journal*; it can profitably be supplemented by his letters. E. Harrison, *Son to Susannah* is a popular biography which does not minimize the bizarre features of the movement. *A New History of Methodism*, ed. W. J. Townsend and others (1909). For those who have access to it, L. Tyerman's old-fashioned *Life and Times of John Wesley*, 3 vols. (1870), contains a great deal of valuable material. Among recent studies of Wesley may be mentioned the following: C. W. Williams, *John Wesley's Theology Today* (1962); V. H. H. Green, *The Young Mr Wesley* (1961) and *John Wesley* (1962); M. Schmidt, *John Wesley: A Theological Biography,* vol. I (1962) A. C. Outler, ed., *John Wesley* (Library of Protestant Theology, 1964) is particularly useful. See also R. Davies and E. G. Rupp, *A History of the Methodist Church in Great Britain* (1965—). Hanoverian bishops have been enjoying a mild renascence. In addition to Dr Sykes's works mentioned above, E. F. Carpenter has given us biographies of Tenison, Sherlock, and Compton, and G. V. Bennett of White Kennett. R. Coupland's *Wilberforce* (1923) is an excellent study of a leading Evangelical.

GERMANY

A. L. Drummond, *German Protestantism Since Luther* (1931) helps the reader to understand a complex field. K. S. Pinson, *Pietism as a Factor in the Rise of German Nationalism* (1934) is wider in scope than its title suggests. On the same subject, see E. Stoeffer, *The Rise of Evangelical Pietism* (1965). W. H. Bruford, *Germany in the Eighteenth Century* (1935) contains useful comments on church life.

AMERICA

There is a good introduction in J. Brauer, *Protestantism in America* (1953). The various works of W. W. Sweet are standard in this field. Perry Miller's *Jonathan Edwards* (1949) is an intriguing study of a very important figure. The same author's *The New England Mind* (2 vols., paperback, 1961) is a work of major importance. So is A. Heimert's *Religion and the American Mind* (1966). Heimert and Miller produced a useful collection of source material in *The Great Awakening* (1967). See also H. Shelton Smith *et al.*, *American Christianity* (2 vols., 1960–63). N. R. Burr, *A Critical Bibliography of Religion in America* (2 vols., 1961) is valuable. For Canadian church history there is H. H. Walsh's *The Christian Church in Canada* (1956).

RUSSIA

P. N. Miliukov, *Outlines of Russian Culture*, Part I (1943); Vladimir Solovyev, *Russia and the Universal Church* (translated 1948); and F. C. Conybeare, *Russian Dissenters* (1921) may be mentioned.

SCOTLAND

Hume Brown, *History of Scotland* (1899–1909) is still the most useful general history. W. L. Mathieson, *The Awakening of Scotland* (1910), Graham, *Social Life in Scotland in the Eighteenth Century*, vol. II, and Balfour of Burleigh, *The Rise and Development of Presbyterianism in Scotland* are valuable.

For the other European countries, English studies are relatively scarce. The great exception is the Papacy, where volumes XXXI–XXXVII of Pastor's monumental *History of the Papacy* (English translation, 1940–50) deal with the papal states during this period.

INTELLECTUAL HISTORY

The following may be recommended: P. Hazard, *The European Mind* (English translation, 1953) and *European Thought in the Eighteenth Century* (English translation, 1953); E. Cassirer, *The Philosophy of the Enlightenment* (English translation, 1951); B. Willey, *The Seventeenth Century Background* (1934), and *The Eighteenth Century Background* (1940); G. R. Cragg, *From Puritanism to the Age of Reason* (1950) and *Reason and Authority in the Eighteenth Century* (1964); C. I. Becker, *The Heavenly City of the Eighteenth-Century Philosophers* (1932); J. M. Creed and J. S. Boys Smith, *Religious Thought in the Eighteenth Century* (1934). R. R. Palmer, *Catholics and Unbelievers in Eighteenth Century France* (2nd edition, 1966) is a very able study of intellectual developments in France.

BAROQUE CULTURE

The best definition in English of the Baroque spirit is perhaps that given in G. Highet, *The Classical Tradition* (1949). For art and architecture in general, H. Wölflin, *Principles of Art History* (English translation, 1932) is good. Sacheverell Sitwell's works on Baroque art are still stimulating; for accuracy of treatment they have been superseded by books like J. Bourke, *Baroque Churches of Central Europe* (1958) and N. Powell, *From Baroque to Rococo* (1959). M. Kitson, *The Age of Baroque* (1966) is an able and richly illustrated examination of the artistic achievement of the period. On Wren there is nothing to compare with the volumes of the Wren Society.

For music, there are M. F. Bukofzer, *Music in the Baroque Era* (1947), H. Leichentritt, *Music, History and Ideas* (1938), P. H. Láng, *Music in Western Civilization* (1941); A. Schweitzer, *J. S. Bach* (1923); and B. Smallman, *The Background of Passion Music* (1957).

Index

Aarau, Peace of, 10
Absolutism, 16, 17, 18, 99, 196, 199, 202, Ch. 14 *passim*
Adams, Parson, 128
Addison, Joseph, 61, 126
Alembert, J. d', 216
Alexander VII, Pope, 27, 29
America, Ch. 12 *passim*
Analogy of Religion, The (Butler), 127, 165–7
Andreae, J. V., 100
Anglicanism, Chs. 4 and 9 *passim*, 182, 183
Anne, Queen, 62, 63, 134
Anti-burghers, 89
Antichrist, 110, 111
Anticlericalism, 242
Anti-lifters, 89
Antiquity, appeal to, 71
Apocalyptic expectations, 111
Apollonius of Tyana, 77
Aranda, P.P.A., Count of, 214, 231
Architecture, Baroque, 256–69
Argyll, eighth earl of, 81
Argyll, ninth earl of, 58
Arianism, 137, 169
Aristotelianism, 70
Arminianism, 66, 144–5
Arnauld, Angélique, 26
Arnauld, Antoine, 27, 28
Arndt, J., 101
Assembly, General, 83, 85, 88, 90, 91
Attendance, Church, 85
Atterbury, Bp F., 118, 119
Augustine, St, 234
Augustinus, 26
Auld Lichts, 89

Austria, 16, 217, 218, 219–24, 260
Authority, 11–14, 71, 239, 240, 241, 245, 247, 280, 281
Avvakum, Archpriest, 111

Bach, J. S., 273–8
Bacon, F., 37
Bahrdt, K. F., 248
Baptist Missionary Society, 138
Baptists, 135, 137, 176, 178, 180, 182
Baroque art, 40, Ch. 16 *passim*
Barrow, Isaac, 66, 70
Bavaria, 92, 260
Baxter, Richard, 51, 66
Bayle, P., 12, 48–9, 234, 237–8
Bellarmine, Card., 23
Benedict XIV, Pope, 210–11, 247
Bengel, J. A., 102
Bentham, J., 171
Bentley, R., 74, 127
Berkeley, Bp G., 13, 119, 164–5, 167, 246
Berlin, 101
Bermuda, 119, 164
Bernini, G. L., 257–9, 264
Bernsdorff, A. P., 229
Berridge, 153
Bible, Holy, 48, 71, 102, 169, 175, 176, 177, 237, 239, 241, 248, 249
Bible Society, British and Foreign, 156
Birmingham, 172
Bishops, English, 57, 102–4; French, 202–4
Blackburne, F., 169
Blount, C., 77
Boehme, J., 101
Bolingbroke, Viscount, 63, 161

Book of Common Prayer, 51
Borromini, F., 257–8
Bossuet, Bp J. B., 23, 30, 31, 33, 35, 36, 44, 47, 48, 49, 203
Boston, Thomas, 86
Boswell, J., 128
Bothwell Brig, 82
Bourbon powers, 212, 214
Bourdaloue, L., 36
Boutron, E., 43
Boyle, R., 73–4
Brainerd, D., 180
Brandenburg, 19
Bray, T., 62, 178
Brazil, 188
Breda, Declaration of, 50
Brienne, Card. Loménie de, 201, 204, 205
Bristol, 145
Brunswick, 208
Bulgarian Church, 108
Bunyan, J., 67
Burghers, 89
Burke, E., 169, 170, 172
Burnet, Bp G., 61
Burns, R., 91
Butler, Bp J., 13, 127, 133, 150, 165–7, 246, 281
Buxtehude, D., 275
Byzantine tradition, 109

Cabal, the, 54
Cagliostro, A., 239
Calas, J., 241–2
Calvinism, Calvinists, 60, 65, 66, 68, 86, 87, 90, 94, 137, 138, 144, 153, 181, 217
Cambridge, Emmanuel College; 163; Queens' College, 154, Trinity College, 66, 127, 267, 270; University of, 67, 136, 154, 170
Cambridge Platonists, the, 67–70

Cambuslang, 88
Cameronians, 82, 88
Camp meetings, 184
Campomanes, 231
Canada, 185–8
Candide (Voltaire), 45
Cantatas, 275
Capuchins, 188, 194
Carey, W., 138
Carlyle, A., 90, 91
Cartesianism, 39
Catherine the Great, 115, 226–7
Catholic Relief Acts, 139
Catholicism, Roman, 44, 55, 58, 66, 82, 83, 88, 91, 94–5, 114, 120, 123, Ch. 14 *passim*, 280
Cecil, Richard, 154
Challoner, Bp R., 139
Chalmers, T., 90
Charity Schools, 131
Charles II, 50, 53, 54, 55, 81
Charles III of Spain, 214, 230–1
Chatham, Earl of, 149
Chesterfield, Earl of, 144
China, the Chinese, 46, 47, 191
Chorales, German, 274–6
Christian VI of Denmark, 228
Christian VII of Denmark, 228
Christian Brothers, 35
Christianity as Old as the Creation, 159, 161, 163
Chronology, 47–8
Church and state, 47, 52, 56, 61, 82, 83, 88, 91, 94–5, 114, 120, 123, Ch. 14 *passim*, 280
Church Missionary Society, 156
Churriguera, J., 258
Clapham Sect, 155
'Clarendon Code', 53
Clarendon, Earl of, 53, 54
Clarke, S., 158
Clarkson, T., 155
Class meeting, methodist, 147

Clement XI, Pope, 30, 210
Clement XII, Pope, 212
Clement XIII, Pope, 214
Clement XIV, Pope, 214
Clergy (French), higher, 202–4; lower, 205–6
Colbert, J. B., 19
Coleridge, S. T., 172
Collier, J., 61
Common Fund, 60
'Communion season', 87
Comprehension, 52, 53, 60, 134
Conference, Methodist, 146
Confessional, The (Blackburne), 169
Confucius, 191, 248
Congregationalists (Independents), 60, 136, 137, 174, 182
Consalvi, Card. E., 280
Conscience, 167
Constantinople, 108
Conventicle Acts, The, 53
Convocation, 51, 61, 118, 150
Convulsionaries, 196
Copenhagen, 228
Copts, the, 107
Coram, Capt., 132
Corporation Action Act, the, 53, 134, 170
Corruption in public life, 149
Cosin, Bp J., 57, 65
Counter-Reformation, the 99, 190, 212, 257, 262
Covenant, Covenanters, 82, 83
Cowper, W., 129, 281
Crabbe, G., 128
Cromwell, O., 50, 79
Curates, 126

Danby, Earl of, 55
Davis, Rev. R., 60
Declaration of Indulgence: (1672) 54–5; (1688), 59

Defoe, D., 130
Deism, deists, 14, 69, 75, 77, 157–63, 164, 165, 183, 222, 237, 239, 247
Denmark, 228
Descartes, R., 37–40, 42, 236
Development, 250
Dialogues Concerning Natural Religion (Hume), 168
Diderot, D., 49, 196, 234, 236, 238, 243, 245
Discipline, Church, 84, 97, 146
Dissenters, English, 52, 54, 56, 57, 58, 60, 133–8, 171; Scottish, 88
Dissenting academies, 63, 136, 171
Divine Right of Kings, 23
Doddridge, F., 136, 137, 281
Dominicans, 31, 188, 191, 225
Dominus ac Redemptor, 214
Doubt, 38
Dragonnades, 20–1
Dresden, 101, 259
Dublin, Trinity College, 164
Dubois, Card. G., 11, 194
Dukhobors, 113
Durie, J., 100
Duttenhofer, 104

Eastern churches, 107–8
Eckhardt, Meister, 101
Edinburgh, 90
Education, 149, 177, 200–1, 218, 220, 221, 223
Education of Mankind, The (Lessing), 250
Edwards, J., 179, 181
Encyclopaedia, The, 236, 238, 246
Enlightened despotism, Ch. 14 *passim*, 279
Enlightenment, the, 106, 218, 220, 221, 226, 229, 231, 237, 248, 249
'Enthusiasm', 14–15, 70, 79, 117
Episcopacy, 51, 81, 82, 95, 202–4

Epworth, 141
Erastianism, 12, 61, 63, 89
Erskine Ebenezer, 89; Ralph, 86, 90
Ethics, 76, 236, 243. *See also* Morality
Eudists, 35
Evangelical Revival, the, 152–6, 169, 281
Evil, 44, 244
Experience, areas of, 252–3

Faith, 39, 42, 68, 73, 75, 252
Feathers Tavern Petition, 169
'Febronius' (von Hontheim), 219
Feeling, 238, 254
Fénelon, F. de S. de la M., 30, 33, 41, 203
Fichte, J. G., 97
Fielding, H., 128
Fleury, Card. A. H. de, 11, 194–5
Florence, 224
Floridablanca, J. M. y R., 231
Foundling Hospital, the, 133
'Four-fold state of man', 85
Fox, C. J., 171
Fox, George, 67, 178
France, Chs. 2 and 13 *passim*, 212, 214, 234, 236, 248
Francis Xavier, St, 190
Franciscans, 189
Francke, A. H., 102
Frederick the Great, 96, 211, 215–18, 219, 227, 232, 241, 244
Frederick William I, 95
Freedom, 252, 253
French culture, 234, 247
French Revolution, the, 15, 16, 172, 187, 201, 208, 210, 218, 233, 245, 254, 279

Gallican Articles, the, 24, 25
Gallicanism, 18, 21–5, 186, 193, 195, 196

Garrick, D., 144
Gassendi, P., 39
George I, 134, 163
Georgia, 119, 142, 145
Gerhardt, P., 101, 274
Germany, Ch. 7 *passim*, 247, 248, 257, 281
Gibbon, E., 170, 171
Gibbs, James, 264, 268, 269
Gibson, Bp E., 66, 120, 123, 129, 130, 134, 138, 150
Glanvill, J., 73
Glasgow, 89
Goethe, J. W. von, 255
Goodwin, T., 66
Gordon riots, 139
Great Awakening, the, 179–81
Grégoire, Abbé H., 196
Grimm, F. M., 235
Grimshaw, W., 153
Grotius, Hugo, 9, 48
Gulliver's Travels, 46
Gunning, Bp P., 57
Gustavus III, 229

'Half-way covenant', 177
Halle, 101–2, 248
Halle-Danish Mission, 102
Hampton Court Palace, 267
Handel, G. F., 273, 275, 277
Hanover, 94
Hanoverian Age, the, Ch. 9 *passim*
Hanway, J., 133
Happy Union, the, 60, 137
Hardwicke, Lord, 135
Hare, Bp F., 122
Hartley, D., 171
Harvard University, 177
Hawksmoor, N., 264, 268
Haydn, F. J., 271
Herbert of Cherbury, Lord, 77
Herder, J. G. von, 98, 100

Heresy Trials, 89, 90
Herrnhut, 103
Hesse, 94
'High Church' faction, 63
History, 243, 244
Hoadly, Bp B., 119, 124
Hoadly, J., 125
Hobbes, T., 70, 167
Hogarth, W., 129
Holbach, Baron von, 216, 243
Holland, 45, 47, 54
Holy Club, the, 142
'Holy Experiment, the', 175–7
Holy Spirit, the, 113, 176
Howard, J., 133
Howe, J., 67
Hudson River, 174
Huguenots, 10, 17–21, 47, 48, 49,
    96, 200, 241
Hume, David, 14, 90, 162, 167–9,
    171, 211, 243, 251, 252, 253
Hungary, 10, 224
Huntingdon, Countess of, 152
Hurd, Bp R., 123
Hurons, the, 185
Huyghens, C., 45
Hymns, 137–8, 149, 273–4,
    281

'Illuminism', 238
Immortality, 252, 253
Indemnity Acts, 118
Independents. *See* Congregationa-
    lists
Independent Whig, the, 119
India, South, 102, 107
Innocent X, Pope, 9
Innocent XI, Pope, 24
Inquisition, the, 9, 32, 224, 225,
    230, 231, 232
Ireland, 139, 164
Iroquois, the, 185
Islam, 108, 115

James I, 78
James II, 52, 56, 58, 59, 66, 79, 82,
    138, 149
Jansen, C., 25
Jansenism, Jansenists, 15, 20, 25–
    30, 186, 193–9
Jerusalem, Council of (1672), 116
Jesuits, 15, 23, 26, 27, 28, 30–1, 41,
    94, 138, 186–92, 193, 194–9,
    212–14, 232, 247, 257, 279
Jews, the, 222, 250
John of Damascus, St, 115
Jones, Inigo, 267
Jones, W., 126
Johnson, Samuel, 129, 164
Joseph II, Emperor, 16, 219–24
Josephism, 215
Jovellanos, G. M. de, 231
Jurieu, P., 49

Kant, I., 14, 97, 168, 250–4, 255
Kaunitz, W. A. Prince von., 222
Ken, Bp T., 57
Keppel, Bp, 123
Khlysty sect, 113
Kiev, 115, 116
'Killing Time', the, 82
Kilsyth, 88
Königsberg, 251

La Bruyère, J. de, 46
Laity, 97
Landrecht, Prussian, 96
Latitudinarians, the 61, 70–2, 153,
    157–60, 169
Laud, Laudians, 50, 70, 79
Laval, Bp F. K., 185
Law, W., 126, 163–4, 167
Lazarists, 34
Le Clerc, J., 49
Leeuwenhoek, A. van, 45
Leibniz, G. W., 43, 247
Leopold, Emperor, 224

Lessing, G. E., 232, 249–50
Lifters, 89
Liguori, St Alphonsus, 282
Liturgical Reform, Russian, 110
Locke, J., 13, 14, 70, 75–7, 79, 80, 157, 159, 167, 168, 234, 239, 247
London, Fire of, 263, 264, 265
London Journal, the, 119
London Missionary Society, 138
Lord's Supper, the, 86–7
Louis XIV, 9, 10, 11, Ch. 2 *passim*, 49, 94, 193, 215, 257
Louis XV, 193, 197, 198
Louis XVI, 204, 238
Louisiana, 188
Louvain, University of, 39
'Low Church' faction, 63
Lowth, Bp R., 150
Luther, M., 101, 103, 217, 273
Lutheran Church, Lutherans, 93, 94, 95, 97, 99, 178, 228, 229, 276–7
Lutheranism, condition of, 99–100

Mabillon, J., 35
Macaulay, Z., 155
Maimbourg, L., 21
Maintenon, Mme de, 20, 193
Malebranche, M., 39–40
Maria Theresa, Empress, 219
Marriage Act (1753), 135
Mass in B Minor (Bach), 277
Massachusetts, 174
Mazarin, Card. J., 9, 17
Melanchthon, P., 100
Mennonites, 178
Methodism, Ch. 10 *passim*, 182, 184, 281
Michaelis, J. D., 249
Middleton, Lord, 121
Milner, I., 154
Milton, J., 67

Ministers, Scottish, 84
Miracles, 13, 160–3, 168, 195, 239, 245
Moderates, Scottish, 18
Molanus, G. W., 100
Molinos, M. de, 32, 33
Monads, 44
Monasticism, 108, 204–5, 223–4, 225, 233
Monmouth rebellion, 58
Monophysite churches, 107
Monothelite churches, 107
Montaigne, M. de, 46
Montesquieu, C. L. de S., baron de, 211, 234, 236
Montreal, 178
Morality, 70, 73, 90, 91, 117, 158–9, 167, 236, 238, 251
Moravian Brethren, 103, 142
More, Hannah, 156
Morley, Bp G., 57, 65
Moscow, 109, 111
Mozart, W. A., 271–2
Mühlenberg, H. M., 102, 180
Music, Baroque, 270–8
Mystery, 78, 239, 283
Mysticism, 113

Nantes, Edict of, 10, 18–21, 200
Naples, 212, 231
Napoleon I, 94, 279, 280
Narbonne, Abp of, 203
Nathan the Wise (Lessing), 250
Natural History of Religion (Hume), 168
Natural law, 236, 237, 251
Natural religion, 71, 160, 252
Nature, 166, 236, 253–4
Neo-classicism, 263
Nepotism, 210
Nestorians, the, 107
Netherlands, 224, 259
New England, Ch. 12 *passim*

New Lichts, 89
Newcastle, Duke of, 121, 122, 128
Newton, I., 14, 73–4, 157, 234, 236, 239, 247, 251
Newton, J., 154, 281
Newton, Bp T., 121
Nikon, Patriarch, 109, 110
Noailles, Card. de, 193
Nonconformists. *See* dissenters
Non-jurors, 61
Non-residence, 126
Non-resistance, 52, 58, 79
'Novalis', 254
Nuncios, papal, 99

Oates, Titus, 55
Occasional Conformity Act, 62–3, 118
Oetinger, 106
Oglethorpe, Gen. J. E., 119, 142
Old Believers Schism, 110–14
Optimism, 44, 171, 222, 243, 245
Oratorians, 39
Oratory, the French, 34
Orléans, Duc de, 193, 194
Ornamentation, Baroque, 262–3, 269
Orthodox Churches, Ch. 8 *passim*, 222, 228
Orthodoxy, 99, 240
Owen J., 66
Oxford, All Souls College, 159; Christ Church, 141; Lincoln College, 141; Magdalen College, 59; University of, 154
Oxford, Earl of, 63

Paine, T., 171
Palatinate, the, 10, 94
Palestrina, 270–1, 273, 276, 277
Paley, W., 128, 170–1, 281
Papacy, the, 21, 23, 29, 31, 209–12, 215, 221, 225, 232, 279, 281

Paraguay, 189–90
Parish life, English, 133
Paris, 234
Parlements, 194–7
Partisanship, 63
Pascal, B., 28, 31, 39, 40–3
Passion (music), 276–7
Passive obedience, 52, 58, 60
Pastors, German, 97–8, 104
Patriarchates, Eastern, 107
Patronage, lay, 81, 83, 88, 97
Pattison, M., 76
Paul, St, 90
Pearson, Bp J., 57, 70
Peasants, 217, 218, 220, 221, 227, 229
Peirce, J., 137
Penn, W., 178
Pennsylvania, 178
Pentland, Hills, 82
Percival, Viscount, 129
Pergolesi, 271
Persecution, 19–21, 53, 57–8, 60, 62, 79, 93, 96, 195, 220, 227
Persia, 107
Peter the Great, 111, 112, 114, 115, 226
Peter III, 227
Philanthropy, 24
Philosophers, Ch. 15 *passim*
Pietism, 14, 95, 99, 100–6, 228, 247, 281–2
Pistoia, 226
Pitt, W., 155
Pius VI, Pope, 215, 222
Pius VII, Pope, 279
Plato, 30
Platonism, 70
Pluralism, 124–6, 223
Plymouth, Mass., 174
Pombal, S. J., Marquess of, 213, 232
Pompadour, Mme de, 197

Pope, A., 15, 158
Popish Plot, the, 55
Port Royal, 26, 28–30
Porteus, Bp B., 154
Portugal, 213, 214, 231–2
Posterity, 245
Poverty, 147
Preaching, Scottish, 85, 91; German, 99–101
Predestination, 26
Presbyterians, 50, 60, Ch. 6 *passim*, 135–7, 169, 179, 180, 182
Price, R., 171
Priesthood, Russian, 114
'Priestist' sect, 111
'Priestless' sect, 111
Priestley, J., 136, 171–2
Probabiliorism, 31
Probabilism, 30–1
Procurator of the Holy Synod, 114
Prophecy, 13, 160, 163, 239
Protestant Dissenting Deputies, 135
Protestantism, 44, 94, Chs. 4, 5, 6, 7, 9, 10, 12 *passim*, 249
Providence, 240
Prussia, 95, 217–18, 255
Pufendorf, S., 10
Purcell, H., 56, 272
Puritans, Puritanism, 50, 51, 54, 57, 66, 79, 174–8, 181
Pyle, E., 124

Quakers, 58, 67, 79, 134, 154, 176, 178, 179, 182
Quebec, 185, 187
Quebec Act, the 186
Queen Anne's Bounty, 62
Quesnel, P., 29
Quieting and Establishing Corporations, Act for, 118
Quietism, 15, 32–3

Raikes, R., 131
Rationalism, 99, 106, 115, 153, 159, 165, 169, 247, 248, 254, 280–3
Ray, J., 74, 75, 171
Reaction, conservative, 233, 279–281
Reason, 13, 14, 38, 44, 68, 70, 71, 76, 78, 159–63, 167, 172, 221, 235, 242, 251, 280–3
Reasonableness of Christianity, The (Locke), 76, 159
Recollects, 185, 187, 188
'Reductions', 189–90
Reform, 15–16, 169, 172–3, 206, 210, 221–6, 232
Reformation, the 212, 215, 273
Reformed Church, the, 93, 178, 180
Regale, 24
Regiminis Apostolici, 29
Reimarus, H. S., 249
Religious Tract Society, 156
Rescissory Act of 1661, 81
Restoration, the (1660), 50, 65, 67, 79, 81, 119, 272
Reunion, 43
Revelation, 13, 71, 78, 160, 238, 245, 280
Revivalism, 179–81, 184
Revolution of 1688, 59, 60, 79; 148
Rhode Island, 176, 179
Ricci, Bp S., 226
Richelieu, Card. A., 17
'Rites, Affair of the', 191
Robertson, W., 91
Rococo art, 256, 262
Rohan, Card., L. R. E., 203, 204
Romaine, W., 154
Romantic movement, the, 172, 253–4, 283
'Rome, the, third', 109, 111
Roubiliac, L. F., 270

Rousseau, J.-J., 12, 14, 238, 251
Royal Society, the, 72
Rubens, P. P., 259
Rulers, role of, 95
Ruskin, John, 256
Russia, Ch. 8 *passim*, 226–7

Sabbath, Scottish, 84–5
Sacheverell, H., 62–3, 118, 119
St Andrews, 89
St Bartholomew's Day, 1662, 52
St Cyran, du Vergier, Abbot of, 26
St Maur, Congregation of, 35
Saint-Médard, 195
St Paul's Cathedral, London, 264, 266–7
Saint-Pierre, Abbé, 243
Saint-Simon, L., duc de, 194
St Stephen's, Walbrook, 266
St Teresa, 32
St Vincent de Paul, 34, 35
Salons, 235
Salters Hall Synod, 137
Salzburg, 10, 96, 260, 262, 271
Sancroft, Abp W., 57, 59
Sanderson, Bp R., 57
Savoy Conference, the, 51
Saxony, Elector of, 94, 101
Schism, Russian, 110–14, 115
Schism Act, 63, 118
Schleiermacher, F., 97, 254–5
Schools, Sunday, 131–2
Schools of Charity, 131
Schools of Industry, 131
Science, 12, 13, 72, 73–5, 241, 257, 282; and religion, 43, 74
Scotland, Ch. 6 *passim*
Scott, Thomas, 154
Sculpture, Baroque, 270
Seceders, 89
Secker, Abp T., 127, 129
Sects, Russian, 113
Seminaries, 34, 223

Semler, 249
Serbian Church, 108
Serious Call to a Devout and Holy Life, (Law), 163
Session, Kirk, 84
Shaftesbury, 1st Earl of, 56
Shaftesbury, 3rd Earl of, 89, 167
Sharp, Grenville, 155
Sharp, Rev. W., 130
Sheldon, Abp G., 54, 56
Sherlock, Bp T., 161
Siberia, 112
Simeon, C., 154
Simon, R., 48
Sisters of Charity, 34
Skoptsy, sect, 113
Slavery, 149, 154–5, 180
Smollett, T., 126
S.K.C.K., 62, 128, 178
S.P.G., 62, 178
Societies for the Reformation of Manners, 62, 129
Socinianism, 153, 169
Solemn League and Covenant, 51
Sophia, Tsarevna, 112
Sorbonne, 26–8, 191
Sorcery, 87
South, R., 78
Spain, 17, 212, 214, 229–31
Spener, P. J., 101
Spinoza, B., 39–41, 48
Sprat, Bp T., 73
States General of France, 196
Sterne, Laurence, 121
Stillingfleet, Bp E., 61, 71, 78
Strauensee, J. F., 228–9
Sulpicians, 35
Superintendants, 95
Superstition, 230, 232, 241, 257
Swammerdam, J., 45
Sweden, 229
Swift, J., 63
Synod, the Holy, 114

Talleyrand, C. M. de, 203
Taylor, Jeremy, 65
Telemann, G. P., 274, 275
Tenison, Abp T., 61, 126
'Territorial System', the, 94
Tersteegen, G., 106
Test Act, the, 55, 59, 134, 170
Thirty Years War, the, 93
Thorndike, H., 65
Three Rivers, 185
Tillotson, Abp J., 61, 72, 77, 78, 159
Tindal, M., 159–63
Toland, J., 78, 160
Toleration, 47, 59, 66, 69, 79, 96, 183, 218, 241, 245
Toleration, Patent of, 222, 223
Toleration Act, the, 60, 134, 137
Toplady, A. M., 153
Tories, 56, 62–3, 118, 119, 148
Travel, 46
Treatise of Human Nature, A (Hume), 168
Trent, Council of, 21
Trial of the Witnesses of the Resurrection, The (Sherlock), 161
Trier, 219
Trimmer, Mrs, 131
Trinitarian controversy, 61, 137
True Christianity (Arndt), 101
Tsar, Russian, 109, 111
Turkey, 108, 209
Tuscany, 224

Ultramontanism, 22, 193, 194, 211, 214
Uniformity, Act of, 51, 52, 53, 79
Unigenitus (Bull), 30, 194, 195, 198, 199
Union, Act of, 51, 52, 53, 79
Unitarianism, 60, 136–7, 169, 184, 222
Universe, nature of, 44

Universities (Oxford and Cambridge), 59, 78, 136
Universities, German, 100
Utrecht, 212

Vanbrugh, J., 264, 268
Vanini, C., 46
Vatican, 211
Venice, 225
Versailles, 105, 259, 262
Victor Amadeus, 210
Vienna, 219, 222, 226, 260, 280
Virginia, 174, 178, 183
Voltaire, 12, 14, 45, 49, 90, 194, 197, 207, 211, 216, 234, 236, 238, 239, 243, 246
Vygovsky monastery, 112

Wake, Abp W., 123
Wakefield, Vicar of, 128
Walker, Samuel, 153
Walpole, Sir R., 11, 118–20, 134
Warburton, Bp W., 70, 120, 150
Watson, Bp R., 122, 170
Watts, I., 130, 137, 281
Wealth, Wesleyan, 148
Wesley, Charles, 141, 149, 281
Wesley, John, 14, 132, 139, Ch. 10 *passim*, 167, 182, 246
Wesley, Samuel, 141
Wesley, Susannah, 141
West Indies, 188
Westphalia, Peace of, 9, 16, 17, 93
Whigs, 61, 63, 119–20, 134
Whitefield, G., 142, 144, 152, 153, 179, 181
Whole Duty of Man, The, 78
Wilberforce, W., 155, 156
Wilkins, Bp J., 57
William III, King (William of Orange), 59, 60, 61, 82
Williams, Dr D., 60
Williams, Roger, 176, 177, 179

Witchcraft, belief in, 87
Wolff, Christian, 45, 248
Wolfenbüttel Fragments, 249
Woodforde, Rev. James, 123, 133
Woodwork, Baroque, 269
Woolman, J., 180
Worship, Scottish, 85

Wren, Sir C., 56, 263-9
Württemberg, 102

Xavier, St Francis, 190

Zelo Domus Dei, 9
Zinzendorf, Count von, 102-4
Zwinger, the, 259

READ MORE IN PENGUIN

In every corner of the world, on every subject under the sun, Penguin represents quality and variety – the very best in publishing today.

For complete information about books available from Penguin – including Puffins, Penguin Classics and Arkana – and how to order them, write to us at the appropriate address below. Please note that for copyright reasons the selection of books varies from country to country.

In the United Kingdom: Please write to *Dept. JC, Penguin Books Ltd, FREEPOST, West Drayton, Middlesex UB7 OBR*

If you have any difficulty in obtaining a title, please send your order with the correct money, plus ten per cent for postage and packaging, to *PO Box No. 11, West Drayton, Middlesex UB7 OBR*

In the United States: Please write to *Penguin USA Inc., 375 Hudson Street, New York, NY 10014*

In Canada: Please write to *Penguin Books Canada Ltd, 10 Alcorn Avenue, Suite 300, Toronto, Ontario M4V 3B2*

In Australia: Please write to *Penguin Books Australia Ltd, 487 Maroondah Highway, Ringwood, Victoria 3134*

In New Zealand: Please write to *Penguin Books (NZ) Ltd,182–190 Wairau Road, Private Bag, Takapuna, Auckland 9*

In India: Please write to *Penguin Books India Pvt Ltd, 706 Eros Apartments, 56 Nehru Place, New Delhi 110 019*

In the Netherlands: Please write to *Penguin Books Netherlands B.V., Keizersgracht 231 NL–1016 DV Amsterdam*

In Germany: Please write to *Penguin Books Deutschland GmbH, Friedrichstrasse 10–12, W–6000 Frankfurt/Main 1*

In Spain: Please write to *Penguin Books S. A., C. San Bernardo 117–6° E–28015 Madrid*

In Italy: Please write to *Penguin Italia s.r.l., Via Felice Casati 20, 1–20124 Milano*

In France: Please write to *Penguin France S. A., 17 rue Lejeune, F–31000 Toulouse*

In Japan: Please write to *Penguin Books Japan, Ishikiribashi Building, 2–5–4, Suido, Bunkyo-ku, Tokyo 112*

In Greece: Please write to *Penguin Hellas Ltd, Dimocritou 3, GR–106 71 Athens*

In South Africa: Please write to *Longman Penguin Southern Africa (Pty) Ltd, Private Bag X08, Bertsham 2013*

READ MORE IN PENGUIN

RELIGION

The Gnostic Gospels Elaine Pagels

In a book that is as exciting as it is scholarly, Elaine Pagels examines these ancient texts and the questions they pose and shows why Gnosticism was eventually stamped out by the increasingly organized and institutionalized Orthodox Church. 'Fascinating' – *The Times*

Islam in the World Malise Ruthven

This informed and informative book places the contemporary Islamic revival in context, providing a fascinating introduction – the first of its kind – to Islamic origins, beliefs, history, geography, politics and society.

The Orthodox Church Timothy Ware

In response to increasing interest among western Christians, and believing that a thorough understanding of Orthodoxy is necessary if the Roman Catholic and Protestant Churches are to be reunited, Timothy Ware explains Orthodox views on a vast range of matters from Free Will to the Papacy.

Judaism Isidore Epstein

The comprehensive account of Judaism as a religion and as a distinctive way of life, presented against a background of 4,000 years of Jewish history.

Mysticism F. C. Happold

What is mysticism? This simple and illuminating book combines a study of mysticism – as experience, as spiritual knowledge and as a way of life – with an illustrative anthology of mystical writings, ranging from Plato and Plotinus to Dante.

Eunuchs for Heaven Uta Ranke-Heinemann

'No other book on the Catholic moral heritage unearths as many spiteful statements about women ... it is sure to become a treasure-chest for feminists ... Uta Ranke-Heinemann's research is dazzling' – *The New York Times*

READ MORE IN PENGUIN

THE PENGUIN HISTORY OF THE CHURCH
Other volumes in this series

The Early Church
Revised Edition   *Henry Chadwick*

The story of the early Christian Church from the death of Christ to
the Papacy of Gregory the Great. Professor Henry Chadwick makes
use of the latest research to explain the astonishing expansion of
Christianity throughout the Roman Empire.

Western Society and the Church in the Middle Ages   *R. W. Southern*

In the period between the eighth and the sixteenth centuries the
Church and State were more nearly one than ever before or after. In
this book, Professor Southern discusses how this was achieved and
what stresses it caused.

The Reformation   *Owen Chadwick*

In this volume Professor Owen Chadwick deals with the formative
work of Erasmus, Luther, Zwingli, Calvin, with the special circumstances of the English Reformation, and with the Counter-
Reformation.

The Church and the Age of Revolution   *Alec R. Vidler*

'A most readable and provocative volume and a notable addition to
this promising and distinguished series' – *Guardian*

A History of Christian Mission   *Stephen Neill*

This volume represents the first attempt in English to provide a
readable history of the worldwide expansion of all the Christian
denominations – Roman Catholic, Orthodox, Anglican, and
Protestant.

The Christian Church in the Cold War   *Owen Chadwick*

In this concluding volume Owen Chadwick surveys the difficulties
encountered by the Eastern and Western churches, from the end of
the Second World War and the era of a divided Europe, to the fresh
global challenges and opportunities facing Christians now.